Rethinking Everything

Also by the Author

Those Who Can: Why Master Teachers Do What They Do

Rethinking Everything

Personal Growth through Transactional Analysis

Neil Bright

ROWMAN & LITTLEFIELD
Lanham • Boulder • New York • London

Published by Rowman & Littlefield
A wholly owned subsidiary of The Rowman & Littlefield Publishing Group, Inc.
4501 Forbes Boulevard, Suite 200, Lanham, Maryland 20706
www.rowman.com

Unit A, Whitacre Mews, 26-34 Stannary Street, London SE11 4AB

British Library Cataloguing in Publication Information Available

Library of Congress Cataloging-in-Publication Data

Bright, Neil, 1949–
Rethinking everything : personal growth through transactional analysis / Neil Bright.
pages cm.
Includes bibliographical references and index.
ISBN 978-1-4758-0878-0 (cloth : alk. paper) — ISBN 978-1-4758-0879-7 (pbk. : alk. paper) — ISBN 978-1-4758-0880-3 (electronic) 1. Self-actualization (Psychology) 2. Transactional analysis. I. Title.
BF637.S4B745 2015
158—dc23
2015000453

∞™ The paper used in this publication meets the minimum requirements of American National Standard for Information Sciences Permanence of Paper for Printed Library Materials, ANSI/NISO Z39.48-1992.

Printed in the United States of America

Without the people I love, whatever else I have
and whoever else I am would mean little.

The unexamined life is not worth living.
—Socrates

Contents

Preface

We knowers are unknown to ourselves, and for good reason; how can we ever find what we have never looked for?

—Friedrich Nietzsche

Looking back, the springboard for this book was an immature attempt to earn a relatively easy three graduate credits to maintain my teaching credential by taking a class on a topic I had neither interest in nor knowledge about. Little did I know, that seemingly unimportant course on Transactional Analysis (TA) would blossom as a more comprehensive psychology elective that I would offer as a reality-changing experience for me and, ultimately, for my students. For during that long ago semester, in finding what had never been looked for, I've lived a life I never could have imagined.

In identifying, naming, and demystifying the often ineffectual behaviors of myself and my students, Transactional Analysis in particular and psychology in general provided me with a Rosetta stone for becoming happier, more in control, and increasingly effective in both my personal and professional affairs. Yet at times criticized as an overly simplistic account of human behavior, it is hard to fathom a clearer description of one's internal world and a more immediately obvious "So that's it!" explanation of why we do what we do than TA.

And that this is so is beyond doubt. For class after class, year after year, and student after student numbering in the thousands, this pragmatic and relatively uncomplicated theory of existence has resonated as true to personal experience.

But in understanding the complexities of the economy, the weather, the solar system, why humans act as they do, or virtually anything else, there *is* genius in simplicity. For while still recognizing the contributions of childhood events to current actions in a general sense, rather than endlessly searching for specific and past causes of dysfunctional conduct, Transactional Analysis in the simplest of terms provides the self-regulating awareness to immediately recognize, label, and examine such failings and to use that awareness to curb self-sabotaging behaviors leading to counterproductive ends.

In fact, greater self-understanding, TA related or otherwise, can have a far more positive impact than merely to preempt problems. Once a fundamental emotional or behavioral foible has been identified and intellectual forces brought to bear to remedy that failing, awareness-inspired correction can lead to an improved life in ways not initially recognized as even remotely connected to the original problem. Thus even lacking certainty as to the historical causes of a behavioral shortcoming, changing how the world and one's reactions to that world are *currently* perceived, has the power to change everything. For if perceptions lead to beliefs and beliefs lead to feelings and ultimately to behaviors, changing the first link in that chain changes all.

In any case, even if an individual's disordered childhood history is known, later actions are still unpredictable. As such, the identification of specific and past events unquestioningly retrofitted as causes for current conduct serves little purpose. In understanding human behavior, just because something has occurred early in life rarely is there any certainty as to its ultimate result or, among countless other possibilities, whether that "something" was the primary or even a contributing cause of later activity.

It's not that past history does not importantly affect current behavior—of course it does. Yet even if an irrefutable cause-and-effect relationship between yesterday's experiences and today's conduct was not elusive at best, definitively *knowing* the historical cause or causes of a detrimental behavior still does not guarantee its cure or even its diminishment. Understanding the cause of a problem is not the same thing as doing something about it. Or as George Bernard Shaw observed: "We are made wise not by the recollection of our past, but by the responsibility for our future."

Most importantly, the shortest distance between emotional pain and emotional health is often not greater attention to what was but greater awareness of and responsibility for *what is*. If motivated to change, one need not initially focus on the genesis of counterproductive behaviors but on current choices and the content of one's inner dialogue. And likewise, one need not possess a doctorate in psychology or rely on esoteric language to do so. To that end, in making psychology more accessible to everyone, the founder of Transactional Analysis said it best in remarking that "if something can't be understood by an intelligent eight-year-old it isn't worth saying."

However, precisely because of its colloquial language understandability, TA was initially rejected by some within the psychological establishment. After all, by postulating that human behavior could be better understood by almost anyone, Transactional Analysis in closing the status gap between the "common man" and uncommonly educated scholars may well have threatened that standing. But whether threatening or not, cynically doubting and well-lettered critics viewing TA as "superficial" or a "quick fix" originally overlooked Transactional Analysis as a "serious" discipline.

Yet whatever the reason for TA's past devaluations, simplifying psychological terms and concepts so that "the masses" can be more active participants in their own healing should not disqualify Transactional Analysis as an important therapeutic tool. Above all things, since motivation requires believing that a goal is worth attaining and that reasonable effort will lead to that goal, TA's focus on self-improvement clearly satisfies the first requirement and its user-friendly vocabulary just as clearly satisfies the second.

And besides, once motivated to eliminate or at least diminish maladaptive conduct, if one still wants to examine the origins of those behaviors, that is perfectly fine. However, presumably uncovering the specific source of one's negative actions should never supersede a healing process when its requisite self-understanding is already possible through such "here and now" behavioral explanations as Transactional Analysis. As the originator of TA also said, "Cure first and figure out why later." And he was right.

In the movie *Raiders of the Lost Ark*, Indiana Jones facing an immensely threatening, scimitar-wielding, and seemingly unconquerable opponent with presumably little more than his wits as protection, at the last moment pulls out a revolver and shoots the guy. End of the problem. Often simple *is* simply better.

In fact, an important research principle posits exactly that. Known as the law of parsimony or the application of "Occam's Razor," whenever several explanations exist for a phenomenon, an event, or a behavior, the theoretical economy of the simplest one should initially gain preference as often the most correct. Said best by the fourteenth-century philosopher whose name is forevermore linked to that concept: "It is vain to do with more what can be done with less." And he was also right.

Thus, in explaining human behavior, *failing to at least consider* the answers offered by Transactional Analysis flies in the face of that venerable and almost universally accepted research practice. In any case, perhaps past "problems" with TA were not that it was an overly simplified explanation of human behavior but rather that more "accepted" answers illuminating the human condition were often unnecessarily complicated.

Moreover, for those still believing that Transactional Analysis rests on intellectual quicksand because every conclusion has not been proven in an absolute sense is to forget that, unlike the physical sciences, there are relatively few settled answers within *any* of the social sciences, such as history or psychology. Looking for airtight certainty in any field involving human behavior may well be a noble quest, but if failing unqualified surety debases an entire school of thought then perhaps one should tilt at other windmills in looking for irrefutable truth.

Absolute truth notwithstanding, upon my initial exposure to what some disparagingly described as "pop psychology," for perhaps the first time as an adult I had the "world is what I make it" sense of personal responsibility and freedom to more fully understand and seize control of behavioral options beyond the confines of my past. Thus in beginning repairs to what was broken, I was also initiating construction of what was not.

At the time, it didn't matter that some viewed Transactional Analysis as a faddish and lightweight theory of human behavior for shallow thinkers incapable of fathoming more complex explanations. It didn't matter that TA was discounted because several forgettable versions of the song "Games People Play" were recorded by artists too numerous to mention and too unimportant to remember. It didn't matter that "I'm okay, you're okay" sounded more like the sickeningly sweet, touchy-feely brainchild of a high-on-acid Madison Avenue copywriter than a serious psychological concept. And it certainly didn't matter that once embraced by the "Turn on, tune in, and drop out" Pied Piper of the hippie counterculture Timothy Leary, Transactional Analysis became guilty by association.

All that mattered was that in studying TA, I first realized that behavioral patterns in a personal *and* social sense were not unalterable traits of personality, that counterproductive habits could be overcome, and that *it was even possible* to take greater control of my life. And I was not alone. The two cornerstone books bringing Transactional Analysis to general awareness, *Games People Play* and *I'm OK-You're OK*, each sold millions of copies with the latter volume being on the *New York Times* bestseller's list for almost two years and the former once achieving the nineteenth-longest bestseller run *of all time*.

If needs do indeed motivate behaviors, obviously those books satisfied the needs of countless people seeking enlightenment about their own lives and the world they shared with innumerable others. To that end, inspiring optimism by its "I'm okay, you're okay" core philosophy while prompting greater understanding of and command over one's actions by uncomplicating human behavior, TA's widespread appeal should not be surprising.

After all, since its introduction, several studies have shown a higher degree of effectiveness for Transactional Analysis than for several other therapeutic approaches, and, more generally, numerous other investigations have linked its major principles furthering life control and optimism with enhanced personal effectiveness and physiological well-being. Moreover, despite being initially criticized as offering little to the understanding of human behavior, Transactional Analysis overlaps with and is supported by many long-standing concepts from so-called "established" psychology. To that end, TA is not some superficial and unfounded doctrine one step removed from alchemy or voodoo. Although its conceptual language may be different, *its underlying principles are clearly confirmed by and aligned with widely accepted psychological research and thought.*

Yet perhaps the most persuasive proof of TA's value and effectiveness is neither based on enduring theories nor ivory-tower research. In fact, the most impressive evidence that Transactional Analysis "works" may well be the millions of people across the globe who on a daily basis use its theories to exorcise personal demons, positively navigate relationships, and realistically visualize better tomorrows. Yet whatever the truth of Nietzsche's observation that those dancing are thought insane by those not hearing the music, these innumerable worldwide "dancers" may well be the best evidence that TA's easily understood and elegantly hopeful message that people are OK and can learn to change dysfunctional behaviors rings true.

If fewer things in life are more common than talented people who are unsuccessful, it is equally so that fewer things in life are more common than otherwise healthy people making themselves depressed, ineffective, and unfulfilled. In point of fact, if as our own worst enemies we have the power to make ourselves miserable, we also have the power to make ourselves well or at least better. And as much as anything else, this foundational principle of Transactional Analysis might explain its therapeutic success and why it has touched so many people over so long a time. For if helplessness does indeed lead to pessimism and despair, then greater control over one's life leads to optimism. And it is this optimism, this hope for a better tomorrow, that leads to emotional and physical health. Period.

Enlightenment is a powerful impetus for change. As such, the enlightened realization that change through purposeful self-direction is even feasible may well be among the most powerful motivators of all. Yet as a tool in reaching that understanding, *Transactional Analysis is not, nor is intended to be, a psychological cure-all.* But then again, nothing outside of oneself is. Emotional healing must ultimately come from within.

However, it was only years after gaining this insight, while teaching an introductory course in psychology, that I first realized that Transactional Analysis combined with more "traditional" but related psychological concepts could and should be offered as a type of "self-awareness manual" for anyone seeking greater understanding of human behavior. After all, if studying TA was a turning point in my life, there was no reason to believe that what had been an epiphany for me wouldn't be an equally powerful awakening for untold others. And just as certainly, if in standing on the shoulders of giants who in sharing Transactional Analysis with me became guides for a more fulfilling life, there was a "pay it forward" obligation to return that favor.

As a result, the following pages as an amalgam of personal experience and numerous resources, TA related and otherwise, represent the current, admittedly idiosyncratic, continuously unfolding, and certainly less than omniscient evolution of that realization. Accordingly, some of my insights, definitions, and explanations may not exactly follow generally accepted TA canon. Yet as a behavioral overview thirty years in the making, it is nevertheless offered as an easily traveled gateway for anyone seeking a more fulfilling existence fueled by insight into one's conduct and the conduct of others. In the world of academics, politics, or high finance, knowledge may indeed be power, but whether one is eighteen or eighty, it also provides the impetus for personal growth.

But whether individual development is the focus for my words or whether it becomes a positive side effect of a more general interest in human behavior, if one is an educator what follows can also be taught in part as an immediately accessible and thoroughly practical foundation for a class in general psychology. Or the subsequent material could instead be offered as a standalone course of a semester's duration or with modifications a ten-week elective for exiting high school seniors or incoming college freshmen.

In the end, the expectation is not for anyone reading this book to save the world but rather for those internalizing its self-regulating insights to rethink everything in saving their own more personal universe. And in offering Transactional Analysis as an updated explanation of human behavior long providing awareness and hope to millions of others, the following pages are humbly written as an ever-evolving impetus for the first steps on that journey.

Neil Bright
Catskill Mountains, New York
Summer, 2014

ONE

Setting the Stage

Where the truth is recognized when it is heard, there is then a feeling of exaltation and heightened aliveness, as something within you says: yes. I know this is true.

—Eckhart Tolle

Based on the conviction that current behavior results from adaptations and perceptions that early in life seemed important to our survival but may no longer be valid, Transactional Analysis is a theory dealing with personality, child development, communication between people, personal responsibility, and the maximizing of one's innate potential. Its goal is as powerful as it is straightforward. And that is, through increased awareness of ourselves and others we can positively change by eliminating what isn't working in our lives for the promise of what could be.

Formulated by Eric Berne, this empowering and easily understood explanation of behavior originally used in the treatment of patients undergoing psychotherapy spread to a more mainstream audience initially through the previously mentioned bestselling books *Games People Play* by Berne, published in 1964, and *I'm OK-You're OK* by Thomas Harris, published three years later. Building on concepts of earlier theorists including Sigmund Freud, Alfred Adler, and Abraham Maslow and contributing to the evolution of relatively recent behavioral schools such as Positive Psychology, the basic elements of Transactional Analysis are as relevant today as when they were first developed.

STRUCTURAL ANALYSIS

Structural analysis is the theory of one's unique and enduring character traits or "ways of being." According to TA, these core attributes forming one's personality are divided into three easily identifiable thinking, feeling, and behavioral systems or ego states. Readily observed, clearly differentiated, and always capitalized, these patterns of personality are most simply the Parent, the primary site of one's beliefs; the Child, the location of one's most elemental feelings; and the Adult, the problem-solving center of one's analytical and objective thought. And being grounded in the perceptions people are internalizing and in the behavioral manifestations of that often-hidden world, knowledge of ego states promotes self-understanding in providing explanations for what people are actually experiencing.

More than abstract concepts or superficial metaphors, ego states as common-to-all-mankind experiential absolutes are unrelated to a person's age. Thus in TA terms, a ten-year-old child can act and feel as a Parent or an Adult and a fifty-year-old man or woman can certainly act and feel like a Child. Moreover, just as all people of whatever age have the potential to change, ego states also have the potential to evolve as a result of natural growth and prior events. And this malleability is a good thing. For "change would be impossible if ego states were forever frozen in the form they had at the time of their creation" (Gregoire 2004, 14).

Yet ongoing evolution of ego states is anything but inevitable. That is, "when rigid expectations and beliefs influence representations of the original [ego-creating] experience in such a way that a self-reinforcing system . . . with more or less strong inertia appears," the likelihood for ego state change is reduced (Gregoire 2004, 14). Hence, ego states have the capability to positively adapt to current experiences or selectively interpret those experiences in stubbornly reinforcing the status quo.

Yet in order to foster growth and adaptation, it is essential to acknowledge that even if not immediately apparent, each ego state is endowed with a reservoir of "bound energy." This source of power can unconsciously be moved as "unbound energy" from one ego state to another due to internal or external stimuli or be *consciously directed* to a chosen ego state as "free energy" (Woollams and Brown 1978). And because such choice of direction is only likely when recognizing that direction of choice is even possible, awareness of ego states in oneself and others is an essential precondition for rationally choosing behaviors in effectively responding to circumstances faced every day.

After all, without ego state awareness and an attendant ability to monitor "where one is coming from," as a rudderless ship in a storm at the mercy of stressful currents, we lack conscious control to steer a more satisfactory course. In any case, without knowledge of ego states as an intellectual foundation, a thorough understanding of the following elements of Transactional Analysis would be virtually impossible.

TRANSACTIONAL ANALYSIS

The social aspect of ego state study, transactional analysis, is the examination of how people communicate or "transact" with one another. That is, in our everyday verbal and nonverbal exchanges, how do our ego states interact with the ego states of people we come into contact with? Once understood, this awareness empowers people to change ineffective or destructive transactional patterns in order to more easily avoid misunderstandings leading to the arguments, hurt feelings, and emotional isolation resulting from such failures of communication.

STROKES AND "STAMPS"

In TA, a stroke is a stimulus sent out and received by another person. An exchange of strokes comprises a transaction or communication. Knowledge of stroke importance and more specifically an awareness of the types and potency values of such stimuli can greatly enhance relationships and one's sense of self.

Psychological "stamps" are the good and bad feelings people collect that are later used to justify some action. In the former manifestation, they are legitimately earned psychic rewards for a job well done, and in the latter they are physically, emotionally, and relationally destructive.

GAMES ANALYSIS

Fabricated unconsciously, psychological games are predictable and learned patterns of social maneuvers with underlying messages inexorably leading to unhappy outcomes. And since their repetitive pattern is a signature component of all games, favored ones are passed down and habitually played within families from generation to generation as "comfortably uncomfortable" and, ultimately, toxic ways of relating to others.

Wherever children receive formal instruction in reading, writing, and arithmetic, they are "home-schooled" in the art and practice of psychological game-playing. Accordingly, because of this connection to familiar feelings and their reoccurring function of structuring time, when playing a game, or as the unwitting victim of one, there is a feeling of experiencing it before.

PSYCHOLOGICAL DRIVERS

With feelings of inadequacy and insignificance so much a part of the human condition, psychological drivers are unconsciously prescribed behavioral imperatives diminishing such insecurity. Yet while these "If only I am this or do that" parentally imposed and compulsively followed directives do indeed replace self-doubt with self-confidence, their relief is only temporary. For as with virtually any mood-altering drug, when addicted to drivers without awareness or limits, their emotional and behavioral benefits over time are far exceeded by their costs.

LIFE POSITIONS AND SCRIPTS

Likely internalized in early childhood, a life position is an individual's most basic feelings about him or herself and others. This mindset supports one's script or unconscious personal story both dictating and reinforcing beliefs, attitudes, and patterns of conduct throughout life. Formed in response to parental expectations between the ages of four and seven, this life-plan narrative initially reflects the child's immature understanding of what he or she must do and believe to comply with those directives. And once internalized as behavioral and perceptual absolutes, these script elements resonate throughout life with little thought, challenge, or awareness.

TWO

Rethinking Thinking

It's not what you look at that matters, it's what you see.
—Henry David Thoreau

Because Transactional Analysis is based on changing how people think, it clearly encompasses a cognitive approach for effective living. And since the aim of such a system is to rethink everything in replacing faulty habits of mind with more realistic and healthy patterns of thought, if that focus is to succeed it must begin with understanding that people typically separate into two basic ways of experiencing the world.

EXTERNALS

Externals believe they have little control over what happens to them. They hold that luck, circumstance, or fate shapes their lives and that personal effort and choice make little or no difference. It is this "at the mercy of the environment" orientation that contributes to a sense of helplessness, making wishful "if only" thinking, behavioral drift, habitual scapegoating, and "to do or not to do" indecisiveness likely, if not all but certain.

However, there is still another reason to rethink one's externally oriented perspective and that is such an ongoing sense of impotency is strongly linked to chronic pessimism and correspondingly to despair. This being so, while a relatively minor degree of contemplative pessimism is related to a more accurate sense of present realities than unbridled optimism (Seligman 1991), when otherwise healthy skepticism becomes an ongoing and pervasive backdrop for one's life, results can be devastating.

That this is so should not be surprising. For if one is destined to be "always helpless" with a "Nothing I do matters" attitude, apathy will replace effort and gloom-and-doom passivity will replace a "can do" willingness to strive for betterment. Thus without attending to what needs improving, placing hope that tomorrow will be better on "uncontrollable whims of fate" will likely lead to an endless cycle of failure, pessimism, depression, and further failure. And with success so rare, improvement so unlikely, and hopelessness so constant, the invariable result is a "why bother" sense of demoralization.

But despite such a "glass half empty" mindset, a helpless and hopeless frame of reference, like all thinking, can be rethought. In fact, one of the most significant findings in modern psychology is that individuals can choose the way they think (Seligman 1991). But ironically, what modern psychology has relatively only recently proven was known to the ancient Greek philosopher Epictetus, who just slightly ahead of his time by some two thousand years stated, "People are not disturbed by things, but by the view they take of them."

INTERNALS

Believing they are largely responsible for their own happiness or misery, internals correspondingly maintain a sense of personal responsibility in choosing how they feel. As Eleanor Roosevelt once said, "No one can make you feel inferior without your consent." Hence the mindset of internals is that a person "can only invite and not stimulate in a mechanical sense a particular response in another. In other words, we are in charge of our emotional lives whether or not we choose to recognize it" (Kahler 1977, 227–28).

Thus adopting an "I am responsible" outlook for their behaviors, internals extend empowerment still further in believing that their *reactions* to everyday life are also largely within their own control. This "life is ten percent what happens to me and ninety percent how I respond to it" code of living is the one thing that potentially changes all things. For once accepted, the motivating conclusion can be none other than "one's present as well as one's future largely depends on oneself."

However, it is crucial to understand that this belief in personal accountability should not be transformed into an instrument of self-devaluation when events inevitably don't unfold smoothly, well, or as desired. Emotionally beating oneself up after every bump in the road or even after more significant failures "because everything is my fault" is a dysfunctional perversion of an internally focused mindset. If indeed one can drown in a glass of milk, that something undeniably positive can be transformed into something negative, then recasting self-responsibility as an instrument of self-denigration is a textbook example of such reverse alchemy.

While in an absolute sense we *are* overwhelmingly responsible for our choices, behaviors, and feelings, this mindset must provide a springboard for greater control over life and by extension an enhanced sense of power, optimism, and hope. Yet when an internal frame of reference leads to catastrophizing that when things go badly "I screw up *everything*," that "Things like this *always* happen to me," or that "It will *forever* be this way because I'm a loser," the positive value of taking greater responsibility for one's life is squandered for a going-nowhere existence of pessimism, self-pity, and despair.

As much as if not more than anything else, how we explain our failures to ourselves determines whether we become depressed and apathetic or hopeful and resilient. And far too many of us choose a futility-promoting explanatory style leading to the former result by claiming that life's inevitable failures are everlasting, pervasive, and due to negative and immutable character traits. According to the brilliant work of psychologist Martin Seligman and others, if one were trying to create a recipe for chronic demoralization and giving-up passivity, one could hardly author a better strategy than that.

In the end, when things don't work out it's okay and certainly beneficial to say "I can make better choices," or "Knowing what I knew at the time, making the decision I made was and is understandable," or "I may have failed in this particular situation but will learn from my mistakes," or, most importantly, "I am making myself unhappy, sad, depressed, and so forth by what I'm telling myself." It's destructive and not okay to say "It's me, I'm a failure, everything is falling apart, it will always be that way, and there isn't anything I can do about it."

Constructive change results from believing that when life's inescapable disappointments occur, they are temporary, confined to specific situations, and optimistically within one's internally oriented control to correct, diminish, or, at least, learn from. With that in mind, the more this perspective is cultivated, the greater one's sense of potency. And the greater one's sense of potency, the greater one's optimistically driven persistence in overcoming challenges is likely to be.

It's not that this sense of "can do" optimism associated with internally oriented mindsets inevitably leads to reckless judgments in surmounting life's inevitable challenges. Of course, making important decisions without serious reflection may well transform a relatively small problem into a disaster. In judgments involving large numbers of unknown factors, equally uncertain outcomes, and when the costs of failure are extremely high, a degree of "look before you leap" *thoughtful* pessimism is, of course, necessary.

That said, whether internal or external in outlook, all people make decisions using the same calculus of whether to reject what clearly isn't working and risk "making a bad situation worse" or to rationalize passivity in accepting an "It could be worse" status quo. However, unlike the chronic lack of control, behavioral drift, and "I am helpless" pessimism associated with externals, the tipping point for action in optimistically inclined "what I do matters" internals occurs at far lower levels of discomfort. For them, "doing nothing" when unhappy is rarely, if ever, an option.

Barring a biochemical or genetic abnormality, emotions are largely generated by what we tell ourselves. This "self-talk" based on habitual perceptions about oneself and the world leads to emotional responses. "Although others may create the stimuli for our reactions, it is our interpretation of that objective stimulus that creates our emotional disturbance" (Steinfeld 1998, 193). An event occurs, a person interprets that event, and that person thinks, feels, and acts in accord with that interpretation.

Indeed, many, if not most, people grow up believing that they have little or no control over their behaviors and even less control over their feelings. These beliefs are regularly reinforced by incessant "*You made me . . .*" statements scripted in movies, on television, and virtually everywhere else where taking responsibility for one's thoughts and actions is largely a foreign concept.

The end result is that habitually indulged feelings such as anger, hurt, or victimization strengthened by countless parental transactions and drama during childhood are later in life rationalized as "normal" and even inevitable. Consistent with cognitive therapies such as Transactional Analysis, such reasoning is challenged by thought-provoking questions posed to replace faulty thinking with more realistic beliefs in a process referred to as "cognitive restructuring."

What if rigidly adhered-to assumptions about ourselves and others were irrational or at the least counterproductive? What if interpretations about life "were merely inaccurate assumptions based on distorted views of the relationship between ourselves and the world we were programmed to believe as small children" (Bright 2013, 44)? And what if with relatively little context to compare differing definitions of "normal" during our first years of life, we blindly accepted whatever definitions were offered whatever their harm or aberrance?

Moreover, what if during stressful events we could find peace by intentionally rethinking our thinking to become more of a thoughtful observer of our lives rather than an endlessly brooding victim? What if by changing our explanations for misfortune or failure, depression could be eliminated or greatly diminished? What if Buddha was right in saying "With our thoughts we make the world"? And therefore as a correctable disorder of thinking, what if emotional pain was largely optional?

Must I be loved or liked by everyone? Must people always treat me fairly? Should I always perform well? What if events did not cause our often-negative reactions? What if reactions to events resulted from our faulty understanding of those events based on irrational premises about life? And if unpleasant emotions were really reactions to illogical thoughts and perceptions, if by changing our thoughts we could also change those feelings, what would such control do for the quality of our lives? After all, as Marcus Aurelius so rightly offered, isn't "our life . . . what our thoughts make it"?

But a cognitively oriented therapeutic approach based on the concept that people *feel the way they think* is more than a pithy quote from a long-dead Roman emperor or a line from Hamlet that "There is nothing either good or bad, but thinking makes it so." After millions spent in testing, the National Institute of Mental Health considers cognitive therapy an effective treatment for depression (Seligman 1991) and compared to other verbal procedures for phobias and anxiety disorders, it, "in particular, has fared well in empirically validated treatments" (Jones and Lyddon 2000). To that end, one such cognitive approach helping people to eliminate irrational thought patterns in order to view the world more realistically was formulated concurrently with TA in the 1950s.

RATIONAL EMOTIVE THERAPY (RET)

In pioneering with Transactional Analysis, a reason-empowered therapeutic design, RET posits that illogical and counterproductive self-talk rather than past events is the primary cause of guilt, anxiety, or depression. That is, emotional responses and their attendant behaviors primarily result not from deeply rooted unconscious conflicts or even from recently experienced unpleasant events but from one's idiosyncratic and often irrational "bad thinking" concerning those events. With that in mind, both Rational Emotive Behavior Therapy and Transactional Analysis focus on helping persons "realize how they have largely created their own disturbances, and then to help them learn how they can create their own changes" (Ball 1978, 19).

While conceptually both approaches also accept the importance of childhood events and current influences on behavior, and both see emotions, thinking, and overall conduct as a unified "package" that people can learn to responsibly control, RET presents a series of thinking approaches unique to that construct. Developed by psychologist Albert Ellis, with a philosophical assist from Epictetus, the most commonly offered of these approaches is the "A-B-C model" of linking unpleasant events with equally unpleasant feelings.

To clarify, troubling or self-defeating feelings are typically elicited by an "activating adversity," or an "A," that triggers an "unrealistic and often habitually accepted belief," or "B," that is immediately followed by an unpleasant "emotional consequence," or "C." And as the most easily controllable element of the A-B-C triad is the unrealistic Parent-centered belief about adversity, Adult awareness in eliminating that connection between the originating experience and its Child-based emotional result changes that depressively "inevitable" consequence. Or, in distilling this truth even further, Cervantes noted: "Take away the cause and the effect ceases."

However, the first step in decoupling that sequence is gaining awareness of commonly held irrational convictions leading to their predictably unpleasant outcomes. Often associated with the Rational Emotive approach, such illogical, counterproductive, and often unconscious mainstays of internal dialogue include:

- I must be liked by everyone.
- I must always perform perfectly.
- If I am rejected, then I am unworthy.
- People must always treat me fairly.
- If I work hard enough, success is guaranteed.
- It is catastrophic when things are not the way I want them to be.
- Something once adversely affecting me must continue doing so.

An example of this behavioral approach that many people can identify with is being sent a proverbial "Dear John" letter of romantic repudiation. Amplifying already-existent self-doubts and undermining already-fragile egos, such a missive is soon followed by feelings of inadequacy at best and severe depression at worst. However, was that painful rejection the irresistible catalyst for transforming "someone doesn't like me" into "I don't like myself," or was the actual origin of that self-deprecating conversion an illogical and *controllable* interpretation of the experience? Yet once one recognizes that emotions are the *effect* of thoughts rather than their ultimate source, there can be little doubt how to answer that question.

Simply put, the activating adversity "A," the letter, resulted in the unrealistic belief "B" of being unworthy and/or that "I must be liked be everyone," which in turn stimulated the emotional consequence "C" of despondency. Conventional wisdom to the contrary, "A" did not directly cause "C." The melancholia was the result of "B," the illogical belief that rejection is evidence of worthlessness. Thus by understanding this connection and replacing the unreasonable belief with more realistic thinking, over time the unpleasant emotional reaction is eliminated or at the very least diminished.

Another all-too-common illustration of the A-B-C theory might be "road rage" provoked by the actions of a tailgating and "irresponsibly reckless" driver nearly causing a high-speed accident. Obviously, the narrowly avoided car crash was the activating experience, or "A," which resulted in the emotional consequence of seemingly justifiable fury, or

"C," fueled by the unsubstantiated belief that the offensive driver must be "some idiot kid" or "some guy high on drugs."

Yet while few would criticize a reflexive show of anger resulting from such a life-and-limb threatening close call, what if the "irresponsibly reckless" driver was neither a "live forever" teenager nor someone with a taste for cocaine? What if the incautious driver was a thoughtful and otherwise responsible son on his way to the bedside of his dying mother? What if he was a distraught parent following an ambulance to the hospital after his child was knocked unconscious during a high school football game? Or what if he was an off-duty police officer summoned to a hostage crisis where time was of the essence? And while it could be argued that none of these scenarios excuses careless driving, wouldn't at least knowing the reason for such an "outrageous" action change one's beliefs about its cause and resultantly its emotional consequence?

The A-B-C theory notwithstanding, is it really so that we disturb ourselves through faulty thinking? Many people raised in a world where scapegoating is too much the rule and too little the exception will insist that one "has to" feel a certain way in response to a particular event. If so, and one really doesn't have a choice in thinking and, as a result, feeling a certain way, then the central premise of internals is flawed.

Yet that is clearly not so. What we tell ourselves *is* a learned behavior. And because what has been learned can be unlearned, we have far more emotional and behavioral choices than we may think. Accordingly, at least in a philosophical if not always in a practical sense, the potential for personal control is undeniable. *For if we are not ultimately in control of our thoughts, who is?* Surely, you have far more power than you believe. We all do.

People are born with infinite possibilities in how to think, how to react to events, and, as a result, how to feel in response to those events. Yet over time, in seeking a predictable world, we come to believe that there is only one way to respond to experiences. However, in doing so our birthright of limitless behavioral choice becomes an incremental inability to view situations with an open mind, and as a result, it is not uncommon for people to stridently insist that they *had* to act and feel a certain way.

But if this were so, then everybody would act similarly in response to a particular stimulus. However, since this is obviously not so, one's unique perceptions actually dictate one's unique responses. "The perceived world is not 'out there' immutably independent of one's distinctive consciousness in interpreting that reality" (Bright 2013, 49). That is, "the environment cannot unilaterally cause particular changes in an organism. If it could, that would endorse the notion of universal causality, . . . [which] in nature . . . never occurs" (Loria 2003, 193–94; Dell 1986, 516).

In an absolute sense, the environment does not in and of itself dictate responses but rather provides opportunities for each person to construct his or her own interpretations. And because perceptions, like so many things, are indeed in the eye of the beholder, *it is not what we look at that matters—it's what we see*. Believing otherwise is to maintain that we all experience works of art, events, one another, and the entire world exactly the same way. Irrefutably, that is not so. Choice exists, and the only reason many people don't choose positively more often is that habitually enslaved by their self-limiting perceptions, they often don't realize that options even exist.

> If the same wave hits two children playing at the beach and one starts crying and the other begins laughing, how could this be if there wasn't a choice in response? A football team winning ten games after winning only one game the previous season results in fan celebrations and talk of future Super Bowls. Yet the same stimulus, a 10-6 record for a perennial powerhouse team, results in depression and finger-pointing criticism from fans. How could this be if there wasn't a choice in how to respond? (Bright 2013, 49–50)

Likewise, "a sixty-degree day in January results in Floridians donning thick sweaters. Yet the same stimulus, the temperature, results in Vermonters seeing evidence of global warming and marveling about a winter's heat wave. How could this be unless how one sees the world prompts one's responses to it?" (Bright 2013, 50) Depending on individual differences—a tragedy occurs, a lottery ticket wins, a car stalls, or a job promotion is given—all result in at least somewhat different responses. To that end, would such variation be even possible if there was only one way to interpret reality?

> Yet even if believing how something is viewed depends primarily on past history and present context, in accepting control over one's thoughts, doesn't one also control how a situation is viewed, *whatever its context?* And if there still is doubt about the power and possibility of perceptual choice, how then can a situation be perceived *by the same person* one way today and far differently tomorrow? After all, who hasn't experienced a "What was I thinking?" change in mindset upon personal reflection, advice from a friend, or even a good night's sleep? (Bright 2013, 50)

"Each of us has the task each morning to recreate the universe from our central focus and this responsibility is unavoidable. Unfortunately, we tend to be habit-ridden and do the same lousy job every morning" (Barnes 1977, 19). Even though we are thus frequently our own worst enemies, the power to recurrently inflict self-imposed pain can also be our salvation. For as John Milton said, the same mind that "can make a hell of heaven" can also make "a heaven of hell."

In daily life, paradise can be perceptually gained in much the same way as it can be lost. "To that end, if we accept that we are primarily responsible for our misery through self-defeating perceptions, we can also accept that we are just as responsible for our joy by learning to change how we view the world and each other" (Bright 2013, 50).

Simply put, the power to decide one way of looking at ourselves and others is the same power to redecide those perceptions. Undeniably, "we alone exercise the choice to retain our old decisions or make new ones, . . . [and] no matter how much we may try, we cannot blame our behavior on anyone but ourselves" (Woollams and Brown 1978, 2). However, if one still has doubts about whether we or others have control over our thoughts, feelings, and actions, wouldn't it be wise to accept the mindset that is more likely to get us where we want to go in life? And inarguably, that mindset is to embrace an internally oriented greater sense of personal responsibility, power, and control.

However, having said that perceptions and feelings *can* be changed is not to imply that such rethinking is easy. In all fairness, because the positive and negative emotions of others "have energy associated with them which sets up a field of influence which . . . is received by people in its physical vicinity," it *is* difficult to withstand such forces (Steiner 1984, 141).

Additionally, it should not be assumed that once we learn a new set of internal sentences resulting in more effective living that regression to a less-in-control perceptual framework cannot occur. To suggest that any behavior, however detrimental and reinforced for a decade or more, can quickly be extinguished, never to return, is to engage in magical thinking.

Even as a child, learning to hit a baseball, play a musical instrument, or write a book report did not result in immediate and everlasting success. Why should it be any different for an adult learning new ways of thinking? Especially for negatively oriented atypical events, setbacks may well occur, resulting in a downward spiral of regret, self-condemnation, or despair.

Even for veteran internals, an unforeseen tragedy can trigger an emotional tailspin. Traumatic events such as a relationship's end, the loss of a job, or the death of a loved one will still likely result in depression. However, for most of us, such tragedies are thankfully not commonplace. As such, it is for the more ordinary everyday hassles that practice accepting responsibility for our internal world will result in a lessening of emotional pain. And then even when tragedy inevitably occurs, such a history of controlling one's internal dialogue *will almost certainly* result in a far quicker return to a greater sense of acceptance, if not well-being. "The good news is that though we cannot stop the bad feelings from coming, we can keep them from staying" (Harris and Harris 1985, 2).

In the final analysis, becoming a happier and more effective person, although not always easy to accomplish, is simple to understand. Unlike psychoanalysis, TA and other predominantly cognitive therapies are not as concerned with the historical antecedents of current and often dysfunctional behaviors as with one's ongoing self-talk leading to those behaviors.

Without necessarily knowing the exact cause of a patient's illness, "Berne wanted to be like a surgeon who precisely cuts out the offending lesion, thereby allowing the body to heal itself" (Woollams and Brown 1978, 206). Yet because other than for the most primitive fight or flight responses, cognition precedes feelings, identifying and eliminating such "lesions" of negative internal sentences is an essential prerequisite for emotional health. It is these perceptual wounds that fill the interval between an initial thought and a "no choice but to feel that way" reaction. It is in this gap that lies one's control to choose happiness over pain, joy over depression, and peace over anger. And recognizing this undeniable and centering truth is the first step toward exercising that freedom.

THREE

Connecting What Was To What Is

The dogmas of the quiet past are inadequate to the stormy present . . . as our case is new, so we must think anew and act anew.

—Abraham Lincoln

As you observe people, you can easily notice that their personalities are really made up of three separate parts. As mentioned, these ego states individually represent a group of clearly defined and observable feelings and behaviors unique to each person. Capitalized, the three ego states of Parent, Adult, and Child are "produced by the playback of recorded data of events in the past, involving real people, real times, real places, real decisions, and real feelings" (Harris 1973, 40).

For example, if you accidentally back into another car in a parking lot and are feeling guilty and more than a little depressed, your feelings are "coming on" from your Child ego state. If you engage in self-talk that is critical of your carelessness, that is your Parent ego state. And if you thoughtfully and unemotionally decide how to handle this problem, your Adult ego has been activated.

It is of little doubt that our ego states are embedded in each of us as young children. Indeed, this concept that one's childhood has a significant and often enduring impact on adult life, that in Wordsworth's verse "the child is the father of the man," is a theme consistent with much of psychological thought. However, for Eric Berne the proof of this link between our past and present, the confirmation that our memories are categorized as ego states, and the evidence that "our history follows us around like a patient dog . . . dropping long white hairs on the carpet of life" (Harris and Harris 1985, 2) was perhaps initially realized in a medical school classroom in 1951. For it was there at McGill University in Canada that he was first exposed to the experiments of Dr. Wilder Penfield, a neurosurgeon and instructor at the school.

Noted for his groundbreaking work in memory mechanisms, when Penfield touched the exposed brains of his surgical patients under local anesthesia with a weak electrical current transmitted through a probe, they reported experiencing a vivid and verifiable remembrance of a past event. Moreover, these specific recollections artificially stimulated by the electrical probe also evoked feelings inextricably linked to that remembrance so that the experience was a relived "reproduction of what the patient saw and heard and felt and understood" (Harris 1973, 27; Penfield 1952). That is, once the memory was induced, so too was the emotion originally experienced. Thus inescapably joined as a biochemical "package deal," one could neither be elicited nor recollected without the other.

No matter how often a single location on the brain's surface was touched, the probe activated an unchanging and "single recollection, not a mixture of memories or a generalization" (Harris 1973, 27). And this involuntarily occurred whether patients chose to elicit the memory or not, and even if without artificial stimulation the recollection had long since been forgotten. To the young medical student Eric Berne, the implications of these "forced reexperiencing" experiments were instrumental to the later development of Transactional Analysis and more particularly to structural analysis, the theory of ego states.

Metaphorically, the Penfield experiments provided evidence that our brain acts like a two-track tape recorder, chemically imprinting without editing every conscious experience of our lives *and* recording the original emotions forever linked to those events at the time of their occurrence. As a result, somewhere in the brain of each of us there is an inerasable, "continuous, ongoing record of the stream of consciousness [of everything entering our awareness] from birth to death" (Milner 1977, 1375). And now, some sixty years after Penfield's original research, additional evidence spearheaded by a neurobiology professor at the University of California also suggests that this may indeed be the case.

For little more than the past five years, Dr. James McGaugh has been studying a handful of individuals demonstrating a kind of memory that until very recently was virtually unknown to science. Exhibiting "superior autobiographical memory," these fifty (or so) people can recall virtually any date in their lives the way most of us can remember yesterday *and* "they can tell you what they were doing that day, the day of the week, sometimes even the weather—all within seconds" ("Memory Wizards," *60 Minutes*, April 20, 2014).

But there is more to this story than what some might call the cerebral gymnastics of a parlor trick mentalist or what others more seriously would label as an ability common to some forms of savantism. And that is, in recalling past experiences these so-called "memory wizards" can not only accurately retrieve events from their distant past, but in doing so they *emotionally relive them as well*. As such, with no greater memory for nonpersonally related events than anyone else, these extraordinary few can willfully access, that is "play," their "two-track memory recordings" without the induced stimulation of an electrical probe or any other artificially delivered catalyst.

Yet what this research also implies is that in a sense these "wizards" may not be so wizardly after all. That is, they are likely not at all unusual in the ability to record memories and their associated feelings but only in their "gift" to recall them at will. Thus, supporting the work of Penfield, the studies of McGaugh and others at least initially suggest that as a naturally occurring phenomenon, *all people* internally archive memories and their corresponding emotions in much the same way. But although such two-dimensional "neural files" are there for each of us, the vast majority of people don't have or simply can't launch the on-demand structural "programs" within their brains to intentionally open them ("Memory Wizards," *60 Minutes*, April 20, 2014). As a result, for better or worse, most of humanity must wait for external stimuli to randomly summon long-forgotten memories and the emotions forever associated with them rather than voluntarily inciting their arousal.

But arguably the larger point of the aforementioned research is that because our brains seem to categorize similar events, daily experiences resembling past happenings are likely classified together in spontaneously triggering thoughts and feelings from our cerebral "archives" that are often inappropriate in light of today's reality. Thus in reflexively connecting what was with what is, "you construct reality . . . with memories and emotions orbiting your sensations and cognition; together they form a collage of consciousness that exists only in your skull" (McRaney 2011, 6).

Seemingly supported by McGaugh, Penfield's conclusion was simple yet profound. The brain records, recalls, and *relives* all that it has attended to (Harris 1973). And no less simple or profound, the young Eric Berne thus concluded that "memories are retained in their natural form as ego states" (Berne 1961, xvii), and continuing to exist throughout life, these "relics" under certain circumstance can be revived (Berne 1961). That is, exposed to categorically similar contemporary experiences, a person emotionally relives "a scene or situation from the past with all its multidimensional components and without losing contact with the here and now" (Gregoire 2004, 11).

Furthermore, because brain cells unlike other cells are relatively permanent, our past experiences and those feelings associated with those experiences remain intact long after they occur and are available for replay long after the precipitating event is no longer remembered. With that in mind, as an unavoidable result of everyday life these feelings periodically reemerge in response to daily events much like an unseen stalker whose presence is never far away.

Referred to in general psychology as "priming," a previously experienced stimulus can profoundly influence the way one behaves, thinks, and perceives current reality. Often defined more immediately when, for example, learning a new word and shortly thereafter noticing many previously unseen references to it, a form of priming can also increase sensitivity to events or experiences over far longer periods of time. Accordingly, what parents do and say and their child's emotions linked to those statements and actions forever embedded as protein "recordings" in their children's brains "primes" who they are, how they experience the world, and who they will become.

But just as past experiences prime responses to current reality, contemporary happenings can reverse that flow by emotionally returning us to an earlier time. And as an experiential form of Penfield's probe, this phenomenon of present-day events spontaneously stimulating the brain's preserved "recordings" in triggering long forgotten thoughts and feelings is known in Transactional Analysis as rubberbanding.

This being so, currently experienced stimuli such as music, tastes, odors, and events can set in motion a biochemical time machine, sending us back even into childhood by generating previously unrecalled thoughts and feelings linked to those stimuli. But rubberbanding often has a far more powerful and negative impact on our adult lives than simply reexperiencing anxiety from the first day of school, during the first day at a new job, or the rush of romantic emotions when unexpectedly hearing "our song" years after a love relationship linked to that tune no longer exists.

Reflexively reliving early childhood feelings of inadequacy in response to a present-day event such as a disagreement with a spouse or criticism from an authority figure may be intellectually irrational at best and counterproductive at worst, *yet the impact of such bygone "recordings" is no less real*. Lambasting ourselves for current mistakes as repeat performances from long ago when failing to please our parents, prejudicial loathing learned as children upon seeing an ethnically or racially dissimilar person today, or excessive fear during a presentation based on performance "failures" early in life are all examples of how archival "recordings" in our brains can make us prisoners of our pasts. Clearly, however priming is defined, however rubberbanding displays itself, and however erstwhile emotions are evoked in the present, "our thoughts and our behavior are influenced, much more than we know or want, by the environment of the moment" (Kahneman 2013, 128).

But that is certainly not the least of our "back to the future" problems. Perhaps more than any other emotion, an exaggerated, immobilizing, and counterproductive sense of rubberbanded guilt haunts us in response to relatively minor daily happenings. Virtually any current misdeed, nonperformance, or indiscretion can transport us back to childhood when parents may have played the "guilt card" whenever we supposedly disappointed, disgraced, or failed them.

A relatively insignificant remark, accident, or negligence today can unsettle one's equilibrium and send him or her spiraling into the past where "We sacrificed for you," "You should be ashamed of yourself," or "What will the neighbors think?" parental comments preceded punishment, a loss of affection, a "Get out of my sight" directive, or a bout of self-loathing. And when rubberbanded guilt, anger, frustration, or hurt creates a period of time when a past event "disturbs normal patterns [of behavior] for an appreciable period" (Berne 1973, 263), it is known as "after-burn."

But guilt-inspired anguish or depression is a learned response that can be unlearned. All the guilt in the world cannot rewrite history. It is one thing to pledge greater care in avoiding the behaviors leading to this largely futile emotion, but it is quite another to waste precious moments sinking into despair and feeling guilty about an event that by any definition is unchangeable.

While true that long-ago recordings in the brain remain and are available for current activation, new imprints empowering greater freedom to choose thoughts and emotions can overlay the old with more effective ways to experience contemporary reality. And only in reacting to the world by accepting that behavioral choice is even possible can maladaptive responses be monitored, counterproductive replies be replaced by more effective self-talk, and the old ways of thinking, feeling, and doing be dismantled forever. Once done, "the world begins to look, sound, [and] feel different, and as the person reacts differently, the world reacts differently towards the person and so on into healthy natural behavior" (Novey 1980, 138).

That current experiences have the power to emotionally transport us back to an earlier time is thus beyond doubt. And what is equally beyond doubt is that the Transactional Analysis identification of this phenomenon as "rubberbanding" was predated by experiments of a Russian Nobel Prize winner more than sixty years earlier.

It is well known that in the 1890s Ivan Pavlov in studying the digestive process in dogs noticed that the mere sight or sound of food was enough to stimulate their salivation. Taking this stimulus-response connection a step further, he began a series of experiments by ringing a tuning fork and then immediately placing meat powder on the tongues of his dogs.

After this was done a few times, Pavlov noticed that salivation would begin as soon as the tuning fork was rung, *even in the absence of food*. And though such stimulus-response links had been observed before, Pavlov was arguably the first to appreciate their significance that throughout life we are greatly affected by initially unconnected stimuli producing involuntary responses such as joy, sadness, fear, guilt, and, yes, even salivation. This learning process of unconsciously substituting one stimulus for another to evoke an involuntary reaction has come to be known as classical conditioning.

What Pavlov recognized was that any initially neutral stimulus (e.g., the sound of a tuning fork) could over time elicit an otherwise unrelated response (e.g., salivation) if regularly presented just before the stimulus (e.g., food) that normally induced that response. And when continually repeated over time, such stimulus-response connections are not easily extinguished. Thus every day the environment presents us with events similar enough to the original experiences as to involuntarily trigger emotional and physical "rubberbanded" replies not directly elicited by those daily occurrences but, as classically conditioned, spontaneously retrieved from our often long-forgotten pasts.

As a result, adult anxiety in a doctor's office has as much to do with the sights, sounds, and smells of the examination room, unconsciously and forever linked to deeply embedded childhood fears experienced during routine and long-ago checkups, as any current health-related concerns. Or a message that "The boss wants to see you at the end of the day" is often enough to summon an anxiety-fueled spiral without any objective reason to fret other than the past and largely forgotten "Wait 'til your father hears about this" memories of being "a bad little boy or girl" after a poor report card, a fight with a neighbor's child, or accidently breaking Aunt Minnie's prized heirloom vase.

Moreover, adult feelings of untroubled youthful innocence may also be aroused by watching a game of catch between a father and son as portrayed in the movie *Field of Dreams*. The carefree joy of family vacations during childhood can be reawakened by the sight of sand and the smell of ocean when visiting the beach as an adult. And anxious childhood feelings of leaving the "safety" of home in returning to school after a vacation can be induced as an adult on Sunday evenings with a "back to the salt mines of work" potency often having little or nothing to do with one's current job-related stress or unhappiness.

And though rubberbanding typically refers to the power of a current stimulus to trigger long-forgotten feelings, while emotions associated with classical conditioning may have been encoded far more recently than that, the two processes are much the same. As such, for either phenomenon it is the environment that "acts upon" the individual and not the other way around.

But, there is another form of learning involving an individual's voluntary choices. And unlike classical conditioning where the environment influences the person, for "operant conditioning" the reverse is true. That is, the subject "operates" on the environment by making conscious choices to achieve desired, if not always desirable, ends.

Thus in classical conditioning, behavior is *elicited*, while in operant conditioning behavior is *emitted*. Put another way, operant conditioning is a learning process in which the probability of repeating a behavior is determined by the consequences of that behavior. As a result, much of our behavior is strongly actuated by one's history of rewards and punishments.

Yet simply choosing one's behavior hardly guarantees that choices will ultimately be in one's best interests. At the very least, this is so because one's choices may be based on inaccurate or incomplete information. Or one's history may have ignored, discouraged, or even punished beneficial behavior and encouraged or even rewarded actions that were detrimental.

However, there is perhaps a more important reason why "voluntary" choice does not ensure positive results. And that reason is that what appears to be discretionary choice may not be so intentional after all. This is so because many emotions and their associated actions result from unconscious forces that often dictate less-than-optimal results.

Thus the vast majority of people make "free-willed" choices that are not so free, and depending on environmental stimuli, they will shift from one ego state to another without much thought as to which would be most effective or even appropriate. The reason for this is simple. Most people are not aware that daily events spontaneously stimulate changes in their "recorded" ego states, and even if they did recognize these clearly defined behavioral changes, they almost certainly would not believe that one can learn to make a conscious and deliberate choice to activate one part of their personality over another.

But such naysayers are indisputably wrong. For if learning to make better choices was not possible, personal growth could not occur, hope for a better life would be a waste of time, and the entire science of psychology, TA focused or otherwise, would have little or no value.

Recognizing the behaviors and the ego state language often associated with those behaviors empowers an individual to make conscious choices in solving problems more effectively, choosing direction over drift, taking responsibility over inaction, and opting for greater happiness over distress. Additionally, because one's ego state will largely determine the ego state of people one comes into contact with, knowledge of each state cannot help but to improve one's relationships.

The simple truth is that in order to formulate goals in how to live one's life, we must first acknowledge that however potent our past may be, it is not inevitably our destiny. Choice *is* possible. And understanding ego states within the larger framework of Transactional Analysis makes the promise of that choice an attainable reality.

FOUR

Understanding the Parent Ego State

No matter how far we come, our parents are always in us.

—Brad Meltzer

The Parent ego state is the location of beliefs about ourselves and the world absorbed from our parents, other emotionally significant figures, older siblings, and even television shows we watched during early childhood. And because our parents are no less reflections of *their* childhood caregivers, what is modeled for children is also a reproduction of attitudes, beliefs, prejudices, mannerisms, and coping strategies passed down from grandparents and, inevitably, even further back than that. Hardly a comforting thought for most people, one's Parent thus represents a behavioral mosaic at least two generations behind the times.

But regardless of who provides its initial influence, the Parent is likely to be modestly fine-tuned through early adulthood and beyond as behaviors are internalized from teachers, coaches, bosses, and all other relevant sources, including "truths" gleaned from parenting one's own children. Similar to Freud's superego, this massive and unique collection of perceptions and behaviors regularly manifests itself in our all-too-often self-righteous traditions, values, preconceptions, opinions, and conduct.

Figuratively a "microchip implant with recorded external messages" (Steiner 2003, 179), the Parent ego state is fundamentally the conditioned reproduction of what a child saw and heard caregivers do and say when very young. And as for the Child ego state, unless a conscious Adult choice is made to update Parent messages, what was recorded, incessantly replayed as "voices in one's head," and continually reinforced during childhood remains a resistant-to-change core force dictating what is "normal" in viewing ourselves and the world we live in. Thus however much an objective and active Adult winnows valuable from invalid caregiver-imposed beliefs and conduct, one's Parent will still at least occasionally express itself in our code of ethics, explanatory styles for success or failure, behaviors toward others, *and* in prompting child-like compliance, rebellion, or withdrawal in ourselves.

As mentioned previously, it's not that it's impossible for the Parent, or for that matter the Child ego state to change after the social birth age of five. It's just that by then, the child's experiences have primarily been repeat performances of what has been heard, seen, felt, and reinforced countless times before. As such, the only way the inerasable Parent or Child recordings can be edited is by "turning [their] volume down by reason of newly developed Adult awareness and choice" (Holloway 1977, 183).

But that's easier said than done because the vast majority of people lack awareness that such revision is necessary *or even conceivable*. As a result, the unaltered Parent and Child states remain relatively intact as predictable, largely unchanging, and often ineffective perceptual constellations of how the world works.

Thus however difficult it may be to do, and as most people are unaware that it needs to be done, the fact that the Parent requires Adult editing is beyond doubt. Other than the sources for one's Parent are themselves flawed, this is so for at least two reasons. At a minimum, parental "must do" behaviors and "no doubt" beliefs are recorded "raw" without initially even questioning their accuracy, benefit, or morality. And secondly, the reliability of this likely faulty view of reality is further compromised because whatever "truth" has been recorded is inevitably a subjectively filtered, distorted, and likely mistaken *interpretation* of parental words and actions through the eyes of a child rather than a precisely accurate account of what was actually said, done, and the rationale for either.

This is so because small children don't understand intense and often punitive parental responses after running into the street, handling a knife, "exploring" an electrical outlet, or lighting a match. Likewise, in seeking consistency, they don't understand that what is often true may not always be so when parents insisting on honesty exaggerate a story, when demanding respect for the law exceed the speed limit, and when requiring "proper language" curse in frustration if an appliance doesn't work or a toe is stubbed.

Moreover, children record and interpret parental actions without backstory knowledge of what caused even questionable conduct. So a parent's seemingly too critical, too punitive, or too detached behavior toward their child, even if traumatic, may have far less to do with the youngster's transgressions than with a job lost, bills unpaid, a friend's illness, or a marriage dissolving. Thus as an amalgam of beliefs, attitudes, and behaviors used to navigate through life, the Parent, for most people, is likely thrice flawed as faulty information, forwarded by imperfect caregivers, originally perceived inaccurately.

Yet early in childhood, the doubtful validity of many parental messages paired with the probable unreliability of their "recorded" transcription hardly matters. For to the relatively helpless and dependent child, presumably omnipotent parents are "magical" people who, in defining reality, seem to know everything. All powerful, they are "six feet tall at a time when it is important to the two-foot-tall child that he please and obey them" (Harris 1973, 43).

Besides, if even supposedly thoughtful and otherwise aware adults are exposed to inaccurate, immoral, or counterproductive "truths" often enough they tend to be believed; children are even more susceptible to such blind faith acceptance. This is so because as an evolutionarily programmed fact since "survival prospects are poor for an animal not suspicious of novelty" (Kahneman 2013, 67), whatever has been frequently repeated and is now familiar will more likely be accepted. And considering that the messages a child receives in the home are far less varied and therefore more familiar than those an adult encounters in the wider world, there is little likelihood that such proclamations will initially be rejected or even doubted. After all, if it is true that to a protozoa in a drop of water the world is water, to a young child in a dysfunctional home that too is all they know.

Clearly, when the life of a child begins so needful of parental regard just in order to live, it's almost impossible for them not to deify their caregivers and to reflexively assume the imposed truth of their endlessly repeated behaviors and pronouncements. And since as a matter of continued survival it seemingly becomes essential for the child to please his or her caregivers, the Parent becomes an instructional manual on what must be thought, believed, and done to accomplish that end. For this reason and because most young children as yet have not significantly experienced any worlds other than their own, they unquestioningly accept the accuracy of the parental universe they are presented with as their "normal."

Thus as parents we indicate to children "how it is: [and] they take up their positions in the space we define." But there is often a self-limiting danger in that definition. And that is that "they may then choose to become a fragment of that fragment of their possibilities we indicate for them" (Steiner 1974, 73; Laing 1971).

Additionally, because children, and for that matter adults, seek a predictable world, once "normal" for beliefs and behaviors is firmly established, incoming data challenging that narrative is likely ignored, distorted, or rationalized as unconvincing. As a result, an initially constructed frame of reference is often maintained no matter how objectively absurd or counterproductive it may be.

This frequently inaccurate, at times toxic, and almost always enduring view of the self and the world passed to the child through parental statements and actions that is originally accepted without question is one's "assumptive reality." Often referred to as an individual's "psychological baggage," this collection of ideas, attitudes, and behaviors existing in one's Parent ego state without editing or updating is, when damaging, figuratively spread to children and ultimately from one generation to the next through "mind viruses" known as memes (Dyer 2009).

From the Greek word for imitation, memes are a general term for toxic thoughts, beliefs, attitudes, or prejudices unconsciously transmitted much like a microbe through mimicry of parents, friends, siblings, and cultural norms. Since the core purpose of viruses is to replicate by contaminating uninfected hosts, early in life each of us has been "infected" with an often-false reality about ourselves and others that, as future carriers for our own children, we spread still further throughout the population. Obvious examples of memes include reflexive intolerance directed toward dissimilar groups or, more personally, thinking that one is destined to always be poor, unlucky, unhealthy, unsuccessful, persecuted, or whatever fill-in-the-blank adverse outcomes memes have preordained.

From a Transactional Analysis perspective, the transmission of memes is metaphorically referred to as the "Hot Potato Game." Named after the childhood pastime of playing music while tossing a supposedly hot potato back and forth between two or more players, the game ends when the music stops and the child holding the spud "loses." So, too, parents and other authority figures (e.g., relatives, teachers, clergyman, and even therapists) can, as "donors," transfer maladaptive feelings, ideas, phobias, obsessions, and compulsions to innocent recipients who then internalize the "hot potato" as their own (English 1998).

As an infected baton in a relay race, chronic depression, hostility, anger, fear, or hatred for certain religious and ethnic groups may be mindlessly passed to innocent others. Or "hot potatoes" may even be directives to perform a future task, to succeed "at all costs," or to take revenge on certain other individuals, families, or groups (English 1996). Slightly different than more broadly defined memes that may be culturally forwarded, the transmission of "hot potatoes" is typically an unconsciously motivated family affair where as part of a perversely oriented "You gain what I lose" zero sum game, the vulnerable target assumes the pathologies its donor self-servingly seeks to unload.

As a modern version of alleviating curses once commonly practiced in voodoo or human sacrifice, the psychological version of the "Hot Potato Game" has the same purely egocentric purpose today. That is, at least in theory, "by passing on to a recipient their personal curses of anxiety, depressive feelings, insanity, or suicidal or murderous intentions, [donors] feel they can liberate themselves of them" (English 1998, 11). As absurd as it sounds, "donors operate with the magic assumption that they can rid themselves of whatever frustrations, fears, guilt feelings, or irrational compulsions they carry by passing on such torments to someone else, just as someone gets rid of the potato in the children's game by passing it on" (English 1996, 124–25).

But whether donors are actually able to completely relieve or eliminate their afflictions is highly doubtful; spreading contagion is more certain when victims are passively dependent like a child or highly suggestible like a blind faith cult disciple. Moreover, in such unequal power relationships, donors may gain added benefits in playing benevolent rescuers by lavishing sympathy, support, and protective attention on their now "infected" targets while continuing to emotionally poison them as newly minted Typhoid Mary "carriers" of pathological behaviors to unsuspecting others.

Difficult to eliminate because memes at least in part become who we think we are, they often dictate an inner dialogue prophesizing one's destiny, which may include persecution, addiction, or failure. And although Eric Berne's aphorism that "people are born princes and princesses until their parents turn them into frogs" may not be universally true, it is true enough.

But whatever a youngster's fate authored by "hot potatoes" or memes, these "infections" are supplemented by parent-authored descriptions defining who the child is and who they likely will become. These early labeling messages or attributions are enormously powerful because "research shows that young people who are attributed with . . . characteristics develop them" (Barrow, Bradshaw, and Newton 2001, 63; Dieser 1997). Thus whether positive, negative, growth-promoting, or growth-inhibiting, attributions create the self-talk that increases the likelihood that a child throughout life will move along a certain path.

Indeed, as self-fulfilling "statements of fact," attributions may well be "the most common, as well as the most . . . powerful way script messages are given" (Woollams and Brown 1978, 157). This is so because attributions tell a child not what to be but, in order to stay in the parent's favor, *what he is* (Steiner 1974; Laing 1971). And what a child is told he or she is fosters an adaptive and self-fulfilling response of what he or she will become.

Once a parent programs a youngster into believing such labels as "You are stupid," or "You are just like Uncle Harry who never amounted to anything," or, far more positively, "You are a good person," certain behaviors become more likely and others become less probable. This is so because unless we generate the reality that is congruent with who and what we think we are, the gap between our beliefs and conduct results in emotional discomfort known as cognitive dissonance.

Avoiding such inconsistency-based distress from an action and identity disconnect, children unconsciously foster cognitive ease by becoming whoever their labels tell them they are. Thus as plants grow toward light, children "live to their labels" in growing toward attributions. As a result, however parents define their children, as "useless," "tolerant," "disgusting," or "clever," continues as a self-perpetuating logic ultimately dictating how the child thinks, feels, acts, and relates.

Virtually everything a parent does influences how a child ultimately experiences the world. Thus initially, the child is largely a "tabula rasa," or blank slate that parental actions write on in amplifying or diminishing genetically predisposed characteristics of temperament. And even more important is the consequent realization that because a child largely co-opts parental beliefs and behaviors, the impact of those actions, both good and bad, is unlikely ever to be completely undone. Thus however seemingly insignificant at the time, whatever parents say, how they say it, how they treat others, and how they respond with optimism or pessimism to inevitable problems resonates as behavioral multipliers throughout a child's life, much like a stone thrown into a placid pond sends ripples of water toward the shore.

In summary, as a collection of childhood impressions, the Parent ego state is negative, positive, questionably accurate, and undeniably impactful as a historical record of our early environment that has enormous staying power. As a recording, it's as if our parents continue to unquestioningly live in our heads rent free throughout our lives, and as their blindly accepting adult landlords we are likely little more aware of such potentially destructive boarders than innocently unsuspecting toddlers. To that end, if as Socrates said the unexamined life is not worth living, the unexamined and often deeply flawed Parent ego state is not worth basing one's life on.

Thus considering how significantly the Parent impacts our lives, it is essential to identify its functions, parts, behaviors, and language.

PARENT EGO STATE FUNCTIONS

- Provide people with a model of how to act as a parent to their own children.
- Protect young children when their parents are not present by instilling rules such as "Look both ways" or "Don't play with matches."
- Make responses to many repetitive activities and commonly occurring situations automatic and, as a result, less time-consuming. Such "how to" behaviors include brushing your teeth, tying your shoes, setting a table, making a bed, using the phone, what to do if lost, or even how to blow your nose.
- Provide individuals with a conscience.
- Author supportive or critical self-talk and accompanying Child feelings of doubt, guilt, and insignificance, or "I can do this" importance, confidence, and adequacy in response to environmental challenges.

- Provide the "do and don't do messages" and attributive labels inoculating one's Child with the raw informational materials from which an individual's life story or script is unconsciously written.
- Provide a frame of reference by defining good, bad, right, wrong, moral, immoral, etc.

The Parent ego state is divided into two main behavioral manifestations: the nurturing Parent and the controlling Parent.

The Nurturing Parent

The part of the Parent ego state expressing concern for others or for oneself is referred to as the nurturing Parent. Typically, it is "Look both ways" protecting, "You can do this" affirming, "I'm not mad at you" forgiving, "Those poor people" empathizing, "You'll do better tomorrow" reassuring, and "I'll make a donation or give my time" supporting.

Implicit in this concern for others, the nurturing Parent, with Adult oversight, engenders moral values concerning the "proper way" people "should" be treated. If sufficiently strong, this sense of the "right thing to do" can translate into compassion for the suffering of others and the backing of unpopular but "righteous" social causes, even if it means standing against ostracism or hostility (Boulton 1978).

However, as much good as the nurturing Parent can do, like its ego state partners in personality it embodies both positive and negative qualities. Thus in responding to others, the nurturing Parent can go too far if support becomes overprotective enabling, if compassion becomes excuse, if a "helping hand" becomes unneeded and unwanted rescue, and if well-meaning sympathy leads to a smothering "let me do that for you" chronic dependency and a crippling lack of self-sufficient responsibility. As a result, it doesn't take much imagination to figure out why a child is untidy when a mother continually picks up after him, a daughter is indecisive when a father constantly disallows her decision making, or why a perpetually rescued son lacks confidence and "getting-it-done" drive when parents unendingly perceive him as unable to stand on his own.

In fact, disempowering and growth-inhibiting caregiver remarks can superficially resemble loving, supportive, and sympathetic messages from the nurturing Parent. This is especially so if parents have a covert agenda of diminishing guilt for providing less than adequate childcare or if they fear becoming unneeded and/or unloved by their children.

Yet lowering a child's behavioral expectations by endlessly repeating the siren song of "It's not your fault" exaggerated sympathy or "I'll fix your problem" unnecessary assistance is a recipe for disaster. For however well-meaning such actions may superficially seem, parents who self-servingly satisfy their own needs by enabling their children to be lazy, irresponsible, and dependently "little" will handicap them for a lifetime of challenges yet to come. And when this occurs, the fruits of disempowerment are little different than other equally crippling forms of abuse.

As if coming from model parents, debilitating comments seductively camouflaged as expressions of support if *continually* made to children such as "I'll do that for you," or "Take it easy," or "Things will work out by themselves" will correspondingly translate as blank-check permissions to be lethargic, excessively needy, and passively ineffectual. Thus in seeking to avoid confrontation with potentially rebellious children and attempting to "buy" their indebted love through overnurturance, parents taking the enabling road position their children on the path of least resilience. In the end, this will likely lead not to a life of "being all they can be" but to an existence of doing as little as possible and being whatever they can get away with.

The Controlling Parent

Serving as a counterbalance to the nurturing Parent, the controlling Parent criticizes, orders, punishes, demands, scolds, nags, sets rules, and provides structure. Additionally, it is opinionated, adversarial, prejudicial, and often sees reality as black or white, good or bad, and right or wrong. When chronically repressive, this part of the "You do this and don't do that" ego state is sometimes referred to as the critical Parent because "it makes people feel not OK and because its function is to force them to do things they don't want to do" (Steiner 1974, 53).

But however the controlling Parent is labeled, it should be noted that opinions are not in and of themselves Parental in nature. That is, beliefs and attitudes based on carefully considered evidence and an open-to-debate worldview rather than on unthinking recordings of rigidly held parental ideas, convictions, and superstitions are Adult in character.

While protectively setting appropriate limits and requiring reasonable expectations for a child are importantly constructive functions of the controlling Parent, doing so can have a considerably darker side. This is especially true when rules and behavioral demands are issued in disturbed directives so that no matter what a child does, they are "wrong." Offering a choice with no good alternatives is in reality offering no choice at all. Leading to a "checkmate situation," such verbal and nonverbal contradictory messages are commonly referred to as "Catch-22" or double bind communications.

As the term suggests, a double bind is a statement or situation constructed so that whatever is done, the target of the message is bound, trapped, and unable to affect a positive outcome. Once considered a contributing cause of mental illness, when common during childhood such conflicting messages often contribute to apathy-driven academic, career, and relationship failures.

This should surprise no one. For when continually caught between the "devil and the deep blue sea," a young child without a sense of direction and control will almost certainly internalize pessimism, passivity, and learned helplessness. As a result, when situations are regularly constructed where pleasing the authority figure is apparently impossible, motivation is undermined and the seemingly only choice remaining is to give up.

A parent demanding a son or daughter to clean their room, severely punishing the youngster when invariably it is not done well enough or directing a child to "go outside and play" and then chastising the "bad little boy" or girl for getting dirty will only serve to fearfully confuse the child into "damned if I do, damned if I don't" inaction. A father frequently ignoring his daughter's affections then criticizing her lack of warmth and a mother often telling her son after an embrace that "You don't really love me, you're only pretending that you do" may well dictate a child's future indecisiveness as an adult. Or perhaps most incongruously, a parent repeatedly *ordering a child to not be so obedient* is still another example of double binding.

Yet such no-win messages are not limited to parents and children. They are also an all-too-common form of communication in dysfunctional adult relationships when one person is allegedly struggling to overcome a problem or detrimental condition.

Known as a "love bind," the implied or at times explicit message in such relationships is "If you *really* love me, you will unconditionally love me despite my current *situation*" (Morris and Morris 1982). The purpose of such a statement is clear, and that is, any criticism of the "situation" will be deflected by claims of "Nobody understands how tough things are" victimization and an "I can't help it" free pass to indefinitely continue self-limiting and often destructive behaviors.

To that end, whenever such conduct is *even questioned,* the "persecutor" will reflexively be accused of "not really loving" or "not being supportive" of the addicted-to-excuses sufferer. After all, insists the "victim," how can anyone be critical of drug abuse, gambling addiction, chronic lethargy, or any other problem when "All I need is a chance to work on it?" Thus when seemingly forced to choose between challenging a maladaptive behavior and then being accused of "not caring" or "demonstrating love" by ignoring such conduct and discounting one's own needs for positive relational change, many choose the latter option. This is, of course, the scenario the person "just getting around to doing something about the problem" wants.

Yet even in the absence of double bind messages, dealing with another's overly controlling Parent ego state is unpleasant at best and a healthy relationship deal breaker at worst. With that in mind, several strategies known as "Parent shrinkers" can defuse an overbearing Parent and guide a conversation or situation toward more positive ends (Mart, Nichols, and Cantrell 1975).

One of the most commonly used of these strategies is to avoid responding in kind to another's critical or controlling Parent. Heeding this guidance makes perfect sense because failing to do so invariably leads to a tit-for-tat escalation, making productive communication impossible. Another effective approach to avoid a going-nowhere and often heated Parent-dominated exchange is to literally "check one's ego at the door" by *legitimately* stating "You're right," "That's a fair point," or "I'll need more time to think about what you said." Still other "Parent shrinkers" include encouraging the other person to feel good by laughing, smiling, or by deftly changing the subject.

Actually, even if a dialogue between Parent ego states becomes explosive, unemotionally stating that "I regret if our disagreement or conversation led to any negative feelings" is almost a surefire method to cool an overly emotional critical Parent exchange. Doing so doesn't imply an acceptance that one is "wrong" or was responsible for a "discussion" gone bad. For even if believing that time has been wasted in ineffectual "debate," one can honestly regret that negative feelings may have resulted. In any event, if one values effective communication and if that includes positively manipulating transactions to "invite" other people to do so as well, so be it.

In any event, when the controlling or nurturing Parent is focused on others rather than on oneself, it is referred to as the "active" Parent. Typically, this active Parent reveals himself or herself in a manner resembling one's mother or father. Thus consciously or not, the active Parent has been cathected or energized whenever a person reproduces and projects onto others the actual or perceived behaviors, personalities, and pathologies of one or both parents. And not surprisingly, because how the Parent is directed toward others is a reflection of how the inner Parent is directed toward oneself (Kahler 1977), observing an individual's active Parent provides insight into their otherwise hidden internal Parent-Child dialogue.

Contrastingly, the Parent ego state, controlling or nurturing, inwardly dictating behavior in a manner one's parents would have approved of or at least tacitly accepted, is referred to as the "influencing Parent." Thus whether one's Child is rebellious, compliant, impulsive, restricted, confident, insecure, or withdrawn is greatly determined by the "self-talk" or inner dialogue of this so-called influencing Parent.

But whether the controlling or nurturing Parent is energized and whether either or both are focused externally or on oneself, the child's actual parents provide the primary models, accepted at face value, for their use. For as previously stated, the young child is highly dependent and relatively helpless, has no point of comparison, and typically has nowhere else to go.

As a result, even for adults life is "safer," that is, more predictable, to blindly accept questionably accurate Parent "tapes" than to potentially challenge those recordings by updating a flawed reality. Thus rather than ultimately believing one's own eyes and ears and possibly perceiving the world and oneself more realistically, many people cling to a past that was reflexively internalized early in life. This out-of-awareness assimilation of parental behaviors and attitudes is referred to as incorporation.

Also known as identification, incorporation is the tendency for a child to unconsciously absorb various personality characteristics from his or her parents. After all, rare is the person who as an adult hasn't caught himself or herself sounding or acting like their mother or father. In fact, incorporation is so universal that equally rare is the stand-up comedian not infusing his routine with stories of doing exactly that. But as no laughing matter in daily life, when manifesting the Parent ego state an individual "will not only use the same words [their parents] used, but will often sit, stand, frown, and carry [themselves] as [their parents] did" (Meininger 1973, 20).

Building our parents into ourselves compensates for feelings of inadequacy or insignificance that are common to virtually all children and, for that matter, many adults. And for identical reasons, as we age we substitute admired people or groups for our parents as models for incorporation. Freud called this behavior introjection and categorized it as a psychological "defense mechanism" discussed in greater detail in chapter 10.

Yet in addition to "recordings" of what one's parents did and specifically said, the Parent ego state also contains more generalized and often unspoken messages that have a powerful impact on life literally from cradle to grave. These messages are injunctions and permissions.

INJUNCTIONS

Sometimes referred to as "stoppers," an injunction is a generalized, internal, and unconscious parental imperative forbidding or discouraging certain behaviors. Varying in harm from the relatively minor impact of "don't question your elders" to the crippling emotional damage of "don't exist," these psychological time bombs inhibiting growth are sometimes considered as "the most lethal or life-limiting [of] script messages" (Clarkson 1992b, 91).

Indeed, for a child seeking survival by pleasing his or her seemingly omnipotent parents, such "don't do" directives, especially if delivered in a terrifyingly aggressive tone, are enormously powerful obstacles undermining potential. "A parent, twice the size of the child, with a contorted face, possibly raising a hand to strike, is going to provide a powerfully potent message which cannot easily be disobeyed" (Conway and Clarkson 1987, 22; Woollams and Brown 1978).

For a child unconsciously facing the decision between complying with continually reinforced and perhaps threateningly conveyed behavioral demands from "magical figures" providing life-sustaining needs and resisting them to theoretically "become all that one is capable of becoming," the choice is really no choice at all. At its simplest and most brutally straightforward level, the calculus for how the little person must act is dictated by uncompromisingly offered parental mandates where the essence is "If you want to survive, you must have my protection (love) and if you want my protection you must not be (—)". Thus entirely dependent, under stress, and without more positive options, it is hardly surprising that the youngster makes the decision "to not be (—)" and the life script has been initiated (Holloway 1972, 33).

Limited only by the number of parental demands restricting certain behaviors, common and highly significant examples of injunctions include:

- Don't Think
- Don't Trust
- Don't Succeed
- Don't Be Close
- Don't Grow Up
- Don't Be Who You Are
- Don't Act
- Don't Be Normal
- Don't Exist

It is important to realize that these pathological messages are rarely, if ever, directly stated as verbatim commands. That is, injunctions are recorded in a child's mind more subtly but no less powerfully than explicitly implanted word-for-word edicts. Children are extremely intuitive and are thus ultrasensitive to a parent's body language, tone of voice, level of tension, spoken inferences, and implied actions. Small wonder, then, that a child's behavior may have as much to do with "read between the lines" messages as by what parents directly say and do. To that end, *parents need to know that what they "merely" insinuate, verbally and otherwise, is often as impactful as what is literally stated*. And if what is consistently suggested is growth-inhibiting, a child's "lights" once extinguished may never again be lit.

If a youngster's ideas are ridiculed or ignored, if she is told to blindly obey and "Don't ask questions," or if disagreeing with or making suggestions to a parent is ridiculed, a vitriolic "Who do you think you are?" response will become "Don't Think." If a child suffers discipline that is overly punitive and/or inconsistent, such actions will be internalized as "Don't Trust." If a child plays a game with a parent who no longer participates if the youngster wins, if accomplishments result in parental disinterest or, worse, if parental "accept what you got" messages become the "it's good enough" soundtrack of the household, the underlying message fostering unresisting inadequacy will become "Don't Succeed."

If a child experiences parenting that is remote, "tactily challenged," and uncaring, "Don't Be Close" will be heard loud and clear. If a parent enables their otherwise competent child to remain immature by discouraging self-sufficiency, decision-making, and/or sense of responsibility, such nurturance, even if well intended, will likely result in a crippling "Don't Grow Up" dependency injunction. And if a child is scolded, or worse, for taking even reasonable risks, questioning authority, asserting oneself, or defying any other restrictive formulation-inducing passivity, the global message of "Don't Act" will contribute to a checkmated existence where growth and potency are surrendered for a life of unrealized potential.

Furthermore, if an increasingly aware youngster having been exposed to the interpersonal conventions of other households challenges aberrant rituals within his own family and is severely punished for "breaking ranks" with an "uppity" attitude, a "Don't Be Normal" command will need no explanation. And if a child is ignored, ordered not to speak unless spoken to, or if there are too many "Go away. I wish you had never been born" moments, the transparent message will be "Don't Exist."

However, as restrictive as all injunctions are, they are not created equal. Arguably, the most malevolent of these self-limiting directives leading in whole or in part to fantasized or actual outcomes of premature death or ongoing aberrance are "Don't Be Normal" and "Don't Exist." And when either or both are internalized, whatever progress is made in eliminating other injunctions, emotional health will likely remain a "bridge too far" until these so-called catastrophic injunctions are resolved as well (Hartman and Narboe 1974).

Yet even when injunctions are not as harmful as "Don't Be Normal" or "Don't Exist," other repetitive and seemingly insignificant "don't do moments" from childhood can also have lasting effects as "shut down events," where implied restrictions are taken literally, limits become unquestioned, and "what could have been" possibilities become "what never will be" potentials. As such, all injunctions potentially hold the power to "contaminate or confuse present perceptions, cognitions, and emotions," (Lammers 1994, 253) and as deeply embedded, endlessly reverberating "sleeper cell recordings," such self-limiting Parental messages play an instrumental role in script formulation and continuance.

But just as not all injunctions are created equal, how they are expressed also affects their potency. Obviously, frequency and intensity of delivery impact their power. However, when they are also suggested through negative attributions, the influence of such injunctions may become greater still. This is so because such parentally offered labels implying what a child should and should not do also define what a child is. And because it is extremely difficult, if not impossible, for a youngster or even an adult to dismiss who they believe they are, injunctions indirectly communicated as attributions during childhood are arguably the most powerful delivery system for such growth-suppressing messages (Holtby 1973).

It doesn't take much connect-the-dots imagination for a child to conclude not to think when labeled as "stupid," not to succeed when identified as a "loser," not to be close when described as "disgusting," not to begin a long and productive life when likened to a relative committing suicide, or passively not to act if repeatedly told "You're a worthless, weak, and hopeless case." Certainly not all injunctions are disguised as attributions, yet because how children are defined invariably leads to their behaviors, injunctions emerging from negative labels are powerful, crippling, and far-reaching in their effects. For child or adult, *if you believe that you are already something,* it is difficult to act in a way belying that identity.

In many households, parents form a partnership with their children in conveying both attributions and injunctions. Typically, the child's opposite-sexed parent is the primary and original source for both messages while the same-sexed parent provides the "program" for their compliance (Steiner 1974). Thus a father encouraging his daughter to be assertive with a "You are tough" attribution and a "don't be weak" injunction will often be supported by a strong-willed wife emulating such aggressiveness. Or a mother fostering cleanliness in her son with a "You are a tidy boy" attribution and a "don't be dirty" injunction will frequently be reinforced by her husband providing an orderly and well-groomed model.

Effective parents not only avoid potential-stifling attributions and injunctions but also *actively seek* opportunities to reinforce potential-amplifying behaviors. To that end, enlightened parents give their children liberating "permissions" to succeed, think, act, trust, grow up, be close, be normal, be who you are, and to exist by recognizing their child's successes, patiently listening to their thoughts, practicing fair and consistent discipline, and exhibiting unconditional love.

PERMISSIONS

As generalized and primarily "read between the lines" parental communications, permissions encourage certain growth-promoting behaviors. Typically, such communications are either a license to *do* something beneficial as in a "You may . . ." or "It's OK to . . ." positive permission, or an approval *not to do* something harmful as in a "You don't have to . . ."

negative permission. But whatever their form and despite being suggested rather than directly articulated, permissions as injunctions are still "heard" by children loud and clear. Common and highly significant permissions include:

- To Think (permission for effectiveness)
- To Trust (permission for intimacy)
- To Succeed (permission to "make it")
- To Be Close (permission for intimacy)
- To Grow Up (permission for maturity)
- To Be Who You Are (permission for individuation)
- To Act or Do (permission to be assertive)
- To Be Normal (permission for sanity)
- To Exist (permission to survive)

If a child's suggestions to a parent result in positive comments, the child has, in reality, been given the green light to think. If a child experiences clear rules, consistently fair discipline, and a predictably positive world, trust likely develops. If a child's achievements result in parental interest, approval, and support, the underlying "make it" message is to succeed. And if a child's home is filled with unconditional love offered by attentive parents, the tacit message translates into being close, to exist, and to ask for what is needed.

There is nothing miraculous about raising successful and empowered children. Thoughtful parents will look for and respond to opportunities that give their sons and daughters permission to think, trust, succeed, be close, grow up, be sane, and to exist. Those opportunities are there for all parents, but as for an unheard dog whistle, being there is not enough. In making a positive difference in the lives of their children, parents must cultivate an ear to hear and an eye to see growth-promoting opportunities that may have previously gone unnoticed.

Moreover, because injunctively stated attributions such as "Don't be such a jerk!" or "Stop acting like a fool!" are said loudly and far too often by caregivers both inside and outside of the home, parents need to offset such negativity. Most simply, this can be accomplished by complimenting appropriate behaviors, framing directives more positively with "Do great things," "Make the most of your abilities," or "Be an excellent person" permissions, and by supporting positively emerging character traits and aptitudes.

Praising and nurturing a child's productive conduct or talents encourages those actions and proficiencies to more fully express themselves. As a behavioral trampoline, such recognition fuels effort and elevates such inclinations far beyond levels reached if otherwise ignored or unnoticed. Yet such "crystallizing experiences" providing the confidence necessary for adult achievements are too often overlooked.

Worse still, such positive learning opportunities may be squandered by "paralyzing experiences" in which childhood gifts are hastily judged, ignored, or actively discouraged through injunctions, criticism, or even punishment. Doing so will virtually guarantee those endowments will "wither on the vine" as never fully expressed what-could-have-beens.

If as Edison suggested, many of life's failures are people not realizing "how close they were to success when they gave up," effective parents in supporting and thereby amplifying childhood abilities are stacking the deck their children will not increase that number. And such responsible caregivers can do little else. For if a tree falling with no one to hear is said to make no sound, the unrecognized gifts of a talented yet unsupported child may likewise fall silent and unnoticed.

IDENTIFYING EGO STATES

Arguably, the most common truism in psychology is that you can't change what you don't acknowledge. While undoubtedly so, it is also true that it is difficult to acknowledge what you don't understand or can't even identify. Fortunately, however, taking the context of each action, the tone and vocabulary of each statement, the accompanying body language, and, when possible, an individual's past history into consideration, each ego state is relatively easy to identify by separating signature behaviors into verbal and nonverbal clues.

PARENT EGO STATE INDICATORS

Body Language/Nonverbal Clues

- Furrowed brow
- Pursed lips
- Disapproving scowl
- Wagging index finger
- Foot tapping
- Arms folded
- Tongue clucking
- Rolling eyes
- Hands on hips
- Affectionate patting

Verbal Clues

- Commands
- Put downs
- Sarcasm
- Prejudicial statements

- Preachy moralisms
- Sympathetic, tender, or comforting language
- Endearments such as "honey" or "sweetie"
- Unthinking use of should, have to, must, or ought to
- Automatic evaluations or judgments such as "stupid," "ridiculous," "naughty," "disgusting," or "vulgar"

Common Parental clichés include:

- "How dare you . . ."
- "I'm going to put a stop to this once and for all"
- "You'll be sorry"
- "If I were you . . ."
- "How many times have I told you . . ."
- "Why can't you be more like . . ."
- "Once and for all will you . . ."

Examples of Parental slogans are:

- "You made your bed, now lie in it."
- "Never trust a stranger."
- "Tomorrow is a new day."
- "Give someone an inch and they'll take a mile."
- "If at first you don't succeed, try, try again."
- "Don't sweat the small stuff."
- "Waste not, want not."
- "Do as I say, not as I do."
- "You are judged by the company you keep."
- "Anything worth doing is worth doing well."
- "Keep your chin up."
- "Always respect your elders."
- "All's well that ends well."
- "Spare the rod, spoil the child."

Even though Parental slogans may sometimes be true, mindless obedience to their dictates without Adult oversight can lead to bad decisions. For example, remaining in a dead-end job or a toxic relationship because "I made my bed and now I must lie in it," reflexively accepting abuse or advice from older people because "I must respect my elders," or beating a son or daughter because to "spare the rod is to spoil the child" are all equally unwise.

Parental slogans are nothing more than general guidelines for behavior, not straitjackets for conduct. Yet by avoiding the psychological discomfort caused when events or enlightenment dictate disregard for blindly accepted slogans, many people lobotomize their Adults in conforming perceptions and behaviors to "one size fits all" inherited slogans.

FIVE

Understanding the Child Ego State

I have a woman's body and a child's emotions.

—Elizabeth Taylor

The only ego state present at birth and the location of one's self-concept, the Child is the permanent recording of one's internal responses to what caregivers said and did from birth through approximately age five. Most simply, as the Parent is the internalized history of what parents *did,* the Child is the archived *reaction* to those experiences. And because the Parent as an activating agent for the Child is thus undeniable, recognizing it as an archived repository of caregiver conduct *that a thinking person can accept or reject* confirms an internally oriented accountability mindset for feelings and behaviors that is equally undeniable.

As the strongest and least easily editable part of personality, the Child is the "want to" location of a person's most basic needs, feelings, instincts, and desires. Fully experienced as the child you once were, when you act and/or feel now as you did when you were little, you are in this most elementally "who you are" ego state.

Good or bad, harmful or beneficial, elated or despondent, there is little doubt that childhood feelings pass through the decades of one's existence and emerge fully intact long after the experience initially generating them. Thus an adult feeling ashamed, guilty, afraid, vulnerably unknowing, anxious, victimized, depressed, grief stricken, insecure needing approval, or persecuted, "reading into" another's comments, has rubber-banded back to their Child.

Yet however inappropriate, unpleasant, or irrational such emotions may be, the Child is also the location of some of our most wonderful feelings, including curiosity, excitement, pleasure, delight, hope, anticipation, and the often creative realizations of "aha experiences." Thus, ironically, whatever our age, the Child in each of us generates many of the same feelings that a child can provide for a family (Meininger 1973). As such, while the Child can be impatient, shortsighted, and reckless in its demands for immediate gratification, it can also create the joy that makes life worth living. But however the Child displays himself or herself, it is divided into three main behavioral manifestations.

THE ADAPTED CHILD

Whenever one unthinkingly modifies basic urges to conform to familial and societal expectations as expressed by the long-ago demands of our parents, the adapted Child is active. Beginning in infancy, and whether resulting from rational or repressive parental limits or care, this is the part of all of us that has been positively or negatively programmed. And to create a socialized being, this is to be expected. For as with all newborns, "any animal must learn to deny its natural pattern of behaving and discharge impulses at times convenient for its masters" (Mescavage and Silver 1977, 332).

"When we are small we adapt to the people around us, who protect and nurture us, and have power over us, in ways that will get us acceptance, approval and [the] acknowledgement we crave" (Barrow, Bradshaw, and Newton 2001, 55). Failing to conform to "appropriate" conduct at their peril, young children quickly learn that in order to get along and gain parental recognition and acceptance, they must learn to go along. Thus in monitoring caregiver pleasure, displeasure, or attention, most children have little choice but to grow toward their expectations. To that end, the origin for much of human behavior is the result of coping adaptations.

As complementary hand-in-glove behaviors, a child may therefore "become mother's darling, always weak and affectionate and craving sympathy. He may weep or fall sick at any reverse, to show how much he needs looking after. On the other hand, he may have outbursts of temper; he may be disobedient or fight with his mother in order to be noticed" (Adler 1931, 127; Wilson 1975, 119). Thus in reconciling daily conduct and natural urges with parental demands, the adapted Child emerges "not because [children] want to, but because they feel they must" (Woods 2000, 96).

Initially, the adapted Child resulted in eating our vegetables, going to sleep when it was "time for bed," and learning to retain or eliminate bodily waste on schedule to please our parents. It resulted in sharing our toys, controlling our anger, respecting our elders, and living in fear of being caught masturbating. And continuing throughout life, whenever a person reflexively curbs natural impulses as once gaining approval from parents, resisting their demands, or escaping their control, the adapted Child has been energized. At the most basic level, these behavioral "adjustments" to parental authority unthinkingly result in the "compliant," "rebellious," and "withdrawn" adapted Child subdivisions.

ADAPTED CHILD BEHAVIORS COMMONLY INCLUDE:

- Compulsive adherence to caregiver values
- Sharing and taking turns
- Excessive submission to authority figures
- Conformity to social norms (manners)
- Punctuality
- Respectful salutations (sir, madam, officer)
- Exaggerated willingness to please others
- Guilt/shame/remorse
- Sexual and/or drug abstinence
- Passivity
- Resistive tantrumming
- Habitual arguing and/or debating rules or requirements
- Physical and/or emotional withdrawal

In most of the aforementioned examples, natural impulses have been modified in commonly identified ways to curry favor with parents. In such instances, the child has become agreeable, cooperative, or even submissive in order to gain approval, leading to whatever tangible expressions of that approval, such as attention or privileges, the youngster wants.

Yet however misguided blind faith submission might seem in a larger sense, during childhood it may understandably be viewed as unresisting ways "of controlling our surroundings and obtaining from [parents] what we need to survive" (Vallejo 1986, 115). But over time, the cost of such impulsive submission is high. For taken to extremes, an ingrained willingness to comply as a child may lead to overadaptation and loss of autonomy as an adult when habitually conforming to how we imagine others want us to act and who they want us to be.

Referred to as the Helpful Adapted Child (Holloway 1977), this lifelong pattern of exaggerated and reflexively compliant "dutiful" behavior dictating a spineless unwillingness to stand up for oneself likely emerged from the early and unspoken quid pro quo agreement trading unquestioning childhood obedience for the emotional sustenance of parental approval. Thus as adults, not expressing pride in personal achievements, projecting a "happy face" after withering criticism, or remaining silent upon hearing an offensive statement or disagreeable proposal are all examples of the adapted Child fearing others will correspondingly read one's actions as conceited, overly sensitive, or inflexibly narrow-minded.

Yet in homes where it is advantageous for compliance to be defined not by submission but by passivity, a Helpless Adapted Child (Holloway

1977) behavioral model frequently emerges. This powerless "I can't do for myself" stance will likely be reinforced throughout adolescence by inviting and expecting deliverance from overly nurturing others all too willing to do so. And still later in life, the pattern as a confused, incompetent, and incapable victim will invariably continue by seeking complementary role players serving as enabling rescuers tacitly encouraging such contrived impotency to persist.

However, in other homes, the child learns that in order to "win" with parents, reflexive compliance through submission or passivity is not the most effective path. In some families, children learn that a desired "payoff," whether it is parental attention, approval, or more tangible rewards, results from resistance to authority. When this is so, the rebellious or so-called Hurtful Adapted Child (Holloway 1977) has gained the upper hand.

In such cases, the child has learned that by whining, raging, or resisting parental expectations he or she is far more likely to "win the day" in getting what they want. At the very least, such opposition results in gaining attention and, at most, parents will eventually acquiesce to the demands being sought. It is results such as these that make rebelliousness as much an adaptation to parental actions as compliance. This is so because if resisting parental directives did not result in desired ends, there would be no adaptive reason for a child to continue such defiance.

In fact, in some homes resistance to authority, parental or otherwise, is actually a highly valued behavior that doesn't go unnoticed, even by relatively young children. In such households, self-aggrandizing parents of "unmanageable" children gush with "my kid is not going to be pushed around" pride in describing a rebellious son as a "chip off the old block," a resisting daughter as "tough-minded," or a defiant child of either sex as "feisty."

Yet as with other adapted Child modes, resistance-influenced coping lessons internalized early in life are learned all too well. For when obeying the letter and not the spirit of parental edicts by interpreting "Don't have sex" as *only* referring to intercourse or "Don't have a party while we're gone" as *only* referring to social gatherings of ten or more, such so-called "legal thinking" provides the basis for reading-between-the-lines adult alibis. And when tantrumming works as a child in satisfying needs, its well-established cause-and-effect pattern survives into adulthood as emotional outbursts directed at family, friends, teachers, colleagues, and bosses.

Still another coping strategy children use in adjusting to parental influences is withdrawal. Whereas compliance is an adaptive response to increase the odds that needs will be met and defiance an anger reaction to frustration that needs are not being met, withdrawal may well result from a depressive resignation that needs, at least through submission or rebellion, will *never* be met. Believing that to be true, the choice to save emotional and physical energy by detaching oneself from a defined-as-futile situation makes understandable if not perfect sense.

Generally speaking, the three most basic adaptive behaviors of compliance, rebellion, and withdrawal are related to "life energies" interacting with and adjusting to the environment. Known colloquially as Scary, Spunky, and Sleepy to describe their functions (English 1977), these forces personified as "muses" are correspondingly associated with those adaptive behaviors. And as with ego states, during certain periods in life and surely at any given time of day, one of these motivational drives holds sway over our thoughts, feelings, and actions.

Hence in focusing on survival, Scary's concern with gaining protection from environmental dangers as an adult has the same motivation as gaining emotional and nutritional support from caregivers during the first years of life. As such, the same Scary-inspired reflexive submission to parental demands during childhood later results in fawning compliance directed at teachers, bosses, and other so-called authority figures, even at the loss of self-determination and personal dignity.

As a starkly contrasting counterweight to Scary, Spunky's adaptive function is to promote individual and species survival through limitless curiosity, risk-taking, exploration, and creativity. Resisting the status quo and impelling challenge, Spunky is exemplified by an impulsive and at times reckless rejection of "what is" as a motivating factor for a "pushing the envelope" fearlessness of what could be. And this instinctive rejection of "business as usual" may also include the reflexive "I can't," I won't," and "You can't make me" dismissal of parental values and demands.

But there's more. In characteristically thinking "outside the box," Spunky also solves problems not through a linear thinking, purely logical process but rather from intuitive breakthroughs by extrapolating patterns in people and events through "approximations, analogies, and incidental juxtapositions of ideas and perceptions" (English 1972, 65). And though originally driving childhood behaviors as a problem solving and motivational force, Spunky continues throughout life creatively represented as part of the Child ego state known as the "Little Professor."

However, while Scary and Spunky compete for dominance at opposite ends of the conservative-progressive behavioral continuum, Sleepy as the drive behind withdrawal expresses itself as the environmental adaptation prompting detachment and status quo inertia (English 1977).

THE NATURAL CHILD

The natural or so-called free Child acts impetuously with naïve unconcern for consequences. Whenever one acts impulsively, selfishly, sensually, and at times dangerously in thoughtlessly seeking the immediate gratification of urges biological or otherwise, this "devil-may-care" state is in control. Roughly equivalent to Freud's formulation of the id, the natural or free Child is devoid of impulse control and is the "I want to" antithesis to the commonly compliant "I have to" behavior of the adapted Child.

Throughout life, these two personality forces compete for dominance on a daily if not on a momentary basis. To that end, the balancing of natural and adapted Child behaviors begins in early childhood as a struggle between the freedom to express oneself "spontaneously on the one hand, and the capacity and willingness to do what the social situation requires and rewards on the other" (Parry 1979, 127).

Although this struggle between natural and adapted Child behaviors is displayed on innumerable fronts, there is arguably no more obvious a contest than that involving drug use and abuse. That is, by diminishing the control of the Parent and Adult ego states, intoxicants allow the often reckless natural Child to "play" without adapted Child interference, Parent approval, or Adult oversight.

Thus on a purely psychological level, it shouldn't be surprising why people enjoy "doing drugs" often to the exclusion of common sense and long-term health concerns. Whether alcohol, marijuana, or far more potent euphoriants, recreational drugs initially silence the Parent followed by a gradual weakening of the Adult's ability to perceive objective reality. And with the Parent anesthetized and the Adult compromised, the adapted Child, no longer taking orders from the one and counsel from the other, gives way to the impulsive, gratification-driven, pleasure-focused, and unrestricted behaviors of the free Child.

However, as with the nurturing Parent, the controlling Parent, and the adapted Child, the free Child has both negative and positive aspects. Thus while the natural Child may indeed be unrestrained, capricious, and often reckless, its living-in-the-moment, joyful exuberance often seen at social gatherings may also provide much-needed if temporary relief from an overly controlled jumping-through-one-hoop-after-another existence.

Yet because as with Longfellow's "little girl with the curl," when good it is very good but when bad it is really horrid, one must limit the free Child's worst lack of impulse control excesses in order to increase the odds of leading a productive and fulfilling existence. And perhaps there is no more seemingly unsophisticated yet compelling evidence supporting this predictive connection than an investigation conducted by psychologist Walter Mischel at Stanford University in 1972.

In the so-called "marshmallow experiment," over six hundred preschool children were brought one by one into a room and expressing personal choice had a marshmallow, pretzel, or cookie placed in front of them. They were then told that if they waited for an adult to return from an errand they could have two of whatever they selected, but if they ate the one in front of them before the adult returned, that's all they would receive. Several of the youngsters ate the treat on the spot, some waited a few minutes longer, and only about one-third of them were able to wait fifteen minutes for the adult to return (Bright 2013; O'Neil 1996). Overall, most children "held out for an average of less than three minutes" (Lehrer 2009).

When the children were contacted years later, researchers found that the "marshmallow test" was an extremely accurate predictor of how they ultimately did in school. The youngsters delaying free Child gratification by denying themselves a single reward for the promise of two "were more emotionally stable, better liked by their teachers and their peers, and were still able to delay gratification in pursuit of their goals" (O'Neil 1996, 7; Bright 2013). And as an unintended test of aptitude, the S.A.T. scores as a predictive measure of college readiness of those less impulsive children *were on average 210 points higher than youngsters exhibiting little self-control more than a decade earlier* (O'Neil 1996; Bright 2013).

But that's not all. In comparing the so-called "low-delaying" children to their self-controlled and goal-driven peers, those unwilling to defer gratification were more irritable, more sensitive to stress, more likely to pick fights, and by age thirty-two were more significantly prone to obesity and recreational drug abuse (Public Policy Implications of the New Science of Mind, *Charlie Rose Brain Series 2 Episode 13*, March 7, 2013). Moreover, when tested with a laboratory task measuring strength of willpower, those subjects who unsuccessfully resisted marshmallows as children generally performed more poorly on tests of self-control as adults (Delaying Gratification, American Psychological Association).

EXAMPLES OF FREE OR NATURAL CHILD BEHAVIORS INCLUDE:

- Unsafe and/or unashamed sex
- Stealing
- Cheating
- Fighting
- Impulsiveness
- Carefree enjoyment of people, places, and/or things
- Overeating
- Greediness
- Drug abuse
- Overspending
- Unwarranted absenteeism
- Inability to delay gratification
- Selfishly demanding that things be "their way"
- Unbridled laughter or joy

Interestingly, under certain situations such as the relative anonymity one feels in large crowds, the free Child appears to get stronger as the Helpful Adapted Child's adherence to "civilized norms" gets weaker. In such gatherings, people seem to lose individuality and with it their sense of morality, responsibility, and concern for what others think of them. And as a result of such deindividuation, behaviors that would otherwise be considered reprehensible may become "acceptable" and even commonplace.

Displayed at crowded sporting events, spring break for college students, rock concerts, large protest demonstrations, or at other heavily populated gatherings, such a loss of personal identity may also lead to a loss of inhibitions restraining immoral and, at times, violent behaviors. In short, the bigger the group, the greater the anonymity and the more defuse the responsibility. And the less one internalizes himself as a responsible *individual*, the greater the likelihood of antisocial behavior. Thus, especially in faraway settings, wearing a uniform as part of a large group also increases deindividuation and its probability of provoking the worst aspects of free Child behavior.

THE LITTLE PROFESSOR

Because young children have a relatively limited amount of Adult ego state data in which to make decisions, they often solve problems based on intuition or on hunch. As such, among an infinite universe of how-to-behave and how-do-I-get-what-I-want questions, children often rely on parental sounds, gestures, movements, and facial expressions to "know" the answers to questions such as "Is mom angry with me?" or "Should I ask dad for an ice cream?" or, even more commonly, "How do I avoid punishment?" The location of this implicit and nonverbal intuitive sense, which as the child's first Adult and primary means for "staying safe" by perceptively figuring out or "reading" the feelings and expectations of caregivers, is the part of the Child ego state appropriately referred to as the Little Professor.

But as the emerging Adult in young children, the Little Professor is not solely a part of childhood personality. As an almost pitch-perfect facsimile of what is now known as "System 1 thinking," it effortlessly guides our subjectively formulated, often immediate, "always on," and frequently flawed impressionistic sense of the world throughout life (Kahneman 2013). This is so because even as adults we regularly make decisions as children, basing our analysis on incomplete information. "This is true of any commitment. It is true of marriage. It is true of voting. It is true of signing a petition. It is true of the establishment of priorities" (Harris 1973, 83). It is also true for any aesthetic undertaking. Accordingly, creative breakthroughs often result from having an almost-mystical sense, inspiration, or feeling without really knowing that a particular word in a paragraph, a certain color in a painted landscape, or a chosen lyric in a song will be "just right."

And while an imaginative, artistic sense is certainly the domain of the Little Professor, this reflexively activated part of the personality also subliminally answers far more mundane and daily questions. "Should I ask for a date?" "Which line in this crowded supermarket will get me to the cashier most quickly?" "Is that advice Parentally critical or forcefully offered as well-meaning support?" "Do I really have enough food for my dinner party?" Or "How do get what I want from my spouse, my boss, or my child without them resisting, getting defensive, or sensing manipulation?" But however used, anytime we make decisions at the margins of our awareness with limited and at times "jumping to conclusions" inaccurate information, as we often did when we were young, the Little Professor is the source of those "don't know how I know" choices.

CHILD EGO STATE INDICATORS

Body Language/Nonverbal Clues/Feelings

- Pouting
- Sulking/downcast eyes/slumping
- Nail biting
- Rocking
- Crying/laughing/quivering lips
- Jubilation
- Defiance/compliance
- Showing off/attention-gaining behaviors
- Selfishness/demanding
- Sex/sensuality
- Cheating
- Excitement/anticipation
- Flirting
- Guilt/shame/remorse
- Creativity/intuition
- Procrastinating
- Anxiety
- Obscene gestures
- Temper tantrums
- Revenge
- Embarrassment

Verbal Clues

- Baby talk
- Whining
- Taunting/teasing
- Victimization language
- Defensive language ("Quit picking on me," "I didn't . . .")

- Absolute statements (never, always, everybody, every time)
- "I wish . . ."
- "I can't," "I won't," "You can't make me"
- "Wow," "Gee," "Gimme"
- Blaming language ("You make me . . ." "You made me . . .")
- "I want . . ."
- Profanities and epithets
- Apathy statements ("I don't care," "Whatever")
- "All about me" self-centered monologues

SIX

Understanding the Adult Ego State

A man has free choice to the extent that he is rational.

—Thomas Aquinas

In an ideal sense, the Adult ego state acts like a smoothly-running, virus-free computer. Unclouded by emotion, it unfeelingly processes data, thinks, predicts, attempts to figure out "what's going on," solves problems by choosing options in light of likely consequences, and, if necessary, revises those options. It is active when a person of whatever age gathers material from the other ego states, evaluates it, and objectively compares that assessment against current data about the world.

Strengthened by formal and informal education, the optimally functioning Adult limits assumptions by dispassionately analyzing reality based on a vast reservoir of information accumulated in the present as well as in the past. And in mirroring the ego in Freud's construction of personality and "System 2 thinking" in far more recent terminology (Kahneman 2013), the Adult also informs decisions regarding the eternal balancing act when "pie-in-the-sky" optimism or unreasoning impulse says "go for it" and overwrought pessimism or parentally imposed injunctions bids us to not even try.

Beginning at about ten months of age, when a child first experiences the ability to walk and manipulate surroundings in accordance with awareness and thought (Harris 1973), the Adult, at least in open-minded people, evolves throughout life. And because everything experienced has the potential to inform the Adult, whether currently as unaware as a child or enlightened as an amalgam of Sigmund Freud, Mohandas Gandhi, and the Dalai Lama, it is the best hope we have to consistently make quality decisions.

As the executive of the personality, a potent Adult resembles an onboard cognitive therapist. That is, by evaluating the objective validity of data in the other ego states, the Adult uses that assessment to cathect, that is energize, the most appropriate response for a given situation. Are Parent beliefs accurate? Are Child feelings appropriate? Are my behaviors reasonable and effective in light of today's reality, or are they recordings from the distant past that need questioning at least and updating at most?

But that's not all. Mindful that ego state contents may well conflict with objective reality and resultantly may foster ineffectual or even harmful actions, the fully functioning Adult continually analyzes the accuracy of its own data while searching for more, utilizes positive elements from the Child and Parent states, and recognizes that understanding the world and ourselves is a never-completed work in progress.

In short, when the Adult is maximally functioning, such an understanding allows it to continually monitor and compare Parent and Child recordings with its "appraisal of reality so that Parent prejudices and Child fears do not masquerade as Adult information" (Woollams and Brown 1978, 36). Thus as a good coach puts his players in a position to win an athletic contest, a well-armed and self-correcting Adult puts its master in a position to "win" the game of life.

Yet however indispensable it is for effective problem solving, the Adult is not without ego state competition. Especially when lacking sufficient time and/or information to make quality decisions, the Parent may well be an effective stand-in. After all, the Parent efficiently handles getting routine and often ritualistic chores done requiring a well-rehearsed sequence of actions rather than complex or original thinking and is also "ideally suited when control is necessary, such as control of children, fears, the unknown, and undesirable impulses" (Prochaska and Norcross n.d., 6). And in reaching those of whatever age who are "stuck" in their Child ego state, the Parent perhaps more than the Adult is typically up to the task.

Then again, the Adult may also play second fiddle to the Child when the creation of new ideas is desired. Because the Child is the source of creativity and intuition, its Little Professor more than the primarily just-the-facts Adult is most effective when inspiration rather than thinking-within-the-box logic is necessary to solve novel problems with no single "right" answer.

However, in addition to its winnowing responsibilities of separating useful Parent beliefs and Child feelings from what is not, the Adult at the height of its powers often exhibits behaviors not frequently attributed to its more traditionally conceived, purely analytical profile. Referred to as the integrated Adult, such behaviors include flexibility, cooperativeness, truth-seeking, and a willingness to be assertive, respectful of others' rights, and ethically responsible (Kuijt 1980).

But arguably a more important function of the so-called integrated Adult is to foster optimism by continually monitoring and, if necessary, editing negative self-talk after life's inevitable adversities. This is so because a person's explanatory style, their internal explanation of why unpleasant events happen, directly impacts one's level of optimism, which in turn "determines how helpless [one] can become, or how energized, when [one] encounter[s] the everyday setbacks as well as momentous defeats" (Seligman 1991, 16).

Yet whatever the Adult should be or is said to do, as often the weakest part of one's personality its relatively impotent processing ability often frustrates ideal decision-making. As previously mentioned, this is particularly due to its inability to generate creative ideas. As a processor of data, the Adult is logical not imaginative, rational not intuitive, and linear-thinking but not inventive.

As such, the Adult must work hand-in-hand with the Little Professor, where the one verifies what the other inspires. Both contribute to effective thinking, but neither can do it alone. Mirroring the different functions of the left and right hemispheres of the brain, "the Adult can test the value, or practicality, or generality of an idea, but it cannot produce a fertile idea. The Little Professor can produce a fertile idea, but cannot systematically evaluate it" (Hughes 1978, 121).

Yet beyond its functional inability to generate divergent thinking, Adult potency is also undermined when offering only token resistance in contesting destructive Child impulses and questioning "How do I really know what I know?" Parent beliefs. That is, since such actions require mental exertion and mental exertion is taxing, it's often easier to obey the "law of least effort" in blindly accepting whatever is familiar, however counterproductive or irrational it may be, than to initiate a more demanding vigilance to continually monitor and eliminate potentially harmful thoughts and actions.

Thus unless there are undeniable reasons overriding intellectual passivity, many people will unconsciously weigh Adult efforts to question and possibly reject long-standing beliefs and behaviors as a cost to be avoided. And with evidence as current as today's news and as obvious as our own behaviors, the sad but simple truth is that because mental exertion is typically so unpleasant, cognitive "laziness is built deep into our nature (Kahnman 2013, 35).

Still another reason for the comparative weakness of the Adult ego state is that its decisions are based on the quality of the data used to make those decisions. And if the Adult's information is woefully incomplete or flawed by archaic Parent beliefs and Child feelings, its decisions will likewise be compromised. Thus for the Adult (no less so than for any other computer)—garbage in, garbage out.

Yet even when Adult determinations based on faulty or incomplete data are objectively inaccurate, there is still great reluctance to overturn or even question their validity. This is so because challenges to accepted beliefs, behaviors, and conclusions not only require effort but also threaten the elemental imperative in all people for safety and security. Translating into the desire for a predictable world, it is this growth-stifling need, arguably more than any other, that serves as a self-sabotaging obstacle to realizing an almost equally elemental self-actualizing need to optimally use and cultivate one's distinctive talents.

SELF-ACTUALIZATION

Formulated by psychologist Abraham Maslow in 1943, self-actualization is the process of developing one's unique potential to its fullest expression. Believing this drive to "becoming all one is capable of becoming" is instinctual and to some degree hereditary in nature, Maslow posited that "a musician must make music, an artist must paint, [and] a poet must write, if he is to be ultimately at peace with himself" (Caracushansky 1980, 322; Maslow 1954). And in reaching this conclusion by studying people leading unusually effective lives, he introduced his "hierarchy of needs" theory: arguably psychology's most elegant and popular model on human motivation and achievement.

The power of Maslow's theory is its clarity in explaining the maximization of one's abilities in terms of satisfying an ordered progression of needs that impel behavior. Simply put, the satisfaction of these predictable and universal needs, diagrammed as a series of steps within a pyramid, dictates our actions. And if a preceding plateau of needs remains frustrated, one will fail to fully move to the next level on a pilgrimage toward self-actualization. That is, unless and until a lower rank of needs is gratified, it will remain dominant in directing one's actions.

Furthermore, the nearer one moves to the self-actualization summit of the pyramid, the less self-centered one is likely to be. Indeed, freed from the tyranny of egocentrically satisfying lower-level needs, the self-actualized few are able to "give back" to others by seeking to remedy the problems and concerns of those as yet unwilling or unable to reach their potential.

From the most primary to the most advanced level, Maslow believed that the following needs motivate human behavior:

- Physiological needs: As its name suggests, this most elemental level of needs includes adequate water, food, and sleep. To this, Eric Berne added the need for human contact, so-called "stroking hunger," as a requirement for physical and emotional health.
- Safety and security: Other than the obvious drive for protection its title denotes, this second step on the hierarchy of needs also implies a universally inherent motivation for a stable, orderly, structured, and predictable world.

  In terms of everyday life, this need impels people to resist change and, even in the face of contradictory evidence, to obsessively confirm, validate, and reinforce long-held perceptions of oneself, others, and of reality in general. And although many people may disingenuously insist that they "like" change, what they really mean is that they'd like *others* to change while they remain rigidly comfortable in doing things they've always done in ways they've always done them.

- Love and belonging: The motivating power of this need can most clearly be illustrated by noting how easily people "go along with the crowd," how pervasive the "us versus them" dynamic is to human nature, how powerfully the desire for acceptance dictates behavior, and how essential friends and family are to emotional and physical health. And along with physiological needs, the love and belonging imperative again supports Berne's contention regarding the importance of physical and emotional "stroking" contact from family, friends, and virtually anyone else as fundamental to personal well-being. It is thus not at all surprising that people often define happiness as spending time with people they love and who love them back.
- Esteem and self-esteem: This emotionally essential need refers to the drive to view oneself highly and to cultivate recognition, status, appreciation, and praise from others. Indeed, this need is so great that many people will do almost anything to satisfy it, including undermining the worth of others in order to comparatively increase regard for oneself. To that end, its unchecked gratification is a primary motivation for many psychological games at least and for discrimination, racism, bullying, and hate crimes at worst.
- Self-actualization: This highest level of need, to realize one's full and unique potential, is difficult to reach and at least as difficult to maintain. This is so because the drive to approach this position can be easily interrupted by the frustration of any lower-level need. Yet this highest, most ultimately selfless stage of need *can* be grasped, even if rarely secured.

  Moreover, those reaching this peak need not be or become famous or even overtly exceptional. Anyone can at least approach self-actualization through a willingness to leave self-imposed limits of the past in order to move ever closer to what they're positively capable of being. And once done, any butcher, baker, or candlestick maker might then come to understand what Mark Twain meant in identifying the two most important days in life as "the day you are born and the day you find out why."

  However, relinquishing the past is easier said than done. This is so because the path to becoming a happier, more effective, and more self-actualized person is often thwarted by resistance to recasting one's perceptions and behaviors in clinging to a comfortably unchanging yet unfulfilling existence. Thus unlike for other hierarchical needs, becoming self-actualized may ironically be in-

> hibited rather than furthered by the realization of a so-called lower-level motivation. That is, since the impulse for the safety and security of a predictable world is often the very factor obstructing the maximization of one's change-driven, self-actualized potential, satisfaction of the one need, *when taken to an apprehension-fueled extreme,* necessarily limits satisfaction of the other.

In such cases, any incoming data reaching the Adult ego state conflicting with earlier information will often be ignored, modified, or rationalized so as to preserve the status quo no matter how irrational, dysfunctional, or antithetical to self-actualization it may be. The past as Shakespeare wrote may indeed be prologue, but for many people it also is a self-limiting prison from which too few escape and hardly more even try.

At the least, such resistance to change may result in relatively trivial behaviors such as an inflexible unwillingness *to even consider* learning a new golf swing, to adopting a different method of study, or to accepting a novel investing approach in the stock market. Yet difficulty in "teaching an old dog new tricks" has far more harmful consequences than strokes over par, declining grade point averages, or diminishing returns on one's stock portfolio.

Self-evidently so, clinging to a well-worn and comfortable plan for existence is undeniably detrimental if such rigidity leads to chronic depression, a seemingly endless series of toxic relationships, and a life's self-actualized promise remaining a "what could have been" potential. And though equally self-evident, many people would still rather convince themselves that they are perceptually "right," however unhappy or ineffective they are, than risk being "wrong" and expose themselves to an uncertain, yet possibly more positive, reality.

Still another reason why the Adult is often less than ideally functioning is that since the Parent and Child states are not dependent on formal or informal education and begin "recording" automatically at birth, as "primary circuits" they overpower the later developing Adult. Thus early in life the Adult falls behind the other parts of personality and for many people it never fully catches up.

As a result, the Adult can often be so strongly influenced by those other states that when one believes they are thinking rationally, it simply isn't so. This tendency for the Child and/or Parent ego states to distort the Adult's view of reality so that a person unquestioningly accepts unfounded Parent beliefs and Child delusions is known as contamination.

CONTAMINATION

Contaminated individuals believe that they are accurately perceiving themselves and the world, but they are not. Put another way, the ideally functioning Adult as one's unobscured eye on reality grows increasingly blind as selective perception reinforces false beliefs and irrational behaviors. Thus one's assumptive reality, the often incorrect views of the self and the world, is rarely challenged and remains firmly entrenched. Simply put, contamination enables the assumptive reality to endure.

But the psychic cost for this often irrational status quo is high in that contradictions between one's beliefs and/or behaviors and objective reality creates an uncomfortable "all is not right with the world" tension previously defined as "cognitive dissonance." And since there is thus greater anxiety from challenges to long-held premises than from maintaining a false reality aligned with those premises, contamination in diminishing cognitive dissonance is the unconsciously dispensed prescription for easing that discomfort.

Yet however damaging a compromised Adult is to effective functioning, contamination of its abilities is neither an uncommon occurrence nor uncommonly difficult to understand. That is, because of the relatively greater strength of the Parent or Child, either or both of those states can undermine the Adult's potency by "leaking through" its overly porous ego state boundaries. As a result, the Adult is often reduced to a relatively feeble, poorly sighted, and irrational observer. And since many people occasionally exhibit at least some form of contamination, this most pervasive of so-called ego state "boundary problems" requires ongoing efforts to monitor.

As such, periodically decontaminating oneself by challenging and, if necessary, replacing inappropriate or unfounded beliefs with accurate information and rationally driven behaviors "is a life-long task" (James 1986, 193). To that end, as good a place as any to begin this undertaking is to decontaminate the Adult from the toxic influences of an invasive, overly powerful, and irrational Parent ego state. And in what amounts to a self-administered form of cognitive therapy, this purification process begins with an awareness of how such contamination reveals itself.

Whenever anyone mistakes Parent opinions and prejudices for facts, they are exhibiting a Parent contamination of the Adult. Additionally, in distorting reality concerning others, such a person believes that they are dispassionately and accurately perceiving the world when in actuality they are seeing reality through an Adult "lens" obscured by an overly powerful Parent ego state.

This condition initially results from parent figures expressing opinions so strongly that to the young child they appear as absolutes. Moreover, because a child as so dependent on parents is defined by his or her early environment, it may feel or even "be safer to believe a lie than to believe his own eyes and ears" (Harris 1973, 59). Over time, these beliefs, having been reinforced by seeing what one wants or expects to see, become unchallenged, immutable, and frequently detrimental.

At the very least, fairly inconsequential examples of Parent contamination of the Adult are seen in petty opinions that there is only one way to do something such as making a bed, mowing a lawn, and cooking a turkey, or insisting on only one brand of cereal to buy, car to drive, or political party to support. However, Parent contamination can and often does exhibit itself in far more seriously destructive ways.

Extreme examples of Parent contamination of the Adult are seen in the behaviors of sexists, racists, terrorists, and zealots of almost any persuasion. Living lives according to their absolute truth beliefs, such fanatics promote and, whenever possible, seek to impose their ideals on others. So invested in their convictions, such individuals are capable of harming or even killing nonbelievers, whatever the moral, religious, or ideological prohibitions on which those convictions are based (Solis 2004).

Commonly afflicting members of prejudicial, radical, and often violent groups, extreme forms of Parent contamination of the Adult are often justified by the "false consensus effect." This distortion of reality is the assumption that one's attributes, values, or behaviors are more widely shared than is actually the case. In so believing, individual views or conduct, no matter how outrageous or malignant, are rationalized as seemingly more correct, acceptable, and mainstream than any more generally accepted definition of morality would suggest.

Thus for those succumbing to the false consensus effect, it is well within the bounds of contaminated acceptability to believe the Holocaust didn't occur, 9/11 was an "inside job," women "should be seen and not heard," persecution of minorities is justifiable, and that such "indisputable truths" are more a general rule than rarely found exception. Obviously, this misreading of reality is an unconscious attempt to normalize one's conduct or impressions as typical, appropriate, and factual, however aberrant they may be.

Still another form of Parent contamination of the Adult, rationalized by what is referred to as the "false uniqueness effect," occurs when an individual underestimates the extent to which others possess the same beliefs, character traits, or behaviors as oneself, particularly when they are positive. That is, viewing one's thoughts and actions as uniquely praiseworthy, an individual irrationally and reflexively assumes that others are less hard working, less dedicated, have less integrity, and are less willing to make sacrifices in pursuit of important goals.

In contrast, when an overpowering Child corrupts the Adult, a person distorts reality not concerning others but concerning oneself. Identified as Child contamination of the Adult, those displaying this condition often confuse wishful thinking, superstitions, fantasies, delusions of grandeur, delusions of persecution, or, more severely, hallucinations with objective facts.

More specifically, individuals actually believing that they have a "good chance" of winning a lottery, that weight can be lost without dieting or exercise, or that high grades can consistently be earned without studying are all common examples of this form of contamination. Equally so, anyone believing that someone or something will always "bail me out," that a good job can likely be landed without experience or education, or that spending money, using drugs, and ignoring health issues with impunity will have no ill effects is also filtering reality through a severely compromised Child-contaminated Adult ego state.

But phrases such as "I'm always unlucky, victimized, or unworthy," that "I can never catch a break," or that "Everyone's got it better than I do" are also common expressions of this condition. However, in a desperate effort to defend, maintain, or augment self-esteem, such statements of persecution may also become self-deluding and contaminated claims of grandiosity such as "I'm always right," "I have a genius-level IQ," "I'm next in line for a big promotion," or, as a tone deaf singing wannabe, "I'm the next *American Idol*." Yet clearly an example of Child contamination of the Adult, this last example of "I'm better than I really am" distorted thinking is known apart from Transactional Analysis as the Dunning-Kruger effect.

Research by Justin Kruger and David Dunning at Cornell University in 1999 clearly showed what fans of reality show competitions have long known. And that is, in grossly overestimating their own abilities, people often badly misjudge their competence when comparing themselves to elite performers. Possibly as compensation for low self-esteem, and not knowing what they don't know, many people inflate their marginal-at-best talents fueled by praise from equally oblivious peers or family members blinded by blood loyalty or an unwillingness to speak ego-deflating truths.

Yet there are other explanations for such delusional thinking having nothing to do with insisting that "my grandmother says I'm the best singer she's ever heard' or "Aunt Sarah is certain that I'm the next Rembrandt." And that is, "the less skilled you are, the less practice you've put in, and the fewer experiences you have, the worse you are at comparing yourself to others on certain tasks" (McRaney 2011, 80). Likewise, knowing relatively little about a subject results in a confidence-enhancing ignorance of what there is to know in total. Truth be told, only through innumerable hours of practice and experience can the understanding be gained as to where one is lacking in comparison to top performers in any field.

In fact, despite some Adult-contaminated writers believing that they're the second coming of Shakespeare or some marginally talented actors claiming they're a reincarnated hybrid of Gable, Brando, and Olivier, success doesn't "just happen." According to some experts, "the key to great achievement in any field is practicing a specific task for at least twenty hours a week for ten years: the so-called ten-thousand-hour rule" (Bright 2013, 97; Gladwell 2008).

But people also exaggerate their abilities for reasons having nothing to do with a Dunning-Kruger unawareness of their talents relative to elite performers or a contaminated ignorance of how much time and effort it takes to become truly exceptional in any endeavor. Because self-worth is often calculated in comparison to the perceived worth of others, many amplify personal value by overstating their talents, skills, and intelligence compared to so-called "average" people. And while as a statistical reality it is only possible for just under 50 percent of people to be better than average at *anything*, this contamination includes the 93 percent of drivers that believe they are better than average (Atasoy 2013), the 94 percent of college professors that rate themselves above their peers (Ghose 2013), and the 55 percent of Americans that think they are smarter than the average American (Koren 2014).

Rationalizing failures and exaggerating accomplishments, this self-serving bias results in a fantasy world inhabited by children who are all above average, sired by parents who are equally exceptional. From the radio series *A Prairie Home Companion*, this mythical place known as Lake Wobegon, where "all the women are strong" and "all the men are good-looking," is visited frequently by those overestimating their abilities in order to falsely distance themselves from the "common herd." Sometimes referred to as the illusory superiority effect, this tendency for many people to claim that among other attributes they are more attractive, ethical, competent, intelligent, popular, tolerant, and less gullible than so-called "average" others is not surprisingly also known as the "Lake Wobegon effect."

More specifically, the belief that compared to others one is impervious to political rhetoric, snake oil advertising claims, and cons in everyday life is referred to as the third-person effect (McRaney 2011). Another form of "self-enhancement bias," this Child contamination of the Adult delusion is founded upon the erroneous assumption that while "everyone else," the aforementioned third person, is susceptible to hoaxes, propaganda, complete lies, and half-truths, one's intelligence and sophistication is an impenetrable shield for such deceptions.

Yet for the most part, this supposition is hubris based on Lake Wobegon's esteem-enhancing prescription that most people don't want to believe that they are like the rest of humanity. But as for much of the human race, when lacking an empowered and uncontaminated Adult ego state, they are clearly wrong.

Still another example of Child contamination of the Adult is the grossly mistaken belief that one's appearance and actions are exaggeratedly noticed by others. As a delusion of grandeur, an amplified sense of self results in believing that every aspect of one's looks and behavior is the source of intense scrutiny, evaluation, and criticism. Known as the "spotlight effect," this distortion of reality is egocentricity run wild. After all, unless one has an exaggerated sense of self, why would anyone think they are so important that others would notice a forehead pimple, a bad haircut, or an extra few pounds? And even *if* anyone did notice, the shelf life of such evaluative thoughts would likely last no longer than a Popsicle on a hot summer's day.

The spotlight effect notwithstanding, the uncontaminated reality is that in the long run we are not so important to most others for anyone to give a rat's you-know-what about our behavioral quirks or physical flaws. Fact is, most people are all too concerned with their own "imperfections."

In yet another manifestation of Child assumptions overpowering Adult objectivity, individuals believing that they are persecuted often hear generally stated comments from others as personal attacks, even when there is no objective evidence for making that connection. But beyond such personalizations, Child-inspired misperceptions of reality might also be exhibited by reed-thin adolescents insisting that they are grossly overweight, political wonks smugly claiming a monopoly on truth, or those seriously believing that wishing or hoping can alter reality. And it is this last form of Adult contamination that is known as the "Santa Claus myth."

By definition, a person embracing the Santa Claus myth naively believes that their hopes can alter reality in a positive way: that, metaphorically, a large man with a white beard and wearing a red suit will, as rescuer, arrive bearing gifts to save the day. That is, if one wishes or dreams hard enough, things will miraculously work out well in the end. But as Eric Berne so correctly observed, waiting for Santa Claus is a waste of time. And because of this, "healthy people learn to resign this quest in favor of what the real world has to offer" (Berne 1964, *Principles of Group Treatment*, 283; James and Jongeward 1971, 134). Yet to failing students hoping to pass with little effort, compulsive gamblers confident "their system" will beat the house, or lottery participants believing that despite astronomical odds their "ship" will soon arrive, irrationality continues without results and without end.

Common to young children and immature adults, such "magical thinking" as an obvious distortion of reality is most simply the belief that favorable thoughts or superstitious rituals can influence events that by any objective standard are beyond one's control. And for some, such irrational thinking is far from an isolated behavior. For as Robert Frost sardonically noted, "A person will sometimes devote all his life to the development of one part of his body—the wishbone."

But the fallibility of an ineffectual Adult may extend beyond poor decision-making, irrational assumptions about oneself and others, or even the belief that wishful thinking can alter reality. Indeed, if Adult impotency results from overly permeable ego state boundaries where "intruding" Parent and/or Child states lead to contamination, it may also result from other "boundary issues." These include inabilities to overcome "rigid boundaries" in activating the most appropriate ego state for a given situation, hypersensitive ego state "lesions" leading to highly exaggerated emotional outbursts, or an almost-total inability to exert Adult control in directing ego state energy due to "lax" boundaries. According to Eric Berne, it is just such boundary problems that result in emotional difficulties people confront every day.

In the first instance of rigid boundaries, the executive function of the Adult is undeniably compromised when an appropriate shift in ego state energy does not freely occur because one or two states are dominant at the expense of the state or states remaining. Of course, this is not to say that in every situation a conscious choice may easily be made to energize a specific ego state to the exception of others; however, when an *unrealized and chronic* ego state inflexibility occurs, an individual exhibiting such "exclusion" will likely be described as a resistant-to-change "constant" Parent, Adult, or Child.

Much as an overly zealous parent attends to their children, the constant Parent is a person who continually criticizes, advises, or takes care of others. These know-it-all people are often duty-bound, preachy, moralistic, controlling, and habitually nurturing or critical of anyone even remotely registering a pulse. Moreover, they "push others to accept their opinions, . . . do not like to take "no" for an answer, . . . [and] seek others who will listen to them pontificate" (James 1986, 195). Such a person is not exactly the consummate employee, an optimal member of a problem-solving team, or the ideal guest to bring home for Christmas dinner.

Contrastingly, with a disproportionate amount of psychic energy "trapped" in the Adult ego state, constant Adults tend to overly analyze every decision and rarely, if ever, act on intuition or "feelings." Typically joyless, sterile, and empathically challenged, such individuals not surprisingly have difficulty forming close relationships. Almost "Spockian" in character and virtually devoid of charm, mirth, and spontaneity, constant Adults make less-than-perfect companions at celebrations, ball games, get-togethers with friends, trips to faraway and exotic locations, or to any other "no jacket required" place where frivolity and laughter are likely to occur.

Often eschewing a sense of personal responsibility and worshipping at the altar of Peter Pan, the last example of rigid ego state boundaries is an unwilling-to-grow-up, destructively irresponsible, center-of-attention constant Child. Frequently feeling victimized and persecuted, such an "all about me" individual is typically an external personality type in orientation, wanting to be "kept, babied, punished, rewarded, or applauded" (Jongeward and James 1973, 87).

Moreover, often lacking impulse control and unwilling or unable to delay gratification, individuals with a dominating Child frequently battle overindulgences in spending, eating, and/or usage of drugs. In doing so, they regularly ignore the warning of motivational guru Zig Zigler that "the chief cause of failure and unhappiness is trading what you want most for what you want right now." And lacking Adult awareness or control, a constant Child missing a strong Parent's conscience may also show signs of the Pinocchio syndrome or even the more destructive antisocial personality disorder.

Superficially similar to ever-immature Peter Pan impersonators, those exhibiting the Pinocchio syndrome have little tolerance for frustration, even less impulse control, and through their words and actions show little evidence of ever wanting to grow up. Yet while Peter Pans are clear in wanting to remain children by escaping from a world unable to fully accept their infantile needs, Pinocchios, mostly middle-aged men, shamelessly lie and manipulate others into believing that if given "one more chance" their impulsive, ill-considered, and self-centered behaviors will become yesterday's news. But in never fulfilling promises to demonstrate greater maturity, a better tomorrow never comes and irresponsibility, unfaithfulness, and the exploitation of others as objects to satisfy selfish needs continues (Novellino 2000).

Once known as psychopaths or sociopaths, those diagnosed with an antisocial personality disorder act without any regard for the feelings and/or the well-being or others. Superficially "normal" yet totally self-absorbed, such individuals routinely violate social norms by engaging in deceitful, immoral, charmingly manipulative, and remorseless acts without appropriate affect, guilt, or anxiety. From a Transactional Analysis point of view, such impairment results from an almost complete absence of Parent-imposed morality combined with the grandiosity, egocentricity, and lack of impulse control resulting from an unchecked constant Child overpowering an impotent Adult.

A third ego state problem referred to as boundary "lesions" is a hypersensitivity to an otherwise hidden emotional issue when "disturbed" by external stimuli. Linked to chronically troubling behavioral concerns or more seriously to traumatic events, such lesions allow ego state energy to impulsively vent in a self-righteous, totally unexpected, and at times explosive fury. Found in only the Parent and Child ego states, such ultrasensitive "hot spots" are triggered by sudden and unexpected stresses that lead to extreme expressions of feelings, exposing their existence (James 1986). Thus in negatively impacting how one exaggeratedly responds to relatively innocuous events, lesions as the irrational impetus for "I'm mad as hell" eruptions are relationally destructive in virtually all instances.

While Child lesions are expressed as thin-skinned outbursts in response to real, imagined, or perceptually exaggerated "attacks" criticizing one's behavior, judgment, or physical attributes, their Parent counterparts commonly emerge after assumed challenges to one's ethical, philosophical, political, or religious beliefs and affiliations. Thus in the former instance, innocently asking about another's dieting results, progress in overcoming a counterproductive behavior, job or academic history, child-rearing practices, or even recreational pursuits might lead to an "I had no choice" explosive response. And in the latter case, questions concerning voting preferences, ethics, social conventions, or views on so-called "hot button" issues such as abortion, same-sex marriages, or gun control might lead to similarly inappropriate and temperamental outcomes.

Parent lesions may also be reflexively stimulated by members of a group one is ashamed to be a part of and wishes to impressionistically separate from. That is, contact with anyone sharing one's ethnicity, family background, or even sexual preferences who exhibits stereotypically "disgraceful" conduct often results in a critical response completely disproportionate to the "inappropriateness" of the behavior triggering the outburst. With that in mind, a conversation with a sibling expressing "contemptible" values or a dinner with a culturally related acquaintance displaying "deplorable" actions may result in explosively exaggerated "that's them, not me" reactions which are likely far more contemptible and deplorable than any behaviors precipitating such descriptions.

But boundary lesions not only express themselves from a responder's point of view as at least marginally understandable reactions to external stimuli such as the mention of troubling "personal issues" or as perceived attacks on one's behaviors, beliefs, or physical characteristics. Individuals with lesion sensitivities may also *initiate* denunciations of innocent targets who are merely commenting *on their own lives* without malice of intent.

Thus a mother contending with an unmotivated child and resultantly suffering from inadequacy lesions as a parent might unfairly claim a friend is bragging for even briefly mentioning the academic success of their child. Or an individual struggling with confidence issues might vociferously label someone as smugly "self-satisfied" for merely stating their beliefs with conviction. Or failing to hold or even look for a job, a person with coach-potato-induced Child lesions activated by shame and guilt might unjustly castigate a family member for innocuously mentioning a job promotion as boastful, materialistic, or overly ambitious.

Having nothing to do with ego state boundaries being overly permeable as in contamination, not permeable enough as in exclusion, or having lesions allowing psychic energy to "hemorrhage" into the environment, the final "boundary issue" results from an almost-total absence of ego state separation. Unable to control the movement of ego state energy, and often unaware that greater control is necessary or even possible, people with "lax ego state boundaries" act in a confused and highly erratic way, which in the extreme is indicative of some forms of mental illness.

Also associated with people in crisis, lax boundaries are often displayed by a disconnect between events and emotions, resulting in a randomness of behavior framed by comments such as "I hardly know who I am" or "I can't seem to function anymore" (James 1986). And when symptoms are chronically severe, such statements express an unintended truth in that independent living is difficult if not impossible.

ADULT EGO STATE INDICATORS

Body Language/Nonverbal Clues

- Focused eye contact
- Thoughtful head tilting
- Calm/confident demeanor
- Nonthreatening attitude
- Erect posture
- Win-win conduct

Verbal Clues

- Unemotional tone
- Statement of facts
- Asking questions
- Giving information
- "What are the facts?"
- "We agree to disagree."
- "According to the research . . ."
- "For me to be comfortable . . ."
- "Would you be willing to discuss . . ."
- "How was that conclusion arrived at?"
- Who, what, where, when, why, how
- "I think . . ."
- "It is probable/possible . . ."
- "What is your evidence?"
- "It is my opinion that . . ."
- "Options to consider are . . ."
- "I hear you saying . . ."
- "I recommend . . ."
- "The facts show . . ."
- "What are the pros and cons of . . .?"
- "Tell me more."

SEVEN

Utilizing Transaction Theory

The way we communicate with others and with ourselves ultimately determines the quality of our lives.

—Anthony Robbins

A transaction is simply a verbal or nonverbal communication between two or more people. It is made up of an exchange of strokes, a stimulus by one person and a response by another. Transactions tend to proceed in chains so that each response becomes a new stimulus provoking still another response from the person the initial stimulus was sent from. And depending on whether a response has been anticipated, unforeseen, or contained a concealed message, the three types of transactions are complementary, crossed, and ulterior.

COMPLEMENTARY TRANSACTIONS

In complementary transactions, the response received was expected. This happens when the response returned to the ego state initiating the transaction comes from the ego state the originating stimulus was directed to. Also known as parallel transactions, the overwhelming majority of daily exchanges are of this type. And although the term "complementary transaction" sounds positive, that is not always so.

Complementary Transaction Examples

Stimulus: "Poor people are just lazy."
Response: "You're right. All they want is a free ride."

This is a Parent to Parent / Parent to Parent complementary transaction.

Stimulus: "What time is the meeting?"
Response: "It is scheduled for ten o'clock."

This is an Adult to Adult / Adult to Adult complementary transaction.

Stimulus: "I wish it were Friday already!"
Response: "This weekend will be so much fun!"

This is a Child to Child / Child to Child complementary transaction.

Stimulus: "Pick up that paper!"
Response: "No! I didn't drop it!"

This is a Parent to Child / Child to Parent complementary transaction.

Stimulus: "I can't do anything right."
Response: "You poor dear. Let me help you."

This is a Child to Parent / Parent to Child complementary transaction.

CROSSED TRANSACTIONS

When an unexpected response is made to a stimulus, a crossed transaction leaves one feeling surprised or misunderstood. This occurs when the response returned to the transaction's initiator is sent to or from an ego state other than the one beginning the communication. Yet however constructed, crossed exchanges, as their complementary counterparts, can foster either positive or negative results. Certainly, a crossed transaction can at times abruptly end a conversation with stunned and uncomfortable silence or even prompt a hurtful "war of words," all but eliminating constructive discourse. However, using the Adult "to cross" a Parent to Child critical communication, a Parent to Parent invitation to gossip, or a Child to Parent "poor me" comment can halt a series of counterproductive contacts by thwarting the opening stages of an argument, stifling a rumor-mongering discussion, or encouraging an externally oriented individual to assume greater control and responsibility for his or her life.

However, the vast majority of crossed transactions do not involve such a positive use of an Adult response to a message originating from the Parent or Child. Rather, most begin with an Adult to Adult initiated communication crossed by a Parent to Child or Child to Parent reply. In fact, the latter example may well be "the most frequent cause of misunderstandings in marriage and work situations, as well as in social life" (Berne 1961, 89). And when such transactions occur as patient-to-clinician exchanges in psychotherapy, they are often identified as transference reactions.

First noted by Freud, transference is the stage of therapy in which patients convey to the analyst emotions such as hostility, affection, resentment, or fear once expressed toward their parents. Thus in some ways, transference is primarily an unconscious reenactment of the caregiver relationship the patient had as a child. This makes sense in that when asking for help, patients often feel vulnerable in rubberbanding or regressing back to a helpless and dependent child-like state.

More generally, however, transference can and often does occur in any relationship in which feelings pertaining to a significant person in one's past are shifted to someone in the present. In essence, whether directed at one's therapist, boss, or spouse, transference transactions often mimic aspects of the original caregiver relationship "that were experienced as frustrating, unsatisfactory, intolerable, or abusive" (Little 2006, 11).

Crossed Transaction Examples

Stimulus: "Teachers are lazy and overpaid."
Response: "That is a stupid comment."

This is a Parent to Parent / Parent to Child crossed transaction.

Stimulus: "You stole my watch!"
Response: "What is your evidence?"

This is a Parent to Child / Adult to Adult crossed transaction.

Stimulus: "Kids today are so immoral."
Response: "I have no evidence supporting that conclusion."

This is a Parent to Parent / Adult to Adult crossed transaction.

Stimulus: "Where are my cuff links?"
Response: "Can't you keep track of anything?"

This is an Adult to Adult / Parent to Child crossed transaction.

Stimulus: "Have you possibly contributed to your current situation?"
Response: "Why are you always picking on me?"

This is an Adult to Adult / Child to Parent crossed (transference) transaction.

Stimulus: "Let's call in sick from work!"
Response: "You're so immature!"

This is a Child to Child / Parent to Child crossed transaction.

Stimulus: "I've got troubles!"
Response: "So do I!"

This is a Child to Parent / Child to Parent crossed transaction.

Stimulus: "Stuff like this always happens to me!"
Response: "Why do you think that is so?"

This is a Child to Parent / Adult to Adult crossed transaction.

Stimulus: "You're an idiot!"
Response: "And you disgust me!"

This is a Parent to Child / Parent to Child crossed transaction.

ULTERIOR TRANSACTIONS

An ulterior transaction simultaneously involves two levels of complementary communications. One level is typically verbal, overt, and obvious while the other is covert and often includes nonverbal actions such as posture, gestures, and facial expressions. But since the underlying psychological stimulus rather than the apparent communication is more strongly felt in determining the transaction's outcome, as business management expert Peter Drucker noted, "The most important thing in communication is hearing what isn't said." And he was right. Other than the simplest, most straightforward transactions, the result of any stimulus-response exchange is determined at the "hidden," or psychological, level.

In fact, the power of ulterior messages in provoking a change in consciousness *and* a temporary decommissioning of their target's Adult ego state may be so potent that the effect of such concealed communications is sometimes described as "hypnotic induction" (Conway and Clarkson 1987). And this power is not some uncommon curiosity of human behavior rarely seen outside of psychology texts and psychiatric wards. For undeniably so, this ability to "entrance" others to act in irrational, counterproductive, or even destructive ways through the use of ulterior transactions is a regular feature of daily life and an ongoing characteristic of many interpersonal relationships.

Accordingly, among an infinite number of ulterior transaction examples of "making" people do things without Adult oversight, people may buy things they don't need, drive others away not knowing why, and elect incompetent politicians. In the same manner, hidden-message communications may also motivate friends to question their worth, provoke heated confrontations among family members, and prompt others to overlook one's self-destructive actions.

"Awareness of the double-level communication and its context within a conversation, a negotiation, a relationship, or a life plan is a crucial factor in analyzing human communication" (Summerton 2000, 212). Indeed, Dr. Albert Mehrabian's seminal work on nonverbal transactions noted that *when there is a discrepancy between words and expression,* only 7 percent of communicative meaning will be in the words spoken, 38 percent in the way words are said, and 55 percent in facial expression and overall body language (Chapman 1995–2012; Calcaterra n.d.).

As a picture is said to be worth a thousand words, equally so wordless actions speak volumes, often negatively ulterior in nature, as to their true meaning. Whether admitted to or not, is there any reasonable "You don't matter" ambiguity for chronically thoughtless gifts, repeated failures to acknowledge major achievements, or continual unresponsiveness to dinner invitations? Equally so, can there be any question whether ignoring someone's presence, needs, beliefs, or requests sends a "You're of little importance" message or worse? Truth be told, except for autonomic physical processes and thoughtlessly programmed everyday activities such as brushing one's teeth or tying one's shoes, *all* actions have underlying meanings. For even without speaking, "one cannot not communicate" (Vandra 2009, 54: Watzlawick, Beavin, and Jackson 1967).

But with human communication so infinitely varied, it is too simple to describe ulterior transactions as primarily nonverbal. In fact, depending on word choice, current circumstance, and historical context, many seemingly explicit spoken exchanges, even if unintentional, clearly have connotative meaning.

When a husband tells his wife that her attempts at writing are "nice" or "interesting," when a wife asks her husband if she looks fat, or when a boss answers the grievances of a once-favored employee by constantly changing the subject, there can be little doubt as to the read-between-the-lines intent of these presumably overt transactions. Additionally, it could even be argued that obviously spoken crossed transactions are *all* covert in nature (Vandra 2009). That is, when a reply to a stimulus is self-servingly redirected by a responder, can there be much uncertainty about the "I don't want to do, say, discuss, or act how you want" ulterior response?

Clearly, several common impediments to effective transactions are often at least somewhat ulterior in nature. These so-called communication blocks include inhibiting maneuvers whereby a person is condescending, abrupt, secretive, and/or evasive (Karpman 2009). Certainly, we've all been on the wrong end of an exchange in which the person we are transacting with tacitly makes clear that it is a waste of time dealing with you or considering your point of view. Even lacking such body language "tells" of eye-rolling or smirking, is there any real doubt concerning what such a person thinks of you, its effect on your emotions, and its negative impact on constructive dialogue?

We have all experienced being repeatedly interrupted by another's "monopoly of truth" facts, statistics, and arguments. We have all attempted to cooperatively solve a problem only later to find out that important information was withheld. And few, if any, of us haven't faced an issue with a person who rarely provides straight answers and continually changes topics. Is there any uncertainty as to the ulterior intent and discourse-stifling impact of such otherwise overtly boorish behaviors? And conversely, is there any question whether replacing the communication blocks of condescension with caring, abruptness with approachability, secretiveness with sharing, and evasion with engagement will positively impact discussion whatever its focus (Karpman 2009)?

Yet despite ulterior transactions as a primary element hindering productive communication, such exchanges are not always dishonest or harmful. To be sure, even many positive intentions are communicated by innuendo on multiple levels in words, actions, and body language. At the very least, well-intentioned concern, sympathy, or even flirting may be communicated in this manner. However, because the primary focus of this book is personal growth through the identification and correction of maladaptive behaviors, the following concealed-message illustrations could only be described as negative.

Ulterior Transaction Examples

- On the surface, a salesperson stating to a shopper that "this top-of-the-line computer might not fit your budget" is an Adult to Adult message. However, the covert communication is clearly a critical "You don't look like you have a dime to your name" Parent to Child ulterior statement designed to engage the shopper's rebellious Child, who then superficially as an Adult will almost certainly respond, "No, it's not too expensive. It's *just* what I was looking for."
- Although the explicit message is Adult to Adult when a person sending a provocative and politically loaded essay to a "friend" claims, "I thought you might be *interested* in this," the underlying stimulus is clearly Parent to Child. In many but certainly not all cases, the actual intent of the message had little or nothing to do with "interest" and everything to do with convincing the "friend," as many parents do with their children, of the sender's wisdom and point of view.
- Similarly, verbally "sharing" some "interesting" research "disproving" the recipient's point of view ulteriorly accomplishes much the same end. Obviously, as with "sharing" a politically slanted commentary, the underlying purpose is often to treat differences of opinion as an "I can be right only if you are wrong" contest to enhance the "sharer's" self-esteem. But whether such "sharing" is

verbal or otherwise, unless the recipient of such "interesting" material is also a true believer, relationship-damaging irritation will almost surely result from the sender's not so thinly veiled "I told you so" paternalism. And this is so whether the hidden aim for offering such "interesting" research was self-promotion or not.

- At a party, a flirtatious encounter results in a lengthy conversation culminating with a seemingly Adult question: "Would you like to come back to my apartment and hear my new audio system?" Obviously the surface-level message, an Adult to Adult question, was in reality a poorly camouflaged Child to Child invitation to romantically "play." The response to this invitation might ostensibly be an Adult statement of fact, "Sure, I'm really into classic rock." Yet in reality, the response is also a Child to Child "let's play" message having nothing to do with the Doors, Led Zeppelin, or the Allman Brothers.
- A husband's question of "Where did you hide my car keys?" precipitates a provocative "In the same place as you hid my laptop" reply from his wife. Superficially, an Adult question is presumably followed by a statement-of-fact Adult response. However, as anyone having been asked a similar question well knows, the underlying motive of this exchange initially expressed in the word "hide" is hardly an innocent request for information followed by an equally innocuous response. In both cases, the ulterior message was a long-simmering, sarcastically couched Parent to Child expression of "Can't you be more responsible with my possessions?" frustration.
- After work, a friend matter-of-factly says to you, "I got really drunk last night and wrecked my car." This comment is followed by a smile and a laugh. You respond by saying, "Really? You did what?" And then taking your cue from your reckless friend, you also laugh.

On the surface, this exchange began as a complementary Adult to Adult informational transaction. However, by laughing, this seemingly innocent conversation morphed into a far more sinister ulterior communication diminishing the gravity of some destructive and/or self-defeating behavior. By doing so, others are invited to also laugh and the real issue, the reasons for such negative behavior, remains unchallenged by the listener's Parent and equally unexamined by the sender's Adult. This form of ulterior communication is known as a "gallows transaction."

Just as witnesses to long-ago hangings often laughed at a condemned prisoner's jokes when mounting the scaffold, "spectators" react similarly today in sharing laughter over the self-imposed misfortunes of someone condemning themselves to more of the same. As such, by responding with a laugh rather than a challenge to bad behavior, current onlookers to gallows humor become unaware accomplices in encouraging detrimental conduct to continue. For in sending a tacit message of acceptance by laughing, inappropriate and counterproductive actions continue unexamined, unopposed, and thoughtlessly enabled. And for the presumably condemned jokester, the story ends badly. The noose metaphorically tightens, doom is hastened, and the trapdoor is sprung not by a faceless executioner but by laughing members of the crowd.

But whichever type of transaction one is experiencing, certain ego states attract, almost like a magnet, certain other ego states. Accordingly, when analyzing communications, one should be mindful of the following principles.

"RULES OF ATTRACTION" FOR TRANSACTIONS

- In replying to a transaction's stimulus, one's ego state response can be consciously or unconsciously activated. If the activation is unconscious, the ego state is said to have been "hooked," and if an ego state reply is consciously made, the ego state has been energized or "cathected." Undeniably, an important purpose of studying Transactional Analysis is to provide the awareness and skill necessary to decrease one's "hookability" and make cathecting the most effective ego state in any given situation not only possible but commonplace.
- Typically, the Parent ego state only sends messages to the Parent or Child of the person it is intended for. If the stimulus is sent to the Parent of the other person, the communication usually involves a message that is either critical, nurturing, or "gossipy" about something or someone else. Complaining, "Isn't it awful" messages, or "Isn't it sad about those poor people" communications are also of the complementary Parent to Parent variety. Obviously, Parent to Child communications are extremely common and involve an initial stimulus that is either critical, controlling, comforting, sympathetic, or warmly helpful.
- The Child ego state usually "speaks" to the Child or the Parent ego state of the person the Child is communicating with. Child to Parent communications invariably involve a rebellious "You can't make me" statement, abject compliance, or a whining message requesting sympathy, support, or absolution. Child to Child verbal exchanges are commonly of the "Let's play" or "Let's be irresponsible" variety.
- For the most part, the Adult ego state only "speaks" to the Adult in another person. However, even though the Adult in the recipient may not respond as expected in a complementary manner, that is where the initial Adult stimulus has generally been sent. And since

most transactions by nature tend to "complementarize," that is, become complementary, *sending a response from one's Adult to another's Adult is an effective way to induce a highly productive Adult to Adult complementary conversation irrespective of what ego state the initial stimulus was sent from.* Generally speaking, repeated messages from one's Adult will engage the receiver's Adult by the third attempt to do so.

Thus even if a critical or inciting Parent to Child message has been sent, by ignoring this stimulus and sending a flatly delivered Adult to Adult crossed transactional answer, a potentially explosive confrontation will likely deescalate. Or if a "feeling sorry for oneself" Child message is sent to one's Parent, by ignoring this stimulus and again responding with a thoughtful and calmly stated Adult to Adult crossed reply, productive Adult introspection can replace the language of victimization for the person initiating the exchange.

- Despite confrontational or counterproductive Parent or Child transactional stimuli received from children, students, colleagues, family members, or unresponsive sales personnel, emotionally increasing the distance from provocateurs and provocations by replying from one's Adult is a potent strategy promoting effective communication. This being the case, one can more easily stay in control and cathect the Adult through the internal process of "reframing."

  Thus rather than seeing relationship problems with others as incomprehensible behaviors or personal attacks, TA-savvy individuals consciously energize their Adults by seeking explanations for questionable conduct that can change the meaning, feeling tone, and the entire "frame" of such events. Although mentioned in chapter 2 as reframing examples regarding romantic rejection and road rage, opportunities to view potentially disturbing or detrimental experiences more positively are hardly limited to "Dear John" letters and "Is my will in order?" internal responses to reckless drivers.

For example, rather than seeing a coworker's criticism as a personal attack that "must" be responded to in kind, depersonalizing such behavior as perhaps a desperate compensation for low self-esteem diminishes the visceral reflex for confrontation. Or rather than inferring a sibling's hurtful behavior is malicious, regarding such actions as "he knows not what he does" unawareness rather than bad-to-the-bone animosity can transform an explosive Parent reply into an "it's not that big a deal" Adult response.

Likewise, instead of dismissively and critically responding to a spouse's child-like fears of going back to school, starting a diet, or looking for a new job, viewing such anxiety as motivated by legitimate hunger for confidence-boosting support changes a potentially destructive "Stop your whining!" transactional response from one's critical Parent to a far more positive Adult or nurturing Parent reply.

In any case, rather than responding in kind to "affronts" with annoyance, anger, or even counterattacks, internally reframing an incitement with an Adult "Will any of this matter a year or two from now" question usually puts things into a healthier, more positive perspective. Hence, by changing the way things are looked at, the things looked at also change (Dyer 2009). And by initiating constructively complementary Adult to Adult exchanges, reframing is the transactional tool making such change possible.

EIGHT

Differentiating Psychological Strokes

There are two things people want more than sex and money . . . recognition and praise.

—Mary Kay Ash

A stroke is a verbal, nonverbal, or physical stimulus sent out and received by another person. It is a unit of attention, recognition, or stimulation as when someone says your name, laughs at your jokes, smiles at you, embraces you, cooks your favorite meal, criticizes your intelligence, applauds your efforts, frowns at you, responds to you verbally, or listens attentively to what you have to say. As a transaction is the fundamental unit of social intercourse, a stroke is the fundamental unit of social action.

Simply put, a stroke is any contact or connection acknowledging another's presence. And such stimulation is more than something people enjoy or simply a form of attention at least marginally confirming one's worth. That is, in nourishing and revitalizing the Child ego state, strokes are essential for the healthy emotional life of children and adults and are even more crucial for the psychological and physical well-being of newborns. So clear is this biological connection that the term "stroke," to caress, was coined because of this inherent need for tactile contact during the first months of life.

Indeed, "infants who are neglected, ignored, or for any reason do not experience enough touch suffer mental and physical deterioration even to the point of death" (James and Jongeward 1971, 45). To that end, people may recall stories surfacing shortly after the Berlin Wall fell in the early 1990s when overcrowded orphanages in former satellites of the Soviet Union led to the retarded physical and emotional development of children denied adequate handling.

But such harm to children has not been limited to nations emerging from Communism nor even to third-world states struggling with poverty. Even in America, a potentially lethal condition commonly known as "marasmus" was once an all-too-frequent occurrence in foundling homes where children, even if well fed and clean but denied sufficient stimulation in the form of ongoing caregiver contact, exhibited a "failure to thrive" due to "maternal deprivation syndrome."

At least as recently as the 1940s, it was noted that infants placed in institutions endured "harm not only from their mothers' absence but also from a lack of sensory stimulation" (McCormack 1977, 1). More specifically, such children suffered significant psychological damage, greater susceptibility to disease, serious physical retardation, delayed development of vocalization and language abilities, and "progressively more serious developmental handicaps [including] depression and listlessness" (Clarkson 1992b, 90; Provence and Lipton 1962). And the damage to such stroke-deprived newborns likely extended well beyond infancy in that the neural fibers of children denied adequate stimulation "atrophy and cannot be regenerated by subsequent stimulation if there is a significant lack in early infancy" (Clarkson 1992b, 90; Melzack 1965).

But whether decades in the past or far more recently than that, at least some children denied adequate stimulation have suffered even greater harm. That is, without sufficient human contact by being held, cuddled, soothed, and spoken to, many children living under otherwise favorable conditions have died apparently due to compromised immune systems, even though there was no other physical cause to explain these deaths "except the absence of physical stimulation" (Harris 1973, 64).

Thus, undeniably so, sensory and emotional deprivation forges a biological chain bringing about or encouraging organic changes leading to degenerative changes or death (Berne 1964a). In fact, it may well be that stroke-producing interactions are so important that five hundred thousand years ago the cranial capacity of our ancestors' skulls doubled in size not only to accommodate larger brains for making tools and weapons but as a necessity for "carrying out . . . effective human relationships" (Seligman 2011, 22).

But adverse effects of stimulation deficits are not limited to infants and young children. Indeed, adults "who lack strong social ties or who have few intimate social relationships are more likely to suffer premature death from heart disease, cancer, or suicide than those who maintain social contacts" (Horwitz 1982, 221). Yet because as adults these deficits cannot always be satisfied by contact strokes, as we grow older "recognition becomes a substitute for physical contact" (Newell and Jeffery 2002, 22).

With that in mind, virtually everyone has heard of cases when the death of an elderly person was quickly followed by the heartbroken and stroke-deprived death of their spouse. In fact, a recent study of people at least fifty years old has found that over a six-year period the loneliest among those surveyed were "twice more likely to die than the least lonely" (Dolor 2014). This should come as no surprise. For when facing actual as well as existential aloneness, if stroking relief is unavailable from recognition-providing friends and family, "giving up" apathy often becomes a self-fulfilling reality.

Moreover, we all know of people who go "on the rebound" seeking another partner shortly after a relationship ends. We have all experienced discomfort when someone ignores us with the silent treatment, the cold shoulder, or simply a lack of attention. And we also know that the stroke denial of solitary confinement is among the most dreaded of penalties because in many cases "control of stimulation is far more effective in manipulating human behavior than [is] brutality or punishment" (Steiner 1971, 9; Berne 1961). Yet what many people likely don't know is that some sixty years ago, in one of the earliest experiments on the effects of sensory deprivation, a study irrefutably illustrated the negative effects of severely reduced external stimuli on a group of college students.

As reported in the *Canadian Journal of Psychology*, most students denied sensory variation by donning translucent goggles, wearing gloves limiting tactile perception, and reclining in a lighted but partially soundproofed cubicle *within eight hours* developed what appeared to be a strong need for stimulation. In fact, exhibiting restlessness, irritability, decreased performances on intelligence tests, emotional volatility, and auditory as well as visual hallucinations, some of the students left well before the end of the three-day experimental period. With well-earned student reputations for a willingness to do almost anything for a few dollars, this was so even though their stipend for essentially doing nothing was more than double what they could have normally earned. Moreover, several subjects reported the persistence of confusion, headaches, nausea, fatigue, and a lack of motivation for up to a full day after their isolation (Bexton, Heron, and Scott 1954; Steiner 1997).

Clearly demonstrating the importance of sensory diversity to healthy human functioning, the aforementioned study and many others provide evidence that the need for stimulation in general and human recognition in particular is so great that an array of superficial and often counterproductive behaviors serve as negative substitutes whenever more intimately positive contact appears to be unavailable (Steiner 1997). And with the explosive birth of the digital world beginning in the 1990s, the variety of such substitutes is arguably now larger than ever.

In addition to the longstanding use of psychological games, debatably positive stroke-generating behavior now also includes compulsive cell phone use, texting even while driving, and endlessly trolling even less-than-reputable Internet dating sites. Additionally, "computer addictions" such as excessive gaming, emailing, and inconsequential social media postings have also become familiar if not ubiquitous methods to virtually "reach out and touch someone" when more directly personal forms of contact are unavailable or nonexistent. And other than obvious financial rewards, the gaining of questionably constructive recognition strokes also includes a fifteen-minutes-of-fame willingness to humiliatingly expose one's behavioral foibles to unseen millions on reality television.

But whatever such "voyeurvision" reveals about our society, it speaks volumes about its "stars" placing themselves in situations where public scrutiny and ridicule are all but certain. That is, if given the opportunity to obtain financial rewards and recognition strokes, there seems to be no limit of otherwise seemingly unexceptional people eagerly waiting to sign on the dotted line. And judging by the apparently endless variety of reality programming, its ever-increasing viewership, and the bottomless pit of those offering themselves as leads in such bread-and-circuses entertainment, that trend is unlikely to end anytime soon.

However, the cultural, anecdotal, and research evidence for our innately insatiable love affair with strokes doesn't end with neglected infants, prisoner punishments, goggle-wearing college students, online matchmaking services, or the *Real Housewives of New Jersey*. And confirmation that strokes are physically and emotionally essential doesn't end with anecdotal evidence that much of adult life is spent pursuing the same "stroke fix" affirmations of personal significance addicted to when young.

In the final analysis, the most undeniable proof that the need for strokes is a foundational motivating force of human life may well be that *there is little people won't do* to gain stroke satisfaction. As such, "if acceptance is not offered we will go for approval; if we don't get that we will settle for disapproval; and *in extremis* we will go for outright rejection rather than be ignored" (Barrow, Bradshaw, and Newton 2001, 58).

Accordingly, when hungry for recognition there is little doubt that negative strokes as emotional food have almost the same "nutritional value" as positive ones. To that end, avoidance of a stroke vacuum might at least partially explain why seemingly rational individuals invite criticism and court relational melodrama by overeating, overdrugging, and overspending at the expense of their physical and financial health. Equally so, the need to offset stroke deficits might also explain why many people provoke disputes with others, continually set themselves up for failure in school or at work, play psychological games, and apparently against all reason remain in abusive relationships.

It is thus not surprising that no less an authority than Eric Berne considered stroke hunger as a primary motivation underlying behavior (Novellino 2005). And in recognizing "love and belonging" on his needs pyramid as only slightly less important than food, water, safety, and security, Abraham Maslow, among countless authors and lyricists waxing poetic about finding love or losing it, would be among the last to disagree.

As with so many behavioral patterns, an almost obsessive willingness to pursue and accept strokes of virtually any variety obviously begins early in life. Accordingly, "where healthy strokes are not available or are infrequent or inconsistent, the child unconsciously begins to accept negative strokes, . . . [and] once the expectation for a certain pattern of stroking is established, it develops a tenacious stability, leading eventually to the child's decision on life position and later evolving into his or her life script" (Bary and Hufford 1990, 214).

Said another way, without Adult oversight *the strokes one currently internalizes and unknowingly generates from others are largely preordained by parental stroking patterns established early in life*. But whether an individual pursues positive or negative strokes or precisely when an adult has been programmed to accept or reject certain strokes as an child, the emotional and biological importance of recognition, contact stimuli, social support, the need to belong, and intimacy with others is impossible to ignore. And because stimulation has virtually the same relationship to well-being as food, when experiencing deprivation it doesn't matter if strokes produce joy or misery. Being life supportive, a negative stroke, just as bad food, is better than no strokes at all.

But while in our daily interactions there seems to be a limitless supply of "bad food" negative strokes, "positive strokes are in pervasive scarcity due to a set of inhibiting social and internalized rules that prevent people from exchanging them freely" (Steiner 2003, 178; Woods 2007a, 32). In fact, traditional sex role expectations are at least partially responsible for this culturally imposed stroke deficit.

Obviously less so today than in the recent past, conventional definitions of what it means to be a man or a woman artificially inhibit the free exchange of strokes. That is, many "real men" projecting an image of toughness and control still can't easily accept or ask for strokes. This is so even when in severe emotional pain. To that end, if "big boys don't cry," in keeping stiff upper lips, big men can do no less.

As for women, traditional gender definitions once fostering stroke inequalities within the home mirror workplace disparities still existent today. This being so, women are expected to be endless providers of strokes but must often be content with accepting recognition for beauty or mothering skills while denied comparable notice for intelligence or leadership abilities.

Thus for cultural reasons or as a result of parental injunctions against asking for what one wants or needs and living in "a state of chronic, biological stroke hunger" (Steiner 2007, 309), most people accept and even manufacture negative strokes, whatever their harmful effects. And in a wrongheaded yet understandable way, this makes perfect sense. For as with any biological imperative, the greater the need the more desperate its drive for satisfaction.

With that in mind, it shouldn't be surprising that with stroke hunger as an inborn motivating force and positive stroke deficits as a common condition, "we can be perversely gratified . . . by the negatives we receive if they reinforce a decision that we deserve them, or that people are basically unfair, or that "you can't win," or some other self-defeating conclusion we have come to" (McCormack 1977, 6). Sadly, there is often dysfunctional security even in misery.

This might explain why some people, feeling incapable of attracting positive notice or even any notice at all, will negatively manipulate reality just to generate any stroking response whatsoever. The unconscious reason is simple. To an ignored and assumed to be "invisible" person, at least bad behavior is likely to provoke immediate regard temporarily satisfying the need for recognition. And thus unknowingly complicit in his or her own suffering, such a person is said to have a negative "stroke economy."

STROKE ECONOMY

Often defined in a "macro" sense to describe our culture-wide system of tacit rules where strokes as commodities are "bought, traded, and stolen but hardly ever given freely" (Steiner 1981, 8), in a more personal "micro" sense, stroke economy refers to the number and type of strokes a person expects and internalizes. Yet while there is a certain constancy to this economy, it lacks perfect predictability in that due to changing conditions in daily life, similar strokes do not always offer the same "nourishment." And if this is undoubtedly true on a personal level, it is equally so on a comparative one.

Just as different people respond differently to other forms of sustenance, they also react as individuals to identical or almost-identical strokes (De Quintero and Boersner 1982). One person may value, accept, and encourage recognition for intellectual pursuits, while another for athletic prowess, and someone else for physical attractiveness. And how all or none of these people filter strokes often depends on their current mood, the circumstances immediately preceding the stroke, or whether strokes contradict or support how their lifelong story or script is written to unfold.

"If a stroke fits neatly into the script then it will be taken in at the value in which it was given. And if a stroke is only close to the script, the [stroke] filter may reject it, or perhaps modify it so it will fit in" (Woollams 1978, 194). Thus a person chronically modifying strokes so as to fit their frame of reference is in actuality retreating into a self-constructed reality show, at least one step removed from authentically reacting to real-world stimuli.

Yet however strokes are defined or accepted, as they are offered during childhood to control behavior, we grow up programmed with unspoken "rules" or expectations dictating how this seeming shortage of strokes is to be given, accepted, and even who they should be prompted from. Such precepts often include not giving strokes when we have them to give, not asking for strokes when we need them, not accepting strokes when we want them, not rejecting strokes when we don't want them, and not giving ourselves strokes (Steiner 1974; Trubshaw 2011).

But because the need for the safety and security of an orderly and predictable world presumably trumps virtually every other need, whatever stroke economy rules one grew accustomed to when little are likely to continue. And this is so even if it would seem a relatively simple paradigm shift to ask for strokes when we need them, accept genuinely given strokes when offered, provide strokes when there are justifiable reasons to do so, and give ourselves positive strokes when circumstances and stroke hunger direct their issue.

Even so, because of self-imposed limits dictated by one's stroke economy, such a supposedly simple and obviously beneficial reappraisal in stroke-related thinking may be easier said than done. This is so because just as a person receiving many positive strokes during childhood seeks to satisfy that need through adult efforts generating that familiar outcome, the reverse is also true. Thus if a person when little grew comfortable with a negative stroke economy, later in life he or she will "extract" unpleasant units of attention from others through actions unconsciously intended to recreate that predictable yet unhappy result.

Thus while important to understand strokes as precursors for an individual's life position and ultimately their script, it's equally important to understand that as reinforcing stimuli, strokes confirming, validating, and reinforcing those personality foundations are more likely to be generated and accepted than those contradicting one's sense of self. For example, a confidently okay person will deflect or devalue negative strokes while an individual suffering from low self-esteem will similarly tend to ignore or discredit positive strokes. But whether one's economy dictates homeostatic satisfaction of positive, negative, many, or few strokes, since the hunger for stimuli is a constant for all people, in order to ensure ongoing recognition we surround ourselves with "stroke banks" and "stroke magnets."

Any person, pet, activity, or memory that an individual extracts stimulation from is a stroke bank. And obviously, the greater the requirements of one's stroke economy, the greater the number of "banks" necessary to provide stimulus "withdrawals." Yet however many banks one has approved as reliable stroke providers, the demand to maintain stroke equilibrium is so great that if for whatever reason a bank "closes," then the need to find another source of attention becomes overwhelming. Accordingly, many people quickly and recklessly rush into ill-advised relationships or "couldn't say no" stroke-generating projects soon after a previously open "bank" closes its doors.

However, sanctioning numerous stroke banks is not the only way to satisfy one's primal need for regard. Obviously, in times of stress recycled withdrawals of affirming strokes deposited in one's memory can help ease disappointment, failure, or depression. Yet still another way to temper the frustration of an unsatisfied stroke economy is to fill one's life with anything or anyone capable of attracting strokes.

When positive, such "stroke magnets" may be a diploma at graduation, good grades as recognition for hard work, a beautiful home as proof of a large bank account, or a successful child as evidence of good genes and effective parenting. However, less positively and perhaps with greater desperation, it may also be an unaffordably expensive car as evidence that "I've made it," an "eye-candy" trophy spouse as proof that "I've still got it," an ancient athletic award chronicling a triumph few revere and fewer may even recall, a car decal telling the world where in the age of dinosaurs one went to college, or with only slight exaggeration a "Kiss me, I'm Irish, Italian, a Yankee fan," or whatever automobile bumper sticker.

And while stroke magnets in an absolute sense are thus not always "good," they are a far better alternative than repeatedly "massaging" the environment to generate all-too-familiar negative strokes through self-defeating behaviors known as "rackets."

RACKETS

A racket is a learned and reoccurring behavioral pattern or "gimmick" in which a person semiconsciously manipulates the environment to provoke negative strokes, foster disappointments, and collect bad feelings in order to confirm a pessimistic worldview. The emotional profits from such manipulations are clear. For in recreating past failures and in orchestrating new adversities, rackets provide verifying experiences, "proving" that one is inadequate, unworthy, victimized, unlucky, not OK, or that life is simply unfair. Thus with little or no realization of intent, a racket "junkie" will not only look for but will unceasingly create unpleasant or counterproductive experiences in order to draw from them an "inference that she must protect herself, that she is not properly appreciated, [or] that she has always been followed by bad luck" (Adler 1929, 91; Wilson 1975, 120).

"Always" persecuted and "always" a failure, "racketeers" will chronically arrive late for work and lose their job. Asserting "I can't succeed at anything" will be their predictable lament after a lack of effort precipitates flunking out of school. Failing to heed an array of "idiot light" instrument panel alerts will inevitably result in "I'm a loser" self-recriminations after a mechanically induced automobile accident. And insisting "No one likes me" will become a self-fulfilling prophecy following boorish and "all about me" egotistical behaviors of chronically talking about oneself, breaking social engagements, gossiping about friends, or failing to return whatever has been borrowed. In the end, racket-addicted individuals aren't satisfied until their "I told you so" prediction of misery is realized and their role of victim has been validated.

Similar to psychological games described in chapter 10, rackets are exploitive in habitually manufacturing "displays" to extort evidence of inadequacy, or worse. But unlike games that are an entirely social phenomena, rackets often enacted as emotional solitaire do not require complementary players. In fact, the self-inflicted pain at their conclusion is always *intended* to be masochistically directed rather than as with games often focused on others.

Additionally, while rackets and games are both repeating patterns of dysfunctional conduct, rackets unlike games are not predicated on predictable, recurring, and well-choreographed patterns of ulterior transactions. But perhaps the easiest way to differentiate these toxic coping strategies is to understand that in games where the pain is focused on oneself, such behavior is by definition a racket, but because rackets can also exist as solitary entities they are not necessarily or even primarily games.

Out of Adult awareness, a "rackety" person thus continually sabotages their life, figuratively shooting themselves in the foot, in order to maintain a predictable "why does this always happen to me" existence. Wallowing in fabricated self-pity, such an unhappy individual would rather manufacture sympathy, lower expectations, and be "right" that the "short end of the stick" is all one can hope for than to risk uncertainty in learning from mistakes and taking positive control of life in more internally responsible ways. And since rackets, unlike games, are often solo affairs, generating rackety pain is often as simple as chronically feeling sorry for oneself by endlessly reliving past disappointments, failures, and injustices or by imagining such misfortune yet to come.

Thus a racket is a behaviorally negative stroke magnet common to anyone continually entering into abusive relationships, inattentive students regularly failing classes, self-obsessed companions consistently sabotaging friendships, and "poor me" job losers habitually getting fired for lack of effort or inattention to detail. And if as Einstein is said to have observed that insanity is doing something over and over again in the same way and expecting a different result, then in not only expecting the *same* result but *ensuring* its painful repetition, racketeers necessitate an unfortunate and commonly observed broadening of that definition.

STROKE TYPES AND POTENCY

Internal/External Strokes

While an external stroke is accepted from an outside source, an internal stroke is obviously self-stimulation involving thoughts of current experiences, inspiration from art or nature, or repetitive selections from one's personal reservoir of memories and fantasies. To that end, in cases involving isolated and chronically lonely individuals, rather than generating new opportunities for memory-inspired strokes, it is not uncommon to endlessly replay real and often exaggerated accomplishments, failures, and injustices from the distant past.

Yet whatever the frequency of internal strokes, externally offered stimuli often seem to carry greater emotional weight than any of the "self-talk" variety. Except for the most deeply held core beliefs about one's worth or the lack thereof, this seems to be so. As such, there is little doubt that on an everyday emotional level we frequently place more value on what others tell us than on what we tell ourselves.

Although we may pretend otherwise, compliments from someone else, especially praise from someone we value, likely has greater impact than any "attaboys" coming from within. Similarly and perhaps even more certainly, a put-down from someone else often triggers far greater sting than any self-imposed criticism. And although the reasons for this are unclear, it may well be due to the all-but-universal feelings devaluing or at least questioning one's worth relative to others. For if this weren't so, why would it be far easier to assume someone else's views of ourselves than our own? In any case, whatever recognition one is inclined to accept, reject, or value, there is an undeniable difference in benefits and potency for positive and negative strokes.

Positive/Negative Strokes

Clearly so, positive strokes, such as compliments, rewards, and expressions of appreciation or affection, "invite" one to feel good. Indeed, by promoting confidence, emotional health, and an overall sense of well-being, the frequency of such positive experiences and symptoms of distress "are inversely correlated variables" (Horwitz 1982, 219). So if you're keeping score, optimally functioning "flourishing" individuals, not surprisingly, receive a ratio of over three positive responses for every negative one (Napper 2009; Frederickson 2007). And just as obviously, strokes of a negative variety, such as criticisms, scoldings, or physical abuse, undermine self-esteem and stimulate feelings of unhappiness, aggression, or doubt.

But in offering positive strokes to others, there is still another more self-directed benefit. That is, *authentically* "singing the praises" of a child, spouse, or friend is not only a growth-promoting act of kindness directed toward somebody of importance, but this positive energy will frequently be directed back toward its initiator. This is so because in seeking confirmation of one's existential outlook on life, "persons who feel OK about themselves and others tend to seek out exchanges of positive strokes . . . [while] persons who feel not-OK about themselves and/or others tend to seek out negative strokes" (Woollams and Brown 1978, 51). Indeed, the TA truism that "what you stroke is what you get" is largely so.

Yet even though the relative values of positive and negative strokes are thus undeniable, we all know that while positive strokes are often hard to come by, the supply of negative strokes is seemingly inexhaustible. That said, commonplace and extremely potent negative strokes devaluing the worth, concerns, beliefs, accomplishments, or even the existence of oneself or others are known as discounts.

Communicated verbally or nonverbally and implying quite literally that someone "doesn't count," daily examples of discounts are both numerous and painful. Acknowledging someone with a wave or a greeting only to have them unresponsively walk on by is a discount we all are familiar with. For teachers, students putting their heads on their desks is a no less unpleasant version of this form of negative stroke as is anyone continuously texting while someone is talking to them. A parent asking an adolescent child to call if they are going to be late only to be told their request is "stupid" has also been discounted. And a husband telling his wife that her political beliefs are ridiculous, or that her taste in movies, music, or books is "immature" is likewise offering discounts of the first order.

Intended or not, in all these scenarios the implied message if not the actual reality is clear: "You are not that important to me. For if it were otherwise, I would notice you, or show you respect by accepting as at least somewhat understandable your request or point of view." Thus more powerfully hurtful than more generally directed negative strokes, discounts always insinuate their target is without value. Yet however obviously destructive such discounts are to relationships, habitually discounting oneself is a no less chronically harmful pursuit.

As with many behaviors, maladaptive or otherwise, once self-discounting is firmly established during childhood it becomes ingrained and represents what is considered as "normal." But as with other long-internalized and reflexively accepted frames of reference, "It is what it is" perceptual certainty may well be "It seems what it's not" perceptual error. To that end, like the constant hum of a barely noticed fan, inveterate self-discounters do not hear their reflexive "It was nothing" or "I was only doing what I'm paid to do" responses to praise as loud and clear expressions of self-devaluation that they undoubtedly are.

Similarly, compliments are depreciated by changing the subject, giving credit to someone else, or not taking the source of the acclaim seriously. And when recognition is accompanied by an internal mantra of "This person wants something in return," or "That person is just trying to flatter me," or "He or she *had* to say that" (Bader and Zeig 1976), like a single drop of white paint mixed in an immense canvas of far darker colors, whatever esteem-building value the stroke might have had disappears forever.

Discounts or otherwise, it seems as if negative strokes or adverse events are far more powerful than their positive counterparts. Anyone doubting this should remember a date, a dinner out with friends, a family gathering, or a day at work that was overwhelmingly a great experience until an ill-advised comment, criticism, or difference of opinion ruined an otherwise "perfect" afternoon or evening. In such cases, several hours of positive strokes were almost instantly nullified by a single negative one. Or similarly, a "harsh" criticism or "deliberate" snub from one's boss or "significant other" is typically far more troubling than virtually any compliment or acknowledgment is satisfying.

The reason for this may simply be that perceiving a negative stroke as an "attack," our primitive survival instinct is "hardwired" with a brain "that is designed to give priority to bad news" (Kahneman 2013, 301). That is, although people *want* positive strokes they are evolutionarily *compelled* to pay greater attention to negative ones because our ancestors who spent too much time focusing on good events when they should have been preparing for bad harvests, bad company, or the snowy days of the Ice Age to come eventually followed in the never-to-be-seen-again footsteps of woolly mammoths and saber-tooth tigers.

However, the explanation for the relatively greater power of negative versus positive strokes may be even more complicated than that. And that explanation may be the same as the one causing someone else's comments directed at us to more powerfully resonate than what we often tell ourselves. That is, even in the best of homes, emotional wounds suffered when we were little, unsure, and needy leave an adult legacy of self-doubt. Thus it shouldn't be unexpected that what someone else says to or about us frequently has a stronger impact than any internal dialogue suggesting otherwise.

Similarly, it shouldn't be surprising that negative stroke criticism reinforcing the sense of inferiority we've carried from childhood typically has greater power than positive recognition that is less likely to be believed or accepted. It would only be surprising if accepting what others say about us more than what we say about ourselves was *not* a common signature of the human condition. After all, even to our own detriment, don't we selectively perceive what we "must" accept in order to foster safety and security based on an orderly and predictable world? And if our orderly and predictable world is defined by feelings of inadequacy and insignificance, there is then seemingly little choice but to give greater weight to what others say about us than what we say about ourselves.

But whether positive or negative, how strokes are communicated can also enhance or diminish their potency. For example, while looking directly at the stroke's recipient, beginning statements with the word "I" or the person's name as in "I love you" or "Bill, you are really clever," delivers strokes more powerfully than "You are loved" or "That's a good solution to the problem." Additionally, present-tense strokes and those clearly expressing specific traits about a person carry far more weight than past-tense strokes stated in a more generalized way. Thus "I enjoy your storytelling" and "I love how you effectively blended color and furniture styles throughout your home" are far more meaningful than "I enjoyed your story last week" and "I like your decorating."

And finally, to the greatest extent possible, time-related modifiers should be avoided when offering strokes. That is, "left-handed compliments" such as "I *sometimes* like your cooking" or "I find your writing interesting *at times*" have little positive value to their recipient and by definition sound ambiguous at best and derogatory at worst (Gladfelter 1977).

Conditional/Unconditional Strokes

As a training tool often used to influence children's behavior, a conditional stroke is given as a reward or punishment for doing something. Thus "You are a good boy when you clean your room," or "You look beautiful when you wear that outfit," or "Your language is offensive when you talk that way" are all conditional strokes. In short, whether positive or negative, criteria-based conditional strokes are offered when satisfying or failing to satisfy performance requirements or expectations.

For children offered a preponderance of "strings attached" conditional strokes, an understandable assumption is that they are only loved when they follow parental directives or achieve certain parentally prescribed goals. As a consequence, later in life there is an adapted Child predisposition to reflexively comply with the requests of others and an all-too-frequent adult willingness to accept whatever guidelines for life parents once offered as absolute truth.

In contrast, unconditional strokes are based on the totality of one's being and therefore cannot be earned. Instead, they are offered as generally stated evaluations of intrinsic abilities or characteristics not requiring special effort. "You are a terrific person," or "I love you," or "You disgust me" are examples of unconditional strokes. More narrowly, when comments allude to relatively fixed behavioral or physical traits such as "I enjoy your sense of humor," "You have no sense of direction," "I admire your optimism," or "You have beautiful eyes," such emotionally powerful statements are referred to as unconditional *attributive* strokes (Oller-Vallejo 1994).

Even smiling at a friend, the level of attention one gives a speaker, or simply nodding to someone as they enter a room are considered unconditional strokes. And because such evidence-of-recognition behaviors as well as the aforementioned characteristic-based comments are focused on the essence of what a person is and not on how they may have temporarily acted, unconditional strokes are typically far more potent than conditional ones. It is for this reason that unconditional negative strokes, attributive or otherwise, such as "You are evil," or "You sicken me," or even "I hate you" are the most damaging of all.

Conversely, combining positive recognition of personality strengths in the form of "You are so intelligent" unconditional strokes *and* the positive recognition of "Your last speech was amazing" performance strengths in the form of conditional strokes enhances self-esteem, competency, and overall "is essential to increase confidence" (Napper 2009, 70; Linley 2007).

Counterfeit Strokes

These are superficial forms of recognition that resemble positive strokes but in reality are neither meant, believed, or, as claimed about Chinese food, likely to provide long-term hunger satisfaction. For example, adjectives such as "nice" or "interesting" describing a creative endeavor are often manufactured and hardly complimentary attempts to feign approval for a painting, a literary work, or a decorating choice.

Similarly, talk-is-cheap "Let's get together" invitations and perfunctory "I love you" farewells coaxing an "I love you, too," response among marginal friends or relatives are equally artificial forms of pretend recognition. And professing to really like someone's new car, outfit, haircut, or choice of restaurant while disdainfully sighing, rolling one's eyes, or looking away are no less transparent examples of "going-through-the-motions" counterfeit strokes embedded in ulterior transactions.

Yet whatever its value as a communication tool, one has to wonder whether the social media explosion of the last twenty years also serves as a counterfeit stroke delivery system. There seems little doubt that Internet-assisted contact stimulation beginning with "chat rooms" and more recently aided through character-limited Twitter messages and even briefer "wall posts" from Facebook friends serves little purpose other than to provide a minimally nourishing stroke fix for those craving "will-anyone-please-respond-to-me" recognition. *But rather than a criticism of such behavior, this seemingly endless appetite to structure time in this manner provides further "it is who we are" evidence of just how important strokes are to emotional and physical well-being.*

Sweatshirt Message/Persona

These terms are synonyms for a type of nonverbal stroke that is the personality impression one wishes to convey to others. In keeping with the easily understood language of Transactional Analysis, "sweatshirt message" was coined by Eric Berne from the youthful fad of wearing slogan-imprinted sweatshirts, while persona, Greek for mask, was conceived by Carl Jung. But whether sweatshirt or mask, it is not uncommon to outwardly express who we claim to be by "wearing" a composite statement of our idealized identity.

Likely an adaptive strategy to diminish personal insecurity, a glorified façade is contrived to shield our true, often uncertain, and seemingly exposed selves from the rest of the world. Thus for those fearing rejection because "who I am is all I have," adopting a seemingly more appealing shorthand expression of their infinitely complicated selves, such as "I'm hot," or "I'm tough," or "I'm a jock," becomes a habitually enacted charade.

Yet whatever image we project to the rest of the world, such deception concealing our authentic nature has enormous power to reflexively dictate, often quite mistakenly, what people think of us. And since what is true in general is often true for ourselves, such an error in judgment frequently colors how we correspondingly view others from classrooms to courtrooms and everywhere in between.

But whether our core perceptions of those around us are based on superficial sweatshirts or on absolute reality, formulating inaccurate assessments about people by unconsciously generalizing the quality of one characteristic to unrelated and often unknowable details of personality is known in "mainstream" psychology as the halo effect. Thus a physically imposing person is apt to be considered a leader, a president whose views are favored will almost certainly be portrayed as honest, and, despite evidence to the contrary, an unattractive individual will more likely be considered blameworthy. Moreover, a beautiful but weak *American Idol* singer is often presumed to have a good voice, an athlete from the "steel city" of Pittsburgh is frequently seen as "blue-collar tough," and a child wearing a school uniform may well be viewed as studious.

Unfortunate but true, among a multitude of other factors, how a person dresses, their ethnicity, how tall they are, what they weigh, and how well they speak form an immediate and subliminal positive or negative stroke–inspired impression in our minds, which is unlikely to be questioned and just as unlikely to be accurate or be reversed. Thus in observing that people *do* tell books by their covers and that disproportionately weighted first impressions *do* matter, it is inescapable that such behaviors are far less empty clichés than undeniable statements of fact.

NINE

Collecting Psychological Trading Stamps

Unexpressed feelings come forth later in uglier ways.

—Stephen Covey

Even a person well-versed in transaction theory may be thrown a curveball when an initially calm communication inexplicably erupts into full-blown conflict. In many instances, such unexpected confrontations result from the aggressor's collection of "psychological trading stamps." As the good and far-too-often bad feelings collected and used to justify later behaviors, grey stamps accumulate from negative experiences while gold stamps amass after positive ones.

Figuratively likening compilations of feelings to collections of stamps comes from the practice common at the time Eric Berne wrote *Games People Play* of merchants offering "trading stamps" to patrons to encourage their purchases. Over time, with more money spent and more stamps stockpiled, customers pasting these trading stamps into store-distributed booklets would exchange them for "prizes" based upon the number of booklets redeemed.

But as free rides in reality are limited to dreams of small children and immature adults, believing that hoarding "stamps" linked to painful experiences engenders no expense is little different than believing in hobbits, trolls, or unicorns. To that end, collecting commercially offered stamps was financially costly in the past just as accumulating grey psychological stamps is emotionally costly today. And though trading grocery or gasoline-compiled stamps for higher-priced merchandise has gone the way of room-sized computers, white-walled tires, and rotary-dialed telephones, the practice of gathering collections of negative feelings only to self-indulgently cash them in for depressive days and ruined relationships continues now as then.

Contrastingly, redeeming gold stamps from a job well done or as the result of complimentary strokes is a relatively positive experience. To that end, gold stamps are often "cashed in" for a vacation, a shopping spree, a celebration, a bottle of champagne, or "pigging out" at a fancy restaurant. As long as redemption is kept within prudent limits by an objectively watchful Adult, the cashing in of gold stamps is a highly pleasurable and rarely destructive experience.

But the value of collecting gold stamps is greater than simply providing convenient permissions for a good time or a "well-deserved" purchase. Aside from the tangible rewards of legitimately earning recognition by "doing good," such an internal reservoir of success-generated feelings can also provide an "I can do this" confidence and optimism when facing daunting challenges or an accentuating "what is good in life" credit to draw from in times of stress and/or positive stroke droughts.

Stating the obvious, grey psychological stamps are the bad feelings collected from a failure, an embarrassment, a disagreement, or simply from a negative stroke. Frequently emanating from ego state boundary lesions, when the potential energy of accumulated stamps reaches an emotional "tipping point," they are kinetically redeemed for an argument, a physical altercation, drug abuse, an extramarital affair, a divorce, or even a homicide.

But that's not all. When continually collecting grey stamps without Adult oversight, the greater is the likelihood of further manipulating real, imagined, or exaggerated injustices as "redeemable opportunities" maintaining a predictably depressed existence. Yet as a perfect example of being sorry for what one wishes for, these "opportunities" inevitably result in still larger numbers of bad feelings collected and, correspondingly, ever more counterproductive behaviors and consequences. This should be expected. For clearly so, *grey stamps are the emotional dividends without which psychological rackets would have little reason to exist.*

Yet whatever the degree of manipulation, the quantity of stamps generated, or the intensity of feelings involved, grey stamps are often collected in one place only to be unloaded on innocent and unsuspecting victims somewhere else. And when this happens, stamp collectors are guilty of displacement in Freudian terms or of "kicking the dog" in the language of Transactional Analysis.

One needn't look very far to find examples of relieving personal frustrations or insecurities by exhibiting hostility and dominance over relatively defenseless victims. After a bad day at work, a woman coming home and yelling at her children or a student bullied by classmates beating a younger sibling after school are all-too-common occurrences. So, too, are more serious examples of displacement, including an adolescent chronically angry and feeling inept over his academic and/or social deficiencies torturing small animals or, on a national level, those having power persecuting those having none.

Certainly, the Holocaust is arguably the most horrifically obvious societal example of collecting grey stamps in one place and "cashing them in" on blameless targets. Clichéd but true, in flowing from the strong to the relatively weak, aggression as water invariably flows downhill.

But whichever type of stamp one regularly collects, the inertia of "normal" dictates the continual accumulation of such feelings. So in order to make sense of things by maintaining a predictable existence, stamps are regularly gathered in alignment with and as reinforcement for one's sense of reality.

Thus perceiving or even imagining the world as unfair, stamps embodying feelings of anger, depression, or persecution are likely to be masochistically hoarded whether circumstances objectively dictate such collections or not. And contrastingly, seeing the world as positive, hopeful, and joyous, events will be generated leading to the accumulation of the success or approval variety of gold stamps.

Moreover, just as people become "addicted" to the comfort of certain existential "truths," they also become habituated to those very feelings their favored variety of psychological stamps represent. Thus for some people, anger, depression, success, or approval become "drugs" dispensed from one's "internal pharmacy" to maintain a sense of equilibrium, and stamps are but a junkie's "fix" to ensure that end.

But fortunately, grey stamps are unlikely to be redeemed on a wrong-time-wrong-place target without at least some warning. Likely so, just before a collector is about to "gunnysack" or unload an accumulation of such feelings (Zechnich 1976) they will announce that action with a "redemption time phrase" such as:

- "I've taken this long enough!"
- "I've had it up to here!"
- "I've taken all I can take!"
- "That does it!"
- "That's the last straw!"

Yet although "stamp collecting" seems to be a pervasive part of the human condition, such actions are not inevitable. Indeed, emotionally healthy individuals collect few grey stamps. Communicating emotions appropriately, such "having-it-all-together" people regulate the very drive to unexpectedly lash out at others that is the unhappy and divisive product of collecting grey stamps. And although the harm of stamp collecting is a construct unique to Transactional Analysis, Daniel Goleman's *Emotional Intelligence* in 1995 voiced similar concerns for people inappropriately expressing their feelings.

Emotional intelligence refers to a group of character traits dealing with effectively managing one's emotions and behaviors. Such traits include: restraining negative impulses, self-motivation, remaining optimistic despite the inevitable "speed bumps" of life, appreciating the views of others, delaying gratification by exercising self-control, and, supporting a prohibition against collecting grey stamps, handling relationships in an effective manner.

Consciously or not and well-versed in Emotional Intelligence, Rational Emotive Therapy, Positive Psychology, or Transactional Analysis or not, people excelling in life recognize that collecting negative feelings is physically toxic, damaging to relationships, destructive to one's career, and morally questionable to practice. And yet as mentioned, even though studies abound linking anger, stress, frustration, and pessimism to illness and premature death, stamp collectors foolishly drink the poison of enmity expecting someone else to sicken. But they are wrong. In a psychic law of energy conservation, negativity aimed at others is neither created nor destroyed but is redirected back toward oneself.

But there is an alternative to accumulating anger, irritation, or resentment. And that is "the healthier the individual, the more [he or] she will directly and effectively express . . . feelings, wants, and needs as they occur, rather than collect stamps" (Woollams and Brown 1978, 146).

However, there is another more purely philosophical reason to seek constructive alternatives to collecting negative feelings in one place and "dumping them" somewhere else. And that is, if real or exaggerated "hurts" resulted from an unpleasant interaction with a particular person, how is it useful or even ethical to focus the toxic fruits of that exchange on someone else? Or if stamps indeed resulted from an argument, insult, or criticism, how is it effective or even moral to initially say nothing, "stew" in one's internal juices, and then unexpectedly lash out against the "guilty" party at a time and place of one's choosing?

Isn't it possible that the supposed injustice was simply a misunderstanding? Isn't it possible that in playing the victim, one is overreacting? Isn't it possible that either you or the "guilty party" was just having a "bad day"? And isn't it possible that the "injustice" was manipulated as a racket precisely to collect the bad but "comfortable" feelings confirming one's "woe is me" victim's outlook? But whatever the possibilities explaining a stamp-collecting event, how is it fair to collect and later redeem stamps for an "injury" that the "guilty" party may be unaware of, quite possibly does not even remember, and hasn't even been given a chance to correct?

With the above in mind, as a noncritical explanation of one's feelings to the "offending" individual, the "call for an accounting" approach is a potent alternative to accumulating and redeeming grey stamps. In doing so at the earliest possible time after the perceived injustice, stamp collecting is avoided, the "guilty" party gains awareness, an opportunity to apologize is offered, and a potentially explosive situation can be diffused.

Expressing the reasons for one's feelings *in the Adult ego state* is essential to the success of the call for an accounting approach. Rather than blaming others for one's emotions, "owning feelings" by *nonjudgmentally* stating why one is upset lessens the likelihood of a defensive and potentially confrontational response. Additionally, avoiding the use of the pronoun "you" helps to ensure that the accounting statement will not be heard as a Parent attack on the "offender's" Child.

In fact, if a call for an accounting is effectively expressed and an Adult to Adult complementary transaction immediately follows, the ensuing responses of the "guilty" party will often be surprise, remorse, overwhelmingly apologetic, and unlikely to be repeated. And yet even if such positive reactions do not occur and those behaviors that led to the call for accounting approach continue, that outcome is *still* not necessarily a bad thing. For however unpleasant it might be, wouldn't it be enlightening to know that a person one has a relationship with isn't willing to *at least minimally* alter their behavior to spare emotional pain to someone they otherwise claim to care about?

As the subsequent examples indicate, call for an accounting "I statements" should be calmly stated, completely noncritical, and *purely informational.* Authentically expressing vulnerability, such declarations should be straightforward explanations of what emotions followed someone's actions. And because their extreme simplicity "merely" establishes that a verifiable action resulted in an irrefutable feeling, "there is no judgment, accusation or reproach, so as not to provoke guilt or defensiveness" (Steiner 2001, 142).

- "Since I'm sensitive about my weight, comments about how heavy I am are depressing."
- "After hearing remarks about my "dead end" career, I felt like a loser."
- "Whenever I'm questioned about my inability to maintain positive relationships, I lose even more confidence in myself."
- "Each time I'm reminded about how poorly my child is doing in school, I feel inadequate as a parent."

And if due to mitigating circumstances the call for an accounting approach is not immediately used, it is emotionally beneficial and morally justifiable to impose the "Seven Day Rule" for employing that strategy. That is, if a "transgression" is important enough to collect and store negative feelings, it also is important enough to force a relatively speedy resolution by enacting a week long "statute of limitations" after which the "wrongdoing" should forever be put to rest. This "now or never" restriction presupposes the requirement to promptly bring the grievance up, talk it up, and wrap it up, as opposed to irrationally saving it up, blowing it up, and mopping it up long after the stamp-collecting "injustice" may even be remembered by the "guilty" party (Karpman 2009).

TEN

Identifying Games and Defenses

You're welcome to play this game if it makes you happy, but for most people, it will make you miserable.

—Seth Grodin

If indeed you can't change what isn't acknowledged, it is essential to recognize the role that nearly universal feelings of self-doubt play in the human drama. Undeniably, much of what we say and do is at least tangentially related to overcoming feelings of inferiority and insignificance on the one hand and confirming those same toxic feelings in fashioning a predictable world on the other.

To that end, how many failed relationships and how much self-loathing and depression is linked to "I'm not good enough" feelings no matter how unrealistic and destructive such thoughts may be? And how often is "all about me" braggadocio, objectively absurd delusions of grandeur, and omnipresent alibis for failure prompted to fend off "attacks' from others and criticism from ourselves? But besides daily questions about self-worth and ongoing struggles offsetting their torment, a strong case also exists that virtually any form of intolerance or outright bigotry stems from inferiority-inspired compensatory needs to elevate ourselves at someone else's expense.

Certainly, the concept that feelings of inadequacy and unimportance as common to and motivators for the human condition is not at all unique to Transactional Analysis. Indeed, whatever its therapeutic focus, much of psychology is devoted to understanding this dynamic and recognizing its behavioral manifestations in denying, distorting, and modifying reality in order to counter ongoing challenges to self-esteem. And although there are numerous behaviors commonly employed to lessen this all-but-universal sense of deficiency, at the very least they include prescriptions as old as prejudice, as commonly experienced as Freudian defense mechanisms, and, in a relative sense, as recently recognized as psychological games.

Described as "the most important aspect of social life all over the world" (Berne 1964a, 49), a game is a learned and repetitive series of superficially plausible ulterior transactions leading to an expectedly negative conclusion exposing the initially camouflaged motivation for playing the game in the first place.

Signaled by an unanticipated and emotionally impactful change in role or ego state "switch," such dysfunctional pastimes begin with a provocatively manipulative "con" covertly intending to lure an unsuspecting foil into game participation. In turn, this "game-within-a-game" provocation is accepted because it invariably incites a hypersensitive vulnerability or "gimmick" such as vanity, hubris, or insecurity in its naïve target. This is then followed by a series of ulterior transactions or "moves" that ultimately end the game with a damaging but perversely satisfying "payoff" result.

Thus because someone almost always gets hurt by the dishonestly hidden intention of a game, the term itself is quite misleading. That is, games are anything but fun or enjoyable because by definition their painful and detrimental grey-stamp payoffs are not meant to be. As out-of-awareness obstacles to intimacy, "they are relationship wreckers and . . . misery producers" (Harris 1973, 146) involving discounts to oneself and/or someone else. Yet because the only way to avoid playing games or becoming their unsuspecting target is Adult awareness, it is essential to understand why they are played and what they look like.

THE REASONS FOR PLAYING GAMES

There are many reasons why people play games, including the "need" to collect stamps, avoid responsibility, relieve guilt or insecurity, or satisfy the biological imperative to generate predictable strokes. However, the overriding motivation for such ulterior pursuits is again likely grounded in Maslow's belief that we all cling to the safety and security of a predictable and orderly existence. And with feelings of inadequacy an almost universally experienced burden, it seems likely that a primary cause for playing games flows from a "repetition compulsion" to provide psychic stability in confirming, reinforcing, maintaining, or compensating for this sense-of-deficiency perception about oneself relative to others.

In fact, such a comparatively focused perspective regarding personal worth is a foundational determinant for which games are played. As such, an individual's "go-to" games are not randomly chosen but out of awareness are specifically selected according to the life position they are designed to validate, sustain, and defend (Berne 1964b; Fine and Poggio 1977).

Undeniably, such frame-of-reference constancy is essential to effective functioning. Indeed, "if an individual changes beliefs frequently, he or she may soon not know what to think, or may stop thinking, or may think wildly and out of touch with reality" (Hine 1990, 36). And as much as anything else, the most valued evidence ensuring such a necessarily stabilizing constant image of the world are the strokes that one receives. Thus in provoking negative strokes for oneself and/or providing them for others, the path to a game's destination may be as important as its ultimate result.

Failing to manipulate reality to align fact, opinions, or behaviors with one's intellectual, moral, or existential compass leads to psychic discomfort caused by a disconnect between what is believed or done and what evidence irrefutably indicates is true or "right." Since people avoid the distress of such cognitive or emotional dissonance like the plague, surefire methods to reduce this tension are either to disavow, misrepresent, or devalue irrefutable facts contradicting one's assumptions or to create additional "facts" supporting them.

The first method implies that an individual "unconsciously and automatically accepts whatever reinforces his or her pre-set views and in the process . . . any evidence to the contrary will be discounted at whatever level necessary to maintain the homeostasis" (Bary and Hufford 1990, 214). However, it is the second method of unmindfully manipulating events and people to corroborate views of oneself and others that is particularly well suited to playing psychological games.

Thus in creating a procrustean bed "confirming" perceptions of oneself and the world, games provide the manufactured evidence for their continuance. It's not only as Santayana insisted that "Those who cannot remember the past are condemned to repeat it." The problem is that in habitually recreating games learned in childhood, players at least emotionally remember the past all too well.

But unlike fish mechanically filtering plankton-rich water for caloric nourishment, people do not passively filter whatever reality-confirming sustenance comes their way. Accordingly, to guarantee greater predictability in an otherwise unpredictable existence, they selectively perceive and *actively create* experiences "proving" the accuracy of their homeostatic frame of reference. And in eliciting the internal and external stroking equilibrium they are comfortable with through games, people are doing exactly that. In fact, games "can become the principle source of strokes for some people" (Steiner 2007, 309).

Furthermore, since evidence confirming one's worldview has been self-servingly fabricated to prove its truth, the games providing such validation are largely determined by how people view themselves and how that value compares with their appraisal of others. And because feelings of insignificance and inferiority stemming from a child's lengthy physical, social, and economic dependency are so widespread, the purpose of many games is primarily defensive in temporarily relieving this sense of inadequacy.

Thus in postulating that once safety is achieved through a predictably secure world the needs of esteem and self-esteem soon follow in motivating behaviors, Abraham Maslow unknowingly made his second contribution to explaining games as a pervasive part of human behavior. For clearly so, their frequent focus to feel better about oneself at another's expense perversely serves this esteem-enhancing purpose quite well. And the short-lived, ultimately destructive, and common-to-many-games approach to realize this aim is "leveling."

Leveling

Fittingly enough, leveling refers to actions directed toward relatively raising one's esteem by simultaneously lowering someone else's. In a general sense, leveling can be accomplished in several ways, but whatever the method of leveling a game player chooses, the underlying purpose is based on a one-upmanship calculus as old as mankind. That is, the easiest way to relatively reduce one's own sense of inadequacy is to demonstrate power by passing self-doubting pain to another in an egocentrically motivated round of emotional "hot potato" (English 1969). And though in any fundamental way no one ever gained in value by diminishing the worth of someone else, game-playing continues as if proving otherwise.

The most obvious way to level someone is to criticize or belittle them so that they begin to question their competence, adequacy, or importance. When this invariably occurs, the game is won. This is so because when someone else feels greater inferiority, the game player, in a purely relative sense, feels greater worth. Thus a common theme of many games is to create a scenario constructed from a series of ulterior transactions with that "I'm smart and guess who isn't," or "I earn six figures and guess who doesn't," or "I'm successful and guess who'll never be" purpose clearly in mind.

Leveling can also be accomplished by refusing to acknowledge another's achievements and/or by building oneself up through conceit, inferentially "proving" the inferiority of one's audience. The first instance results from the scarcity logic that, in a relative sense, strokes given to others somehow diminishes the availability of strokes for oneself. Moreover, as a form of passive leveling, withholding recognition of another's accomplishments avoids comparative reminders of failings, shortcomings, and "I should have but didn't" regrets from one's own life. And the second instance occurs when "casually" mentioning the size of one's income, by subtly interjecting a personal accomplishment into an unrelated conversation, or by offhandedly mentioning with hidden-agenda motivation the achievements of a spouse or child.

Another form of leveling involves delighting in the suffering or the misfortune of others. The media is rife with "feet of clay" stories regarding athletes, movie stars, and politicians. And because such schadenfreude can be accomplished quite easily without an ongoing series of ulterior transactions, experiencing "joy" in the misery of others while a result of many games is not in and of itself inextricably linked to such ulterior activity. Indeed, schadenfreude need not involve any transactions at all.

But while relishing in the agony of others is often a solitary activity akin to emotional masturbation, it too can be the dominant reason for at least some games and a psychological side effect for others. But whatever way schadenfreude is exhibited, its evolutionarily programmed emotional result is always the same. That is, when someone else experiences adversity, those viewing such setbacks as self-serving "what is bad for others is good for me" survival opportunities (Smith 2013) feel better about themselves. And by any definition, this, too, is a form of leveling.

Whereas leveling is primarily enacted to at least temporarily relieve feelings of inferiority by comparatively raising personal regard, many games are also played simply to avoid put-downs by others or condemnation from oneself. In such instances, their common premise is to avoid responsibility for mistakes or misfortune. After all, by artfully constructing "It's not my fault" explanations, game players can delude themselves and hopefully others into believing such fiction and at least briefly reduce feelings of inadequacy. And while doing so, if one can also undermine another's self-esteem by blaming someone else for their shortcomings, all the better.

Although many games are thus designed to inflate one's sense of worth by rationalizing failure or persecuting innocent targets, others are initiated to do the reverse. That is, some games are specifically enacted to actually *confirm* one's presumable lack of value: most notably those played to avoid taking positive action. And though such self-sabotaging sounds counterintuitive, as previously mentioned many people would rather be "right" and cling to a predictable world of self-inflicted victimization than to be "wrong" and risk change in positively moving forward.

In fact, in varying configurations the comfortable, if growth-inhibiting, roles of victim, persecutor, and rescuer commonly cast by ancient Greek playwrights are also common to modern psychological games. Known as the "drama triangle," people typically exhibit two or more of these negative behavioral characterizations, often within the same game (Karpman 1968). Serving to advance a game's moves, such roles also serve to confirm and reinforce foundational life position beliefs about the intrinsic worth of oneself relative to others.

However, while most people have a favorite role in games, as in some twisted variation of musical chairs, participants often move from one interchangeable role to another until the odd man out confirms his or her portrayal of victim. Thus whether for drama, games, or for the wider stage of life in general, "after a character starts a scene with an assigned role . . . action proceeds by means of role shifts from one point of [the] triangle to the next one . . . until a new scene within which action might generate the next role shift, right on up to the end of the play" (English 1977, 323). For example,

> Rescuers who get tired of putting out and not getting their needs met begin feeling victimized themselves and finally end up persecuting the Victim with impatience. Or, Victims get tired of being patronized and feeling matters are out of their control . . . start to persecute the Rescuer. Or, Persecutors move into rescuer because they feel guilty for being so awful or into Victim because people get tired of being their Victim and retaliate by being nasty. (Choy 1990, 43)

But the tendency for people to alternate from one role to another should not surprise anyone. Learned early in life in the "drama school" incubator of the home, family members adopt then change roles with relatively impotent children playing the part of victims overseen first by one parent and then the other alternating as persecutor and rescuer.

Adjusting to such theater, children adopt a favored role with the Hurtful Adapted Child as precursor for persecutor, the Helpful Adapted Child as future rescuer, and the Helpless Adapted Child as prototype for victim (Holloway 1977). Yet as parents of some teenagers know all too well, whatever mode of adapted Child was initially embraced, later in the story as the no-longer-powerless child enters adolescence, the hitherto oppressed coming-of-age "victim" turns the tables as a difficult-to-control persecutor.

It should also be noted that the aforementioned game roles, though played out of awareness, are manipulative in nature. That is, rather than the appropriate role of "persecutor" as a judge in legitimately enforcing laws, the role of victim for someone denied equal treatment, or the actions of a rescuer in helping those truly needing assistance, drama triangle characterizations are ulterior façades exploitatively confirming a person's life position and furthering their script.

Yet maintaining the role predictability of a game-initiated drama triangle existence ensures more than status quo security and ultimately unhappy results. For however reality may be negatively influenced, games can also stimulate superficially "positive" side effects. And these less obvious so-called "secondary gains" derived from a menu of self-defeating behaviors are fruits of the "neurotic paradox."

The neurotic paradox is the tendency for some people to counterintuitively resist overcoming dysfunctional conduct because such outwardly irrational actions serve ulterior aims in their lives. That is, many people often have an underlying purpose in maintaining behaviors leading to failure and depression because they offer compensatory advantages. To that end, the "hidden benefits" of games are not inconsequential. As a result, despite their destructive impact on relationships, games as anxiety-relieving and addicting "behavioral drugs" are difficult to surrender.

As the primary value of many games is to offer psychological "escape hatches" from threats to self-esteem, it is easy to understand how undermining the worth of others through leveling, or by refusing to accept personal responsibility for failure, furthers that end. However, what is less obvious is that in maintaining self-imposed obstacles to a better existence, games also compensate players with many of the same secondary gain "benefits" arising from imagined or exaggerated illnesses. This is especially true when, as is often the case, the favored role of the game's instigator is a pitiable victim.

With the star of the game thus portrayed as victim, sympathy is aroused, expectations are diminished, attention is gained, hostility seems excusable, and personal irresponsibility becomes counterfactually more acceptable. This being so, Freud's observation that "neurotics complain of their illness, but they make the most of it, and when it comes to taking it away from them they defend it like a lioness her young" could just as easily have been said about players of psychological games. So, too, the spirit of this assertion was echoed by Freud's colleague Alfred Adler.

> The chief occupation in life [for a neurotic] is to look for difficulties, to find some means of increasing them, or at least of increasing his own sense of their gravity. The most ordinary difficulties of life, common to everybody, are carefully collected by him and kept on exhibition. He does this more to impress himself than others, but naturally other people take his burdens into account and do not expect much of him. Any success he may have, moreover, is magnified by this heavily advertised handicap, so that it becomes his most useful possession. By it he wins his way to a privileged life, judged by a more lenient standard than others. (Adler 1929, 49; Wilson 1975, 121)

But for the neurotic, the hardcore racketeer, or the chronic game player, the secondary gain "rewards" of their "privileged life" are fool's gold. For in self-sabotaging existence, their free-ride ticket of excuse and inaction is revealed as hardly a bargain in stopping at "pity parties" where negative strokes are the "coin of the realm" in purchasing a reality that confirms, maintains, and reinforces not-OK feelings about themselves and the world.

A SAMPLER OF PSYCHOLOGICAL GAMES

Mine Is Better Than Yours

Likely the first game most people learned to play, "Mine is Better," often continues throughout life. Clearly, this is a leveling game intended to "prove" that its initiator is superior to his or her target. Once accomplished, such a result is a tonic for temporarily relieving feelings of inferiority common to many people. Thus not so paradoxically, the underlying impetus for Mine is Better Than Yours is the same as so many leveling-inspired pastimes. And that is "I am not as good as you."

On the surface, the opening move of Mine is Better is a superficially Adult-sounding statement of fact such as "I have more baseball cards or dolls than you do" during childhood, to "I have more video games or can do more bench presses than you" during adolescence, to "I have a larger house or a bigger bank account than you" as an adult. But whatever the evidence used as a basis for comparison, the barely disguised message can be none other than "I am superior and guess who isn't."

A variation of Mine is Better is "Mine is Worse Than Yours." In this game, players try to outdo each other's story of personal hardship. Following someone's tale of woe, the player's response in this perverse competition is often something like "So you think that's bad. Have you heard what happened to me?" That story is, in turn, followed by more details or by greater "tragedies" as each player attempts to trump the other and thereby "prove" who is complaining unnecessarily and who is really more deserving of lowered expectations and victim-status sympathy.

Yes but

Said to be the "most common game played at social gatherings, committee meetings, and psychotherapy groups," (Berne 1964, *Games People Play,* 58) Yes But is launched by people who ask for advice but don't really want it. The game begins when a player as victim requests help in solving a problem. This plea hooks the target's nurturing Parent, who responds "Why don't you . . .?" Yet, whatever suggestion or solution is offered, the insinuating-its-inadequacy response is always "Yes but" followed by a fill-in-the-blank nonactionable reason. Indeed, over time an accomplished player can hold off advice-givers with why-suggestions-won't-work rationalizations longer than the three hundred Spartans held off the Persians at the Battle of Thermopylae.

Interestingly, virtually every parent has been baited into playing a version of this game by their young children, who despite endless suggestions of amusement possibilities continue to wander aimlessly and zombie-like through the house complaining that there's "Nothing to do." But whatever variation of the game is played, while the initial request for assistance is seemingly plausible, players of Yes But have a far more ulterior agenda. And that is to remain chronically infected with a case of "It's not my faultism."

In addition to leveling advice-offering rescuers with "It won't work" rejections, Yes But enthusiasts want to "prove" that since there is no solution to their "issue," they can continue to do nothing other than to persist in feeling sorry for themselves. In this way, the self-generated evidence that "no one can help me" or "I guess there's no solving my problem" is overwhelming and secure. Moreover, since "we are driven more strongly to avoid loses than to achieve gains" (Kahneman 2013, 302), Yes But offers players the preferred option of failing to try than trying and failing.

But whatever rationalizations such manipulated evidence provides, the end result is inaction, self-pity, and the added benefit of "proving" that the unable-to-help patsy hooked into offering suggestions is just as inadequate as oneself. And the silence following the rejection of all advice signals the game player's triumph of that "going nowhere fast" leveling strategy.

I'm Only Trying to Help You (ITHY)

With players offering advice rather than asking for it, ITHY might be described as Yes But in reverse. The game's initiator begins play as a seemingly well-meaning rescuer whose ignored, misinterpreted, paternally overbearing, and frequently failing counsel leads its recipient to "persecute" the newly martyred "helper." Now as victim, the game player then embraces that role with an entirely self-serving "Nobody listens to me" all-knowing and all-good "So this is the thanks I get" portrayal of Mother Teresa.

Played by parents, friends, and family members giving aid to those neither needing nor often wanting it, ITHY is initiated to provoke self-imposed sympathy by proving that people are ignorant, ungrateful, and inherently not OK. After all, if rejected as a competent and good-to-the-bone helper, can there be any other conclusion about the disappointing nature of people? And the predictable and equally ignorant answer of the ITHY player is "of course not."

An interesting and all-too-common variation of ITHY is played by parents with their "failure-to-launch" adult children. Previously mentioned as one of the dangers of an overly nurturing Parent ego state, the game begins early in life by presumably responsive parents satisfying every desire, solving every problem, and meeting every need of their child. Yet masquerading as completely selfless acts of love, the underlying reason for such exaggerated parental "support" may well be just as much motivated by regard for oneself. That is, by continually rescuing their children, insecure parents hope to self-servingly trade such "only trying to help them" efforts for "only trying to help ourselves" behavioral compliance and everlasting affection.

However, for both parent and child, this exchange is a Faustian bargain. This is so because in enabling a perfectly able child to become perfectly disabled, parents may indeed temporarily manufacture a child's loving response, but as basic training for powerlessness, it will often undermine the youngster's spirit of self-sufficiency. And when this dependency extends beyond adolescence, the financial and emotional costs of ITHY, for even well-meaning parents, will likely be felt for years to come.

But in gaining a relatively free ride early in life, the ultimate expense for the child will be no less damaging. For in unconsciously internalizing an entitlement worldview where "normal" means that "others do for me," the child never experiencing the personal potency of "making it on their own" will predictably grow into adulthood waiting for Prince or Princess Charming to rescue them. Yet while they're waiting, parents who were once placeholders for those same roles will often choose another part to play. And that is, in subsequently gaining "Our child's a slacker" sympathy from friends, they will portray themselves as "We just don't know how this happened" victims.

Rapo

In this popular bar game, the Rapo player gives their victim a romantically oriented "come-on," and then when the "pigeon" takes the bait and makes an advance, they are quickly brushed off with a humiliating "Where did you get the idea I was interested?" response. Simply put, Rapo players are persecuting teases gaining gratification by suggesting interest and availability, only to then reject those same but genuinely advanced behaviors from someone else.

Coincidentally, as Yes But is scripted as a "help me" solicitation followed by a rejection of assistance, in enticing and then dismissing people Rapo offers much the same service. And that is by leveling an unsuspecting and totally innocent target, the player of either game can temporarily raise their sense of worth by diminishing someone else's.

A current Internet version of Rapo is sometimes referred to as "Catfishing." In this online game, the player fakes an attractive and romantically available identity as a means to ensnare an unsuspecting patsy into a nonexistent relationship. Over time, the pigeon becomes emotionally involved in an illusory courtship only to eventually discover that what seemed to be a blossoming connection was in reality a cruel joke played at his or her expense.

Yet online or in person, Rapo needn't have sexual undertones. A version of this game may also be played by dominant members of a group when rejecting the advances of anyone seeking entry into their inner circle. In this Rapo variation, a marginal group member makes a suggestion or might innocently dare to disagree with an alpha member of the clique. Bad idea. Such naiveté is rewarded with a rebuke at least and exile at worst. And in flexing their territorial muscles, group leaders relieve camouflaged insecurities by reasserting dominance at the expense of an easy and "overly aggressive" mark.

Wooden Leg

As has often been said, people generally do what they want to do or will frequently invent a reason for not doing it. That being so, there can be no better game illustrating this truism than Wooden Leg. Commonly seen, the player of this game uses an exaggerated or imaginary impediment, a "wooden leg," as a victim's excuse or "crutch" for losing a job, failing a class, ruining a relationship, or not doing or achieving almost anything else.

Yet fabricating self-handicapping alibis is a pact with the devil. For in protecting self-esteem with rationalization for inaction or excuse after failure, the Wooden Leg player may indeed briefly ease their burden of self-doubt and condemnation, but in *believing* and *insisting* "countless deformities . . . were externally imposed fates rather than self-selected destinies" (Prochaska and Norcross n.d., 25–26), such fantasies only guarantee additional "misfortune."

In the language of Transactional Analysis, Wooden Leg is a game because in stating a rationalized and fictional "If only . . . I would have been able to . . ." narrative for failures to act or problems unsolved, the surface transaction is Adult to Adult. However, the more covert and esteem-saving dynamic is a Child to Parent plea, not to be blamed for a business-as-usual disappointing and self-pitying outcome.

Moreover, in seeking absolution through excuse, there is the secondary gain of lowering future expectations. With that in mind, the ulterior message is clear. "You can't blame me today for you see I have a handicap" and "You can't blame me tomorrow because my handicap precludes being judged as those not so burdened." After all, when failure results from "unalterable" situations, "immutable" character traits, or "that's the way things are" happenstance, and when choices, efforts, and intelligence cannot therefore be criticized, self-worth remains secure in a predictable-yet-make-believe world. And in that self-limiting universe, positive action is rare, excuse is the norm, virtually nothing is within one's control, and personal existence is ultimately measured in "I should have but couldn't" days.

Mindful that examples of Wooden Leg are as infinite as mankind's ability to construct justifications for failure, an extremely common version of this game is to endlessly blame some currently unfavorable or unpleasant situation on a past event. It's not that long-ago and adverse experiences cannot affect one's present reality. Of course, they can. However, *indefinitely* insisting that academic inadequacies, career "setbacks," or relationship disasters are by-products of events long since receding in the rear view mirror of time is, with few exceptions, not only self-diminishing and absurd on the face of it but is also a certain recipe for continuing a painful and unlikely to change status quo. At times, everyone's story is difficult to accept and depressing to experience, and because that is undeniably so, the only question that really matters is not whether one's has suffered hardship but how one responds to it.

But there's another variation of Wooden Leg where its "Don't blame me" theme is exhibited in claims of justified noninvolvement by onlookers who when in a position to help someone in need or correct an obvious wrong do neither. In such "It's not my responsibility" immorality plays, modern-day Pontius Pilates add a fourth role to the drama triangle as do-nothing "bystanders" who by "washing their hands" of any ethical accountability to resist injustice allow wrongdoing to continue as passive co-conspirators with its persecuting authors. And with rationalized inaction unconsciously legitimized by a crowd-inspired diffusion of responsibility, not-so-innocent bystanders initiate do-nothingism with a seemingly inexhaustible number of Adult-sounding excuses including "It's none of my business," "I don't want to rock the boat," "I want to remain neutral," or "I don't have all the facts" (Clarkson 1993).

However, such plausibly stated Adult to Adult justifications for accepting the unacceptable without opposition are frequently "don't blame me for not acting" Child to Parent messages masking a fear of confrontation, a taste for schadenfreude, or an "I can't do this" lack of self-confidence. And as is true in most games, if such verbalized alibis for looking the other way are challenged, "shoulda, coulda, woulda" bystanders will reflexively switch their drama triangle roles from misunderstood victims to self-righteous persecutors.

Kick Me

Common to job losers, school failures, and relationship saboteurs, Kick Me players continually set themselves up to induce "Why does this always happen to me" rejections, punishments, and put-downs. Provoking compassion from others and victimization for themselves, such "can't do anything right" individuals continually "screw things up" in order to collect grey stamps, lower expectations, reinforce their "I'm inadequate" life positions, and deflect criticism with implied claims of becoming a human piñata for the esteem-eroding hits of omnipresent "persecutors."

But that's not all. Going-nowhere Kick Me games are often supplemented by Yes But displays to seek out advice only to label even well-intended recommendations as "will never work" solutions (Breen 1973). Thus surrendering to "whatever will be, will be" pain by ignoring any and all suggestions, in spirit if not in words the inner dialogue of unable-to-tolerate-success Kick Me players is simple: "If I look like a loser, sound like a loser, and act like a loser then . . . surprise! I *must* be a loser."

Yet whatever their blunders or breakdowns, Kick Me players almost always sound exaggeratedly contrite when apologizing for their indiscretions. But in doing so, their underlying motive is more absolution than penance for their "I can't catch a break" worldview willingly reinforced by anyone accepting the complementary role of persecutor while playing this game. In fact, the induced behaviors of respondents to Kick Me provocations will often resemble that of the gamester's actual parents when during childhood the self-sabotaging moves of the game were first perfected.

Schlemiel

Yiddish for cunning, the Schlemiel player continually makes destructive messes and then by appearing exaggeratedly remorseful invites forgiveness from the victim's nurturing Parent. As Kick Me's property-damaging twin, Schlemiel is structured so that in a perverse sense its initiator can't lose. That is, after spilling red wine on a white carpet, burning a cigarette into a leather couch, denting a borrowed car, or knocking over grandma's antique umbrella stand, if a "Don't worry about it" pardon is still grudgingly offered, the game's now-rescued player can continue his or her Child-satisfying irresponsibility. And if rebuke is understandably forthcoming, a sense of "But it was only an accident" resentment or "Everybody makes mistakes" victimization confirms an existential "life is unfair" theme, energizing a perpetual feeling-sorry-for-oneself mindset.

Harried

Enacted from the position of victim, players of Harried impossibly juggle far too many balls, overscheduling themselves in order to generate "poor me" pity and "effort respect" from family, friends, and co-workers. And in fishing for "I have so much to do" sympathy as much as for compliments, Harried is at least somewhat similar to Mine is Worse Than Yours.

However, the meager and short-lived "I'm busier than anybody" recognition payoff from an unwillingness to reject "do this" requests from others and "must do" demands from oneself is anything but positive. For multitasking into exhaustion through "superhuman effort" followed by "I'm overwhelmed" depression when inevitably falling short of unreasonable expectations, Harried players trap themselves in an endless effort-dissatisfaction-effort-collapse martyrdom loop leading to only more of the same.

Blemish

In this game, players feeling flawed attempt to diminish insecurity by "proving" that someone else is more imperfect, that is more "blemished" than they are. In so doing, persecutory Blemish players "innocently" and often matter-of-factly point out minor defects in others by asking questions criticizing their appearance ("Have you put on a few pounds?"), their intelligence ("You don't read the *New York Times*?"), their decisions ("Your apartment is nice, but isn't it on the small side?"), or their inconsequential choices ("Thanks for the pizza but why the anchovies?").

Superficially, such questions might be at least somewhat plausible queries for information generated by the Adult ego state. However, we all know, feel, and see these "little murders" for the transparent and leveling-prompted personal attacks they undoubtedly are. And if the target of Blemish expresses outrage in accurately comprehending a criticism rather than an innocuously trivial question or comment, the game's initiator can then quickly morph into an "I never meant to hurt you" victim or a thin-skinned and overly defensive persecutor.

Blemish can also somewhat resemble a more belligerent form of Yes But when its target's sincerely offered responses to problem-solving questions are met with a player's aggressively critical "Are you nuts?" incredulity. Whether the foil is asked to suggest a movie, a restaurant, the best car to purchase, the safest investment, who to vote for, or the next vacation destination, we have all seen arrogantly blemishing know-it-all bosses, colleagues, and even friends respond to thoughtful recommendations with a "What's wrong with you?" shrug, an exasperated sigh, or an eye-rolling rejection.

Now I've Got You (NIGY)

The theme of this "gotcha" game is getting even. As such, Now I've Got You is inarguably a variation of Blemish where the target is unfairly "persecuted" for a mistake, a misstatement, a "hypocritical" action, or an "incompetent" performance rather than for a physical "imperfection," an intellectual "shortcoming," a "questionable" decision, or a "half-baked" suggestion. And while Blemish typically targets any patsy happening to cross its player's path, NIGY, as commonly a transference-inspired activity, is particularly well suited for "getting back at" authority figures such as parents, bosses, teachers, or elected officials.

But whatever the status of the game's target, in looking for oversights and "injustices" the NIGY player waits for their about-to-be-leveled pigeon to make a minor miscalculation or an innocently stated inaccurate, "hurtful," "two-faced," or "prejudicial" remark and then takes perverse pleasure in responding with sanctimonious indignation. It's only good to be "wronged" when one can repay the "offense" in spades. And for the target of the NIGY player's outrage, that is exactly the plan.

When cutting an authority figure down to size, the opening move of the game is usually a supposedly Adult comment or question. To illustrate, there is little doubt of intent in stating to a politician that "Your statistics highlighting crime and poverty in minority communities *seemed* to have racist overtones." Likewise, the underlying motive of a leveling student is equally clear when mentioning to a teacher that "Didn't you once say that you would *never* assign homework on a Friday? And now you are asking us to study over the weekend for a test on Monday. How is that fair?"

And carrying such "caught you" behavior to an absurd extreme, NIGY is the obvious inspiration for a caller to a radio talk show peppering the host with a series of "gotcha questions" such as "How can you say that you'd *never* hit a woman? What if a morbidly obese, frothing-at-the-mouth, high on drugs woman was attacking your wife and child? Wouldn't you *then* be forced to hit a woman to protect your family?"

Hardly an isolated behavior, the recurring rhetoric of NIGY players is not intended to expand knowledge, gain clarification, or even state an honest and thoughtfully offered opinion. Rather, the ulterior purpose of NIGY gamers is none other than to hopefully expose their victims as ignorant, deceitful, hypocritical, or even bigoted frauds. Yet in asking questions or making statements that superficially seem to be sincerely posed but in retrospect are highly transparent ploys at one-upmanship, NIGY players ironically expose themselves as those lacking sincerity and with something to hide.

Whereas in its simplest form, NIGY often involves a thinly veiled critical response delivered immediately after the target's "indiscretion," its hardcore version is often planned well before its extremely unpleasant and unfairly staged dénouement. Indeed, in this more malevolent form of NIGY, fault-finding is not a response to a solitary "blunder" but rather is an orchestrated and precisely timed stamp collector's dream as a *cumulative* result of past events. Fittingly enough, in this version of NIGY, the "N" is closer in definition to "at last" than it is to "now" (Zechnich 1976, 175).

Thus the underlying "Come to think of it" message to the victim leaves little room for misinterpretation. "*Come to think of it*, some time ago you did this thing which displeased me. I did not do anything about it then, but I will *now*. Pow!" (Zechnich 1976, 175). And because the blind-sided "pigeon" had over time been deliberately uninformed as to his "faults," and since nothing can be done to change what has already happened, the "pow-related" impact of the game creates both surprise and despair.

To say that schadenfreude-inspired joy in the misery of others is an important motivation for "NIGY" is stating the obvious. And equally so, noting that this persecution game also plays an important role in the media's leveling relationship with Hollywood celebrities or political leaders is just as evident. But there is still another variation of NIGY that neither involves silver-screen icons nor Oval Office occupants. It involves anyone who has ever been inflexibly dealt with by a bureaucrat or anyone else playing TWIC or "This Window is Closed" (Mossman 1981).

Named for the all-too-common experience of being denied assistance when arriving at a service window a microsecond past closing, there are endless examples of such everyday TWIC frustrations. As such, few haven't experienced failing a school assignment for submitting a paper twenty words short of the minimum length requirement, receiving a ticket for driving five miles an hour over the speed limit, or being "grounded" by a parent for returning home ten minutes past curfew.

In response to such "egregious" violations of rules, the TWIC player "justifies" their uncompromising behavior as necessary to avoid a slippery slope erosion of their authority. And at times there is truth in that "give someone an inch and they'll take a mile" position. However, *even when there are legitimate and clearly reasonable circumstances* for allowing an exception to such edicts, the person "in charge" wields power with an iron hand, rationalizing inflexibility by enforcing the letter if not the spirit of the regulation. In the end, they display authority with a dismissive "You know the rules" discount, and their now thoroughly leveled victims have little choice but to accept a decision from a "letter of the law" official who comparatively speaking makes Grand Inquisitor Torquemada seem not so bad after all.

I Like You But (ILYB)

Related to Blemish and I'm Only Trying to Help You, this game begins when a player in the guise of a well-meaning "only telling it like it is" rescuer prefaces highly persecutory comments with a "You know I really like you, but" diversionary smoke screen. Potentially offering immunity from counterattack, such "Surely you must know I love you to death" comments provide cover for the ILYB player to morph from "good guy" helper to a "This hurts me more than you" verbal assassin.

With deception thus initiated by such introductory statements, the now "licensed to verbally kill" 007 impersonator can't lose. For if in response to the assault the unsuspecting target expresses outrage, the "totally altruistic" and "totally misunderstood" ILYB gamer is seemingly justified in switching roles to victim in feigning "Don't shoot the messenger; I was only repeating what I've heard," or the equally ulterior "I was only kidding when I said that," or even "What I said from a 'good place' hurt me more than you" self-righteous indignation. And if the game's target expresses no offense, the ILYB player can likely enjoy another round or two of leveling without reprisal.

I Told You So (ITYS)

Similar in motivation to Now I Got You and I'm Only Trying to Help You, players compensate for feelings of inadequacy by "proving" the conduct or beliefs of others is incorrect. As unrelenting "right-fighters" unable to understand how anyone could believe or act as they do, ready-to-level ITYS gamesters can't wait for "inferiors" to be "proved wrong" after ignoring their "well-intended" advice or contesting their ulterior-in-purpose personal opinions and "innocently shared" secondhand commentaries. However, what superficially appear as selfless suggestions or "food for thought ideas" are in reality supercilious cons likely rejected by perceptive targets sensing the covert intent of such "I know and you don't" parentally offered guidance.

Yet counterintuitively, the rejection of their counsel is exactly what ITYS players want. For once ignored, *whatever events later indicate about the value of their recommendations*, game initiators can't lose. That is, in again proving that "success has a thousand fathers, but failure is an orphan," when their "sincerely offered" opinions are exposed as flawed and self-serving nonsense, ITYS players rarely if ever admit their errors. But when an ITYS gamer chances upon a "right" conclusion about sports, politics, world affairs, interpersonal advice, or virtually anything else one could hardly be certain about, the only truly predictable certainty will be their triumphantly announced "I told you so" response to anyone within ear-shot.

See What You Made Me Do (SWYMMD)

Most simply, this "buck stops elsewhere" game is played to avoid responsibility by blaming others for one's actions. The opening move of "See What You Made Me Do" is to accept another's suggestion. If things turn out well, one can plausibly claim most of the credit. Yet if things turn out badly, self-esteem may temporarily be salvaged by predictably disavowing accountability in claiming "See what you made me do!"

But as any internally oriented person knows all too well, such an "It's not my fault" statement hardly squares with objective reality. For except under threats of physical harm, there are few instances in which someone can really "make" someone do anything. That is, when a wife accepts her husband's well-meaning but ill-conceived suggestion to wear a formal dress to a casual party, a recipe is altered due to a friend's recommendation that results in a culinary disaster, or a driver is prompted to take an alternate route leading to a "middle-of-nowhere" dead end, the only people responsible are those accepting the advice.

Although beginning with an overtly stated Parent to Child criticism of "calamitous" advice, SWYMMD is a game because the sub-rosa message is a Child to Parent plea not to be blamed for an unsatisfactory outcome.

Thus the motivation for SWYMMD is an attempt to relieve feelings of inadequacy by absolving oneself of guilt for a negative result and, reinforcing that purpose, persecute the unsuspecting Good Samaritan who legitimately offered "just wanting to help" advice in the first place.

If It Weren't For You (IWFY)

Perhaps the most common marriage game, "If It Weren't For You" is actually SWYMMD in reverse. That is, in the latter game the scapegoat is blamed for advocating that something be done and in the former is condemned for supposedly encouraging that something *not* be done. But whatever the case, using someone as a handicapping prop for failure in doing or not doing something is little different than other versions of Wooden Leg.

In long-term relationships, the veteran IWFY player commonly faults their partner for an ongoing problem or situation such as "If it weren't for you, I could have gone to college" or "If it weren't for you, I could have had a career." Obviously, the "coulda" possibilities in IWFY are infinite. But blame for not getting in shape, not making a fortune, or not having a good job are typical comments in a game illustrating that by not doing something that clearly provokes anxiety, the best defense is often a good offense.

However, since the only way for IWFY to continue is for one member of the relationship to supposedly thwart the other's attempts at improvement, the best way to halt the game is to refuse to play. This can be done most easily *by aggressively encouraging* the game's initiator to make the positive change they have falsely claimed to have been prevented from accomplishing. And once such "go ahead" support is offered, the IWFY enthusiast has little choice but to end play and seek whatever opportunities have supposedly been denied or continue an unhappy existence with no one to plausibly blame but themselves.

Interestingly, in toxic associations there may be at least some validity in claiming that a spouse may actually try to undermine the other's efforts to lose weight, start a business, continue schooling, accept a job, or do virtually anything else that may well have a positive impact on life. And while philosophically an "if it weren't for you" excuse *is* unjustifiable, on a purely experiential level it is not uncommon for partners to engage in a collusive "dance" where the background "music" is a drumbeat sabotaging the other's efforts for self-improvement.

Such subversion might simply be the purchase of ice cream to thwart a spouse's diet, or an exaggerated rationale for one's partner not to seek a better job or additional education, or even encouragement to "have just one little drink, snort, or puff" for a husband or wife struggling with substance abuse. But whatever the tactics for sidetracking someone's positive actions, the motive for such insidious behavior may well be that misery does indeed love company.

That is, if one member of the couple makes positive strides without a correspondingly equal effort from their counterpart, the status-quo equilibrium of the union becomes challenged. This is so because the positive actions of a husband or wife implicitly pressures their more-reluctant-to-change partner into matching those constructive actions or risk doing nothing and thus spotlighting themselves as the "real loser" in the relationship. Prone to inaction yet faced with such esteem-threatening choices, many decide on a third option and that is to egocentrically undermine the self-improvement efforts of someone they otherwise claim to love.

GAMING NO MORE

As in "If It Weren't For You," an effective way to more generally end gaming is by refusing to play. Most simply, this is done by throwing its initiator a crossed transactional "curve ball" and not responding as expected. That is, a good antigaming approach is to *remain calm*, consider the underlying theme of the game, and thoughtfully *answer its ulterior message from the Adult ego state* so as to reply in a manner the game's initiator is unaccustomed to receiving.

Yet while understanding a player's "con" and "switch" combined with a "been there done that" awareness that a game is unfolding is certainly a preemptively effective antigaming approach, such realizations are often too little too late to stop a game that is well underway. As such, in short-circuiting a game at its onset, it is thus also imperative to recognize early physiological alerts such as the buildup of tension in one's body signaling that what initially seemed to be an innocent and innocuous series of transactions was neither innocent nor innocuous. To that end, a greater awareness of one's unique set of early-game affective and somatic cues can become a "canary-in-the-mine" warning for preventative control.

While the specific emotional and physical signals that one is becoming a game's target vary from person to person, initial moves as rescuer, victim, or persecutor almost universally "have an urgent, no-choice, on-the-spot, have-to, must quality" (Hesterly 1982, 145). In turn, this response urgency is physically followed by a sense of stress or discomfort including but not limited to dryness of mouth or throat, a tense jaw, tightness in hand or arm muscles, or just an uneasy feeling (Hesterly 1982). And as early signs that gaming is about to begin, these behavioral cues if triggering a reframing of internal dialogue can halt their physiological momentum before game entrapment becomes all but inevitable.

Moreover, once awareness that a game is beginning has been established, it is essential to refuse whatever drama triangle role is offered by exchanging it for a less conventional but far more positive part. Thus when necessary, constructively substituting an "assertive" role for persecutor, a "caring" stance for rescuer, and an honestly "vulnerable" but thoughtful persona rather than a hangdog "can't catch a break" victim's portrayal should disrupt whatever game one has been "invited" to play (Choy 1990).

Less comfortable than more typically enacted game roles perfected over countless "performances," such positive characterizations are beneficial whatever their initial discomfort. As such, a self-assured "asking for what is wanted" demeanor is far more effective than a triumphantly punitive "others are fools" persecutional stance. Equally so, a sincerely caring and respectfully empowering "others matter" approach is superior to that of a patronizing rescuer saving those neither wanting nor needing help. And sincerely expressing "I need advice" openness in asking for Adult-inspired guidance is far more preferable than wallowing in self-pity as a perennially helpless and seemingly lobotomized victim.

Further, to avoid "foot-in-mouth disease" when invited to play a game, it is also helpful to thoughtfully determine what you're feeling, what you're reacting to, and what you're thinking and doing to continue feeling as you do (Meininger 1973). Since impulsive actions are linked to feelings and feelings are linked to thoughts, a better understanding of why a game is played, why we react as we do, and what thoughts led to those reactions will inevitably change one's responses in tacitly directing a gamester to find a patsy elsewhere. And as a last resort, simply bringing the game's theme into the open with a flatly delivered "What's your intention?" question sends that empowered message loud and clear.

Conversely, in stopping one's own games the first task is to identify them by asking "What unpleasant and dysfunctional patterns of behavior involving other people keep happening to me?" Once done, the Adult should answer the two equally essential questions of "What payoffs do the games provide?" and, even more importantly, "What is their cost?"

Yet above all things, the sunshine of self-awareness is a disinfectant for ulterior transactions as well as for their psychological game progeny. To that end, an important Transactional Analysis goal is educative in bringing otherwise "hiding in plain sight" game dynamics under conscious control. "Through rational decisions, game players [then] have the choice of continuing the game playing and accepting the consequences or finding a reasonable option for each step of the game so as to live happier lives" (Summerton 2000, 209). And once aware of the detrimental impact of game playing, why wouldn't one make the second of those two choices? After all, isn't "winning" the game of life the only game that really matters?

But in accomplishing that goal, as helpful as it is to recognize that games are largely unconscious and ultimately destructive maneuvers used to maintain constancy in one's world, it is equally instructive to understand another group of "coping strategies" identified some sixty years before TA and serving nearly identical purposes.

DEFENSE MECHANISMS

According to Freud, defenses are unconscious behaviors safeguarding a person from perceived imperfections in personality and from emotional and physical stress reactions when threatened by their exposure. Resembling fear, these feelings of tension or apprehension labeled as anxiety are responses arising in the absence of, or greatly disproportionate to, any objective danger. And in denying, distorting, or modifying reality, defense mechanisms, as self-administered and out-of-awareness psychological analgesics, offer temporary relief from these feelings. With that in mind, the first such defense identified by the "Father of Psychoanalysis" was repression.

Repression

Foremost among equals, repression is the most basic defense used to prevent painful, threatening, or disturbing thoughts and/or memories from reaching a conscious level. As such, it is only when the shield of repression "springs a leak" and past or present failures, embarrassments, tragedies, insecurities, or abuse reach awareness that other defenses serve as reinforcements to halt the rising tide of anxiety. However, there is still another reason that Freud considered repression to be the key ego defense.

Since early childhood is filled with anxiety-producing experiences for all children, repression is said to account for the almost-universal inability to remember one's first few years of life. Thus it is far easier for a sixty-year-old to remember life at thirty than a fourteen-year-old to remember life at four. Yet one needn't look at childhood fears to find targets for repression. As an adult, a near-fatal car accident that cannot be remembered, a crime committed that cannot be recalled, or a middle-aged mother not consciously recognizing attraction for her teenage daughter's handsome new boyfriend are all examples of this most common defense.

Reaction Formation

When one's inclinations are so disturbing as to represent a threat to self-esteem, such unsettling thoughts or actions are not only repressed but are often exchanged for their exaggerated opposites. This unconscious substitution of anxiety-producing beliefs or conduct for excessive demonstrations of contrary behaviors is a reaction formation response.

Thus an adolescent male having concerns about his sexuality acting the role of a gay-bashing macho man, a woman enjoying pornography leading a crusade to censor it, a parent resenting an unwanted child showering the youngster with gifts, or an insecure and depressed student failing a class acting super cool as if unconcerned are all examples of the reaction formation defense. Yet despite the infinite variety of reaction formation possibilities, many examples, which significantly overlap with the defense of rationalization, may be categorized as either a "sour grapes" or a "sweet lemon" attitude.

Sour Grapes Attitude

In this variation of reaction formation, something a person wants but can't have is characterized as undesirable. A teenager whose amorous advances are rebuffed claiming that the indifferent party "was ugly anyway," an executive failing to land a desirable job dishonestly insisting that "I was really overqualified for the position," a co-ed refused acceptance into a popular sorority alleging that "I wasn't really interested since the girls were snobs," or a student denied admission into a prestigious university falsely asserting disinterest in "such a competitive atmosphere" are all examples of the sour grapes attitude.

Sweet Lemon Attitude

Whenever a person maintains that something that is bad is actually good, a sweet lemon attitude has been expressed. Thus a dispirited husband stridently describing the quality of his marriage as "an eight out of ten," a woman unhappily employed in a dead end job alleging that she "can't wait to get to work each day," or a sleep-deprived, resentful, and burning-the-candle-at-both-ends young parent falsely professing that changing diapers is "the most enjoyable thing I've ever done" are all examples of the sweet lemon attitude.

But whatever form a reaction formation takes, in differentiating it from a person's "real deal" beliefs or attitudes it is important to note several characteristic "tells" of the defense. That is, if the suspected reaction formation behavior is single-minded, inflexible, and/or inappropriate, the person is likely camouflaging true feelings by amplified expressions of their opposite.

Rationalization

In this defense, one justifies questionable behavior by providing plausible motives for actions rather than admitting to their actual, more embarrassing reasons. Thus, as in the aforementioned sour grapes and sweet lemon examples, by placing oneself in a more favorable light, excuses provide a self-deceiving remedy for the guilt and/or insecurities that are often by-products of uncomfortable or painful realities. In the language of Transactional Analysis, one is trying to relieve the burden of un-OKness by justifying anxiety-producing behaviors frowned upon by the Parent ego state. But whatever the underlying motivations for rationalization, when confronting a person with the truths behind their alibis the response will almost always be an exaggerated and emotional denial.

Common instances of blaming circumstances rather than ourselves for failures are far too numerous to mention. Yet, when an adolescent boy reads an adult magazine for "literary content," a father beats his children "for their own good," a selfish person single-handedly eats an entire chocolate cake "so that it wouldn't spoil," a student smokes marijuana because "everybody else does it," or a man "justifiably" cheats on his taxes contaminated by the same false consensus "I'm no different than anyone else" reason, one can be sure that rationalization is lurking just below the surface. And as with several other defenses, rationalization has its counterparts in psychological games. Clearly, the ulterior motivation for Yes But, Wooden Leg, If It Weren't For You, and See What You Made Me Do mirrors rationalization because their purpose in deflecting responsibility for esteem-sapping failure is purely defensive in nature.

Projection

A truism of human behavior is that character traits people like least about themselves are often attributed to others. Known as projection, there is little doubt that this unwillingness to recognize personal shortcomings by casting them elsewhere is an attempt to draw attention away from questionable beliefs and behaviors, disown problematic conduct and, most fundamentally, protect one's self-esteem. Yet in the extreme, when inner shortcomings become outer concerns, issues, or fears associated with blameless targets, this "best defense is a good offense" dynamic may result in attacking others without guilt. Hence in its most destructive form, it is easy for projection to morph into an excuse for racial, sexual, ethnic, religious, or gender-based bias.

However, even if less destructive than full-blown discrimination, daily examples of projection are often no less painful, or at least no less damaging, to relationships. A wife who desires infidelity unfairly accusing her husband of having affairs, a son unjustly insisting that his father hates him instead of confessing that it is he who hates his father, a man asserting that others don't "listen" in lieu of recognizing that behavior in himself, or a teacher falsely claiming her students are lazy and unprepared rather than admitting her own incompetence are in their own way all deal breakers to forging strong connections between and among people.

Clearly, even if not directly ascribing self-doubt to others, games such as Rapo, NIGY, and Blemish, in aggressively shifting personal insecurities onto unsuspecting victims, are projective in nature. That is, more than simply attributing one's sense of inferiority to unwitting pawns, in prompting self-doubt in others, the players of such leveling games actually plot moves *to ensure* the orchestrated accuracy of their projections. In doing so, power is exerted over scapegoats, the joy of schadenfreude is experienced, and, perhaps most importantly, by inciting vulnerability in others, one's own sense of inadequacy, at least in a relative sense, is temporarily diminished.

Regression

When an individual confronted with a difficult task, conflict, or threatening situation retreats to an earlier, more immature level of functioning, regression is at work in protecting self-esteem. And as for any defense, if regression is overly relied upon its temporary benefit in reducing anxiety is compromised by its long-term result of diminishing one's urgency to fully face reality.

Yet precisely because regression is a mood-altering behavioral "drug," if used in moderation by otherwise healthy people it is not considered evidence of maladjustment. Thus occasional episodes of sleeping too late, eating too much, saving too little, or "surfing the net" too long, if monitored and limited, should not be cause for concern. However, the abuse of intoxicants, throwing tantrums, pretending one is sick, sleeping all day, habitual procrastination, or any other regressively "getting little" behavior used to *chronically* avoid adult responsibilities or unpleasant realities should not be taken lightly.

Of course, this "getting little" theme is also prominently displayed in self-discounting games such as Yes But, Kick Me, and Schlemiel. In all cases, the underlying "woe-is-me" motive is to avoid responsibility, lower expectations, extract strokes from oblivious victims, and gain absolution for failures, "accidents," and unwilling-to-act inertia.

Introjection

Also known as identification or incorporation, introjection is the unconscious or semiconscious absorption or imitation of an admired person's or group's characteristics as compensation for low self-esteem.

Thus by building who or what is valued as powerful into ourselves, we diminish our sense of inferiority.

Obviously, children mimicking their parents in dress, affectations, speech patterns, beliefs, and overall behavior are forms of introjection commonly observed in others as well as in ourselves. Similarly, we have all seen people joining groups, however questionable their conduct, in order to diminish personal insecurities or *habitually* wearing "look at me" clothing representing elite colleges or successful sports teams to accomplish that same end.

Displacement

As mentioned, displacement often resembles TA's "Kicking the Dog." That is, in both behaviors an individual shifts anger or resentment from one person or group to another person or group that is relatively less powerful. In Berne's explanation, such a behavioral transfer results from collecting grey psychological stamps in one place and, in venting hurt, anger, or frustration, "redeeming" them somewhere else. And in the Freudian model, displacement frequently results from desires to satisfy elemental needs such as aggression or hostility by whatever means necessary, however immoral such gratification may be.

Yet in either case, since fulfillment of such nefarious ends frequently results in guilt-inspired anxiety at least, punishment at worst, and resistance by targets more often than not, compromises are often made by finding less satisfying but "safer" victims. And as much as anything else, these "wrong time, wrong place" scapegoats act as living palliatives, easing personal insecurities through their abuse as highly vulnerable substitutes.

But whatever one's theory to explain displacement, in its most destructive forms the result is always the same. And that is the immoral victimization or persecution of a relatively defenseless person, group, or animal with little or no remorse. In the end, when a child angry at his parents tortures his pet, a woman mad at her boss beats her children, or German National Socialists defeated in World War I and suffering economic hardship kill Jews with impunity, it doesn't really matter what label is used to identify those behaviors. At the simplest need-satisfying psychological level, their wellspring is much the same.

Denial

Whereas the Santa Claus Myth refers to the contaminated belief that wishful thinking can positively affect reality, denial is wishful *nonthinking* in failing to even acknowledge irrefutable yet unpleasant realities concerning death, illness, or failure. That is, by refusing to recognize or accept a disturbing situation, the problem is minimized and its attendant anxiety is temporarily reduced. Thus the doctor is mistaken in misreading x-rays, a child holding the school record for disciplinary suspensions is according to parents "really an angel," heroin is "not that addicting," and with a week to go in the semester and an average south of thirty percent, a student insists "*Of course* I can still pass this class."

Sublimation

Said to be the only truly positive defense, sublimation is a more ethically acceptable form of displacement. That is, in redirecting aggressive urges into substitutes considered socially appropriate or having higher cultural value, anxiety is reduced and unused energy from the objectionable but blocked urge is rechanneled into positive or even creative endeavors. Most simply, a man angry at a politician writing a critical letter to the editor of a local newspaper, a teenage boy after arguing with his girlfriend going for a run, or a contentious woman becoming a literary critic are all examples of sublimation.

Yet still another defense is not attributed to Sigmund Freud but to his associate Alfred Adler. Best known for founding the school of Individual Psychology and postulating the inferiority complex as a prime motivator of behavior, Adler identified still another common approach for at least temporarily relieving feelings of inadequacy and self-doubt. And in consistently maintaining the position "that a basic dynamic force behind all human activity is a striving from a felt 'minus' towards a hoped for 'plus,' from a feeling of inferiority, towards one of superiority, perfection, [and] totality," he termed that strategy "compensation" (Wilson 1975, 117).

Compensation

In this defense, people feeling inadequate in a certain endeavor diminish insecurity by turning such "weakness" into a strength or by offsetting that "imperfection" through recognition in other pursuits. Thus as a tactic to improve one's self-esteem, the constructive value of compensation depends upon the situation. For this reason, if anxiety stemming from one's poor speaking ability is overcome by efforts resulting in flawless diction and confident presentations, then compensation served a positive purpose. However, if one's academic failings are camouflaged through efforts at becoming a class clown or a bully, then the results of such compensation are inarguably less constructive.

EVALUATING DEFENSES

With the utilization of psychological defenses as a universal strategy for coping with anxiety, their use begs the question as to whether such self-deceptive practices are beneficial or even harmful. Yet as for many issues in human behavior, there is no easy answer. For if defenses simply provided temporary relief from anxiety and thus shielded one from being overwhelmed during emotional crises, their use would be undeniably positive. However, if defenses in successfully distorting reality also undermine one's ability to realistically solve those very issues stimulating anxiety in the first place, then their use would just as surely be detrimental. But as Ayn Rand noted, since "you can avoid reality but you cannot avoid the consequences of avoiding reality," on balance the latter more negative evaluation seems clearly so.

After all, though defenses are largely successful in temporarily diminishing anxiety, in reducing such feelings and not their source they are much like the proverbial "Band-Aid on cancer." That is, in concealing the root of a problem, short-term well-being is achieved through a live-for-today bargain where the cost of immediate comfort is long-term addiction to inaction. For in temporarily reducing anxiety, defenses also create large blind spots in awareness and in doing so diminish the urgency to constructively face one's difficulties. And when continually sweeping "out of sight, out of mind" problems under the rug becomes a way of life, defenses ultimately create far more problems than they solve.

ELEVEN

Internalizing Life Positions

We must let go of the life we have planned, so as to accept the one that is waiting for us.

—Joseph Campbell

Well before children enter the wider world of public school and probably by the third or fourth year of life, they have unconsciously decided issues of self-worth and the worth of others. In its formative stages, such a conclusion is likely "one of the first functions of the infant's Adult in the attempt to make sense out of life, so that a measure of predictability may be applied to the confusion of stimuli and feelings" (Harris 1973, 74). Known as a life position, such an all-encompassing outlook dictating a person's most basic convictions about themselves and others also determines behavioral choices including what rackets are favored, what games are played, how the world is experienced, and how life is lived.

Thus providing a foundational point of view for ever more numerous relationships with others (English 1977), these deep-seated and permanently recorded life positions are frames of reference for the initial draft of the child's life script directing the path existence will take. In all likelihood, as a perceptual center of existential gravity, *no unconscious vestige from early childhood has greater staying power and impact on life*. That is, as an anchoring definition for an individual's relative place in the world, whatever life position is initially assumed will profoundly influence how one thinks, feels, acts, and relates to others.

In fact, this positionally relative view of one's place in the world "Whether you think you are valuable and deserving, or worthless and hopeless . . . is the hallmark of whether you are an optimist or a pessimist" (Seligman 1991, 44). To that end, since hopefulness as in the former outlook or markedly less so as in the latter impacts conduct and even health in significant and omnipresent ways, there is arguably no greater proof of the immense role one's psychological position plays in life.

Adopted from early experiences as the foundation for the child's developing script (English 1977), life positions are "offered" to children by parental stroking patterns as a type of subliminal logic for how to make sense of the world and one's place in that reality. That is, the type of strokes received early in life become the out-of-awareness evidence that is used as the basis for the unconscious "decision" of which position one gravitates toward for all the years to follow. And that decision as the cornerstone for later decisions endlessly reverberates throughout life in profoundly affecting the quality of existence.

Are we worthy? Are we inadequate? Are we acceptable? Are we powerless? And what about others? Are *they* worthy, inadequate, acceptable, or powerless? And can others be trusted? Do they deserve respect? Or are they without virtue, integrity, or decency? For the young child, caregiver criticism strokes lead to one position, abuse strokes lead to another, abandonment strokes lead to a third possibility, and unconditionally loving and acceptance strokes likely lead to "I'm worthy and so are you" psychological health.

Thus as a practical reality, children are largely "stroked into whatever basic position they assume" (McCormack 1977, 10). And while even in the most negative of environments some children show remarkable resilience in overcoming the harmful effects of such an early existence, many if not most in learning what they live and living what they learn will not.

> "It's a good world, someday I'll make it a better one" . . . "It's a bad world, someday I'll kill myself"—or kill someone else, go crazy or withdraw. Perhaps it's a mediocre world, where you do what you have to do and have fun in between: or a tough world, where you make good by putting on a white collar and shuffling other people's papers; or a hard world, where you sweep or bend or deal; or wiggle or fight for a living; or a dreary world, where you sit in a bar hoping; or a futile world, where you give up. (Berne 1973, 84–85)

So with only a slight exaggeration, it can be said that "the most damaging social injustices are those perpetuated not by the culture but by parents who stroke their children into feeling not OK about themselves, others, or both" (McCormack 1977, 17). And once those perceptions are firmly established, it is all but universally so to unthinkingly guarantee their continuance through a daily regimen of selective blindness and spin control. This is so because in satisfying the elemental need for a safe, secure, and predictable existence, most people will tenaciously ignore even unmistakable evidence to the contrary in generating the positional reality they think is true and that they deserve.

As a consequence, whatever beliefs, coping strategies, and feelings children have been stroked into accepting as "normal" will, as self-reinforcing realities, be obsessively maintained. In fact, once established, the basic positions "can rarely be changed by external circumstances alone. Stable changes must come from within, either spontaneously or under some sort of therapeutic influence" (Berne 1973, 88).

Indeed, the grounding comfort a life position offers in providing a reassuring if often dysfunctional predictability is so great that if these convictions start to dissipate, children as well as adults will do whatever they can to restore them. And if successful, whatever discomfort exists in correctly perceiving life's roll-of-the-dice uncertainty will be diminished if not completely eliminated. Yet ironically in seeking escape from the anxiety of an unpredictable world, people often confine themselves to an existential straitjacket, predictably limiting their freedom to positively experience life and each other.

Thus manipulating perception if not reality, one's life position is often an unconscious and self-constructed prison. In essence, this "window on the world" frame of reference filters out data that doesn't fit basic opinions about oneself and others on the one hand and scans the environment looking for positionally aligned confirming opportunities to feel inadequate, confident, superior, tolerant, or victimized on the other.

It's not that on any given day or moment we can't temporarily shift positions. And it's not that on any given day or moment environmental circumstances and perhaps our level of physical well-being cannot dictate one's "place" *within* a life position. Certainly, at times we all feel differently about our sports teams, favorite restaurants, or the furniture we recently bought for our living room. Change is a part of life, and there are few fixed values for how *anything* is perceived. Why then should it be any different for how relatively okay we feel or believe ourselves or others to be at any given point in time?

Moreover, just as no two snowflakes are the same, no two of anything, least of all individual perceptions about the comparative worth of oneself and others, is identical. Thus other than in a general sense, "no two people have the same life position any more than they have the same life experiences" (Jacobs 1997, 200). It's just that overwhelmingly so, and especially under pressure, when it is common to regress to an earlier more comforting state, each of us centers on our initially "decided" position. And it is that perception of reality that is largely maintained throughout life as the dominant foundation on which our personality evolves.

With that in mind, it might be useful to view this relatively unchanging "core" frame of reference as one's "character" position and the far more volatile day-to-day reaction to the environment view of oneself and others as the "surface" position (White 1994). Certainly, these positions are not mutually exclusive. That is, the daily and far more reactive "surface" position is influenced by one's "character" worldview just as the primary "character" position *over time* may be reinforced, softened, or even reassessed due to the daily experiences of its "surface" counterpart.

Yet by continuing to color or to "cherry pick" only what we want to see, one's initial and continually reinforced core position, even if negative, has enormous staying power in maintaining psychological equilibrium. This is so because even if such unconscious close-mindedness counterproductively stifles growth and life fulfillment, it provides a predictably comforting mindset concerning the relative worth of oneself and others.

Thus depending on positional frame of reference, if someone compliments one's loss of weight, the self-deprecating response might be "I'm still too fat." If members of a lower economic class are arrested, an "I am superior" mindset reflexively provokes a "They can't be trusted" evaluation. If a colleague praises one's work, the "critical of oneself and others" reply is likely "That idiot has low standards." If tragedy befalls a member of a different racial or ethnic group, a "They got what they deserved" judgment reinforces a "They are inferior" outlook. And if someone says, "You're really smart," one's fault-finding Parent may well offer a "Yes but, I'm homely" rebuttal.

However, there is still another reason why life position assumptions are so resistant to change or even to reevaluation. And that reason is that by generating the reality we accept as true, we not only affect our own behavior but *also* influence the behaviors of those around us. Thus to satisfy our "position hunger," we may not only unconsciously associate with like-minded people sharing our existential outlook but also, from the briefest of encounters to fully scripted psychological games, may even "manipulate others into reinforcing our basic psychological stance" (McCormack 1977, 4). This being so, the end result will inevitably be a further validation of our primary position decision as others are chosen or influenced to act in ways congruent with our beliefs.

Resulting more from natural occurrence than from conscious intent, when believing others to be hostile, aggressive, egocentric, or more generally not okay and then treating them as if that were so, those behaviors will likely be directed back at oneself, "confirming" that initial evaluation. This "You get what you give" behavioral dynamic in which "second by second [and] transaction by transaction we are inviting each other into OK behavior or not-OK behavior" (Kahler 1977, 242) is more formally known as the principle of reciprocity.

Fittingly enough, the principle of reciprocity is the tendency for people to treat others in ways mirroring their own treatment. Thus low opinions and toxic behaviors directed outwardly are as unstamped mail returned to their sender, who, in forging a mutually validating and reinforcing chain of negative strokes, continues the cycle. So, while viewing a "despicable person" with contempt likely inspires hostility confirming that evaluation, regarding a "good person" favorably will just as often promote conduct "proving" that perception. Thus positively treating people "as if they were what they ought to be" may be as much a good idea based on the thoughts of Goethe as on a good-for-others and good-for-oneself behavioral truth.

Additionally, since "people tend to give the strokes they want to receive" (Woollams and Brown 1978, 62; Samuels 1971), when reality is manipulated as in a psychological game to confirm one's pessimistic worldview and negative actions are resultantly *directed back at oneself*, the principle of reciprocity is also evident. However, in a more general sense the likelihood that behaviors in others are predisposed to conform to one's anticipations is sometimes referred to as the "Pygmalion effect."

Also known as a "self-fulfilling prophesy," the Pygmalion effect is the tendency for people to perform in ways similar to prior expectations. Thus treating people as worthy and capable "invites" positive conduct as does treating them as valueless and inadequate correspondingly inspires negative actions. And when self-directed, the power of the Pygmalion effect is no less capable of influencing behavior.

Since the creation of a predictable world is such a strong motive force, the more convinced that something such as personal success or failure will occur, the more likely one's behavior will increase the probability of that outcome. Thus for most people, such expectations for themselves and others leading to anticipated results combine with selective perception to ensure that over time one's life position becomes hardened and virtually immune from reevaluation, question, or even doubt.

Yet, there is still hope for change. And that hope is, with increased self-understanding fostered by an empowered Adult ego state, the most basic feelings about oneself and others unconsciously "decided" as children can be consciously redecided today. That said, the tragedy is that many people never reevaluate these early conclusions and literally pay for that perceptual purchase with a self-imposed inertia leading to uninspiring and uninspired lives.

First described by Hippocrates some 2,500 years ago as "temperaments," there are four possible psychological life position combinations (Graff 1976). However, as mentioned, even though one can temporarily shift from one position to another within any given period, people typically settle on one default "window" or "home base" in viewing themselves and others.

Internalized early in life, at their simplest level these "windows" (Hay 1993) can be summarized as "Everyone is good," "I am good but others are not good," "I am not good but others are good," and "No one is good." In our relationships, these ways of seeing ourselves and others correspondingly translate as "If I feel OK about myself and about you, we will get on with each other. If I feel OK about myself but not about you, I will try to get rid of you. If I feel not-OK about myself but see you as OK, I will probably avoid you. And if I feel not-OK about both of us, we will go nowhere" (Leveson 2011).

In the language of Transactional Analysis, life positions are listed as:

- I'm OK, You're OK
- I'm Not OK, You're OK
- I'm OK, You're Not OK
- I'm Not OK, You're Not OK
- I'm OK, You're OK (adult)

I'M OK, YOU'RE OK

As their primary lens for seeing the world, those internalizing this most mentally healthy outlook have a realistic acceptance of the inherent worth and uniqueness of themselves and others. Yet it's not that such a fortunate few gravitating to this position are Pollyannas seeing even the most heinous people as good and worthy of respect and trust. There is thus no OK equivalency between Hitler and Mother Teresa, Joseph Stalin and Gandhi, or Jack the Ripper and Jack the guy next door. None whatsoever. After all, in accepting the basic value and rights of people as an existential ideal, one can still despise, fear, and recoil at obvious contradictions to this rule.

It's just that in separating a person's intrinsic worth from their actions, I'm OK, You're OK people tend to evaluate others in the best possible light as "a statement of their essence [and] not necessarily their behavior" (Corey 2009, 16). And with that frame of reference, their logical conclusion regarding human nature can only be that with relatively few exceptions, *unless and until there are compelling case-by-case reasons suggesting otherwise,* the vast majority of people are fundamentally OK and if provided with Adult-enhancing tools of self-enlightenment, they can positively change.

Thus rather than reflexively viewing others as innately sick or beyond hope, those internalizing the I'm OK, You're OK position *at least initially* reframe behavioral explanations in a manner changing the entire meaning and feeling tone of even negative actions. And so doing, their optimistic determination is that overwhelmingly people are not by nature evil. Yet equally by nature, they may sometimes lose their way.

Difficult for many to accept when posited by Eric Berne more than fifty years ago, the belief that virtually all people are intrinsically OK and if given an effective approach for change can greatly improve their lives is still hard for many to internalize and for many more to achieve. Indeed, even some TA therapists and authors have found it difficult to embrace the I'm OK, You're OK position as the original and universal view of oneself and others. However, Thomas Harris was not one of them.

> I am a person. You are a person. Without you I am not a person, for only through you is language made possible, and only through language is thought made possible, and only through thought is human-

> ness possible. You have made me important and you are important. If I devalue you, I devalue myself. This is the rationale of the position I'm OK—You're OK. Through this position only are we persons instead of things. (Harris 1973, 257)

Yet even if questioning the validity of this "equality of worth among people" position, the principle of reciprocity assures that it is in one's best interest to give others the benefit of the "You're OK" doubt. For in behaving toward those around us as if they are worthy of respect, compassion, and consideration, we invite those favors in return.

Moreover, viewing oneself and others more favorably combined with the positive emotions such an outlook engenders fuels "psychological resiliency . . . and it may be that resilient people use positive emotions to achieve effective coping strategies, such as humor, creative exploration, relaxation, optimistic thinking, amusement, and hope, all of which can create positive emotions in oneself and others" (Napper 2009, 67). And research clearly indicates that people exhibiting such "looking on the bright side" approaches associated with an I'm OK, You're OK outlook "do much better in school and college, at work and on the playing field" (Seligman 1991, 5).

But there are even greater benefits to an I'm OK and so are you "glass half full" frame of reference. A growing body of evidence "has shown positive and negative emotion-related attitudes and states to be associated with physical health, mental health, and longevity" (Danner, Snowden, and Friesen 2001, 804). With that in mind, since it has been statistically confirmed "that the more bad events a person encounters . . . the more illness he [or she] will have" (Seligman 1991, 173), *at the most obvious level* the link between emotions, outlook, and health may not be very complicated at all.

That is, once accurately recognizing a potential problem involving health-related issues or otherwise, internally predisposed "taking the bull by the horns" optimists often attempt to aggressively preempt adversity while externally oriented and passively inclined, "It is what it is" pessimists just as often do not. Hence if the less control one believes one has leads to a sense of helplessness, and if this impotency results in avoidable misfortune occurring without opposition, at-the-mercy-of-the-environment pessimists will more likely experience greater hardship and greater illness. And they do.

However, the evidence linking health and mindset goes well beyond such a common sense cause-and-effect explanation. At the very least, it also includes a study that found that optimism "was associated with a lower risk of death in 839 Mayo Clinic patients observed over a 30-year period" (Danner, Snowden, and Friesen 2001, 805; Swenson, Pearson, and Osborne 1973). It includes research conducted at the Harvard Medical School, discovering that brain chemicals producing "good thoughts improve our immune system and negative thoughts suppress our immune system" (Priya 2007, 287; Holism 2001). And it includes the nearly universal belief that psychological factors can encourage the onset of cancer in that "negative emotions produce negative changes in body chemistry and decrease natural killer cell activity" (Priya 2007, 288; Del Casale 2001).

But now, evidence linking mindset and physiological well-being also includes research over the last decade revealing that exposure to stress can accelerate the degradation of protective caps at the ends of our chromosomes known as telomeres. Acting like a cellular candle, it is now clear that the shorter the length of these DNA segments the shorter the lifespan of cells so compromised. Moreover, even though telomere length indeed "correlates with chronological age and also [to] morbidity and mortality" (Shaley 2012), the ticking of these chromosomal clocks does not inexorably tick in only one direction. That is, studies conducted at the University of California suggest that enhancing well-being by adopting a healthier diet, a more active lifestyle, *and a more positive mindset* can help maintain *or even lengthen* telomeres (Saul 2013).

But that's not all. A finding from a study at Ohio State University also suggests that "ongoing bitterness, dissatisfaction, frustration, chronic anger, and envy are the . . . harbingers of disease" (Rosenfeld 1999, 364), in that stress triggers a "master switch" gene that corrupts the body's immune system, allowing cancer to more easily metastasize throughout the body (Robertson 2013; Sinpetru 2013).

The conclusion of such recently conducted research can be little other than continuing to view oneself and others negatively is a likely ticket to an unhappy, unhealthy, and relatively quick end. And while it is not implied that adopting an I'm OK, You're OK life position is a guaranteed fountain of youth, few could argue that such a positive frame of reference may well be a self-initiated version of what Ponce de Leon was looking for but never found.

Yet as convincing as these contemporary studies are, linking emotional and physical health, an equally impressive yet older investigation was conducted not on subjects observed at a prestigious university but with data provided by a group of 180 nuns housed at a convent. That is, in strongly suggesting an inverse association between positive emotions and mortality risk in later life, Catholic sisters expressing the most positive emotions in autobiographies composed in their twenties *lived an average of almost seven years longer* than those expressing the least positive emotions.

Written in 1930, these life stories evaluated for positive or negative content were thus "strongly related to survival and longevity 6 decades later" (Danner, Snowden, and Freisen 2001, 804). In fact, "for every 1% increase in the number of positive-emotion [autobiographical] sentences, there was a 1.4% decrease in mortality rate." And as importantly, "the relative risk of death *increased in a stepwise fashion*" as the number of positive comments decreased (Danner, Snowden, and Friesen 2001, 809; emphasis added).

Rather than criticizing this research as relatively unimportant due to the small size of the sample studied, its finding of a meaningful correlation between the content of a comparatively few autobiographies written a year after the Stock Market Crash with longevity for their authors some sixty years later is anything but insignificant. For although the number of handwritten impressions of life evaluated was indeed small, what makes the so-called "nun study" results so compelling are the circumstance-related similarities among the women composing those stories.

In drawing a relationship between attitudes and/or actions and physical health, rarely are investigators able to completely "tease out" all behavioral and environmental variables that might impact a study's ultimate results. However, researchers would be hard-pressed to find a more homogeneous group of subjects as those 180 Catholic sisters sharing the same occupation, similar socioeconomic status, identical access to medical care, equal avoidance of excessive drug or alcohol consumption, and, obviously, the same gender. And it is these similarities in lifestyle, environment, and exposure to everyday stressors that make the statistically significant results of this study inversely linking early-life optimism and risk of later-life mortality so persuasive.

But even though a positive outlook is thus undeniably central to one's physical and emotional health, the I'm OK, You're OK position is a perceptual house where few consistently live. Nevertheless difficulty in reaching and maintaining this mindset should not devalue the irrefutable gains of striving for an ever-closer approximation of its ideals. For arguably more than any other perceptual orientation, the I'm OK and so are you mindset, as the positional embodiment of an optimistically confident worldview, is the *single most important disposition leading to a long and fulfilling life*.

Yet however difficult this most beneficial of positions is for some to accomplish or even accept, the behaviors it implies are easily defined. That is, the portrait of an I'm OK, You're OK person is painted with a palette of mutual respect for oneself and others, an unwavering sense of personal responsibility, a confidently lived "find a way" sense of "I can do this" self-empowerment, a win-win imperative dictating conflict resolution, a refusal to engage in psychological games, and an ongoing commitment to self-actualization. Moreover, descriptors consistently associated with the I'm OK, You're OK personality also include cooperativeness, honesty, respectful assertiveness, and compassionate support for those less fortunate (Fine and Poggio 1977).

Said to be the initial orientation of newborns, it would seem that this most optimistic I'm OK, You're OK life position conflicts with the long-held belief that at birth we enter the world with a "perceptual tabula rasa" that experience writes upon. And although we now know that since certain behavioral and personality traits are inborn that is not exactly so, it may well be so in a sense. That is, as TA theory suggests, lacking any preconceived notions and any prior events to draw from that people can be "bad," infants *at least initially* have no cause to doubt the worth of themselves or anyone else.

Thus it is likely that infants responded to by caregivers with a lovingly predictable satisfaction of needs for sustenance and stroking, and as yet lacking evidence to the contrary, initially internalize the optimism prerequisite for this healthiest of life positions. And if people are indeed "born OK," in their "innate state [they] tend to health, healing, and a benign expectation and trust in others" (Steiner, the Transactional Analysis Corroboration Project).

To that end, admittedly suggestive evidence over the last half century supporting this optimistic view of mankind's future perfectibility indicates unmistakable, but obviously still unfinished, worldwide progress in the direction of egalitarianism, collaboration, philanthropic pursuits, universal human rights, and democracy. Furthermore, as selfish and destructive as humans can be and as often as they fall short of moral ideals, "many of us [still] care about strangers in faraway lands . . . many of us care about the fates of nonhuman animals . . . [many of us] see racism and sexism as evil; we reject slavery and genocide . . . [and] we try to love our enemies" (Bloom 2010).

However, for the vast majority of people this positive and presumably instinctual view of oneself and others is soon corrupted by an early life environment melting such optimism as quickly as snow in spring. But unlike snows inevitably returning the following winter, unless there is a conscious adult decision to embrace the same I'm OK, You're OK mindset existing before any childhood socialization damage occurred, it is unlikely ever to return. And while this TA theory suggesting that children are born "good" only to be inevitably corrupted by their environment is more than fifty years old, recent research reveals that this may indeed be the case.

THE "BABY LAB" EXPERIMENTS

In 2007 at Yale University, newborns were presented with a "puppet show" scene involving a square, a triangle, and a circle, each brightly colored and each with movable eyes. As one of the shapes struggled to climb a hill, another shape attempted to push from behind as a "helper," while the third shape tried to prevent that action by pushing back from above as a "hinderer."

When after the "show" the infants were given a choice in reaching for one of the shapes, they were far more likely to reach for the "helper" shape, the "nice" one, than for the "hinderer," or "nasty" one (Stafford 2013; Hamlin, Wynn, and Bloom 2007). In fact, the preference expressed by the infants "wasn't a subtle statistical trend; *just about all the babies* reached for the good guy" (Bloom 2010; emphasis added). And since common sense and research agree that grasping for an object, and for even younger babies gazing longer at some objects than at others, indicates preference, this act of reaching as a reliable indicator suggesting partiality toward those displaying prosocial behaviors is highly significant.

Thus seemingly in forming judgments about the character traits of the "hinderer" and the "helper," infants *as young as six months old* overwhelmingly found the behavior of the latter to be more appealing. While this is hardly definitive proof that even infants have expectations of proper conduct and a preference for supportive intentions over sinister ones, it does suggest that unlike Freud and Piaget positing that we begin life as amoral beings, Eric Berne may have been right that "the most basic assumption of TA theory and practice" (Woollams and Brown 1978, 1) should be that, at least initially, most of us are born OK.

But however questionable some may consider such evidence of "I'm OK, You're OK babies to be, a more recently conducted series of Yale University experiments also suggests that infants are not, as Rousseau insisted, "perfect idiots . . . knowing nothing" but rather evolutionarily programmed beings having at least an incipient sense of right and wrong. And as with the earlier "baby lab" experiments, infants again watched a thematically similar "puppet show" involving a helper and hinderer.

The morality drama played out before babies once thought of as little more than blank slate "blobs" was simple. At stage center, a puppet was shown struggling to open a transparent box with a toy inside. At first, a yellow-shirted character came over to help open the box and then the scene was repeated with a blue-shirted puppet slamming the box shut. To adults, it was obvious that one puppet was mean and the other was nice. But would five-month-old babies once thought to understand little and infants even younger previously believed to know even less be able to comprehend the principled significance of what they were observing?

While obviously neither group of infants could talk, they could indicate a preference for the good or the bad puppet by either reaching for their puppet of choice or, for the younger infants lacking sufficient arm control, by staring longer at whichever puppet they liked. And by all accounts it was immediately clear what puppet the diapered-audience preferred. For in study after study, *an overwhelming majority* of the older babies consistently reached for the "nice" puppet and apparently also feeling positively toward helpful people, infants just three months old looked at the "good" character far longer than the unhelpful one (Born

Good? Babies Help Unlock the Origins of Morality, *60 Minutes*, July 28, 2013).

But if understanding the difference between right and wrong and preferring the former is part of our inherent nature, then where does not-okay misconduct come from? Undoubtedly, some of it likely develops as compensatory behavior for feelings of inferiority stemming from a child's relative sense of weakness and dependency during early childhood's socialization process. Exhibited throughout life as "I'm OK and guess who's not" leveling in the home, at school, on the job, and far more seriously as ethnocentrism displayed on far grander stages, the origins of such relationship-compromising reactions are thus not completely escapable even for children raised in homes where love is unconditional, tolerance is modeled, and morality is valued.

Yet further experiments involving infants seem to indicate that the childhood socialization answer to where You're Not OK wrongdoing comes from may not be complete. Namely, in addition to leveling and at times prejudicial seeds planted during the upbringing process, discrimination against dissimilar others as a contrasting behavior to our moral core may *also* be genetically predisposed from birth. This seems so because babies at Yale's Infant Cognition Center showed an unmistakable preference for puppets who appeared to like the same snacks they did. That is, babies liking Cheerios preferred puppets seemingly mirroring that choice, and babies liking graham crackers clearly favored, and indeed had a bias for, puppets apparently enjoying them as well.

But preference is not bias until it results in negative feelings and/or behaviors directed at others perceived as unlike ourselves. Thus the deeper question is not only whether even infants have a sense of "us and them" but instead whether that partiality results in, or at least is correlated with, negativity toward those seen as different. And based upon the suggestive findings at the "baby lab," that indeed appears to be so. For when puppets liking a different food struggled to open a toy box and were alternately helped and hindered from doing so by two other puppets, *almost nine in ten babies* in showing a preference for the unhelpful character seemingly wanted the puppet with a dissimilar taste in food to be treated badly (Born Good? Babies Help Unlock the Origins of Morality, *60 Minutes*, July 28, 2013).

So it appears that in theorizing that we are all born with a rudimentary I'm OK, You're OK frame of reference only to be later subverted by the environment, Berne was only partially right. As a whole, research does suggest that at birth babies *are hardwired for a sense of morality* or at the least for characteristics prompting morality, such as concern for others and an understanding of another's goals. However, that moral sense appears to favor those perceived to be of their own kind (Bloom 2010). And if a fully developed sense of morality-inspired tolerance presupposes a sense of impartiality, for children not socialized to at least accept if not celebrate differences among people, it is too often but a small step from within-group inborn preference to prejudice, and from prejudice to hate.

But whether infants are initially born OK only to be debased by inadequate or worse caregiving, there seems little doubt that unless genetically and/or biochemically compromised, given quality attention all children have at least the *potential* to assume the I'm OK, You're OK frame of reference. To that end, if one accepts that overtly abusive or absent care leads to catastrophically negative life-position results, why wouldn't high-quality upbringing contrastingly promote the basic trust in others and the implied OKness in oneself to foster the positive opposite?

Thus other than for perhaps the previously cited hopeful evidence concerning the future perfectibility of man, the debate over whether children are born OK or that only through excellent care they become that way is relatively unimportant. As few things are either all black or white, it is probable that by early childhood people exist on a continuum neither all OK nor all the reverse. Due to genetic predisposition, upbringing, and experiential happenstance, they are in varying degrees potentially both. And since of those three factors the most controllable *is* upbringing, it is essential for parents to provide consistently positive strokes *whenever* or *however* children assume the I'm OK, You're OK worldview.

For if the mindset that we are all unique, valuable, and worthy of respect exists at birth, then high-quality nurturance will only reinforce that. And if an ultrapositive core perception of oneself and others partially or even completely results from high-quality care, imbuing children with that "gift that keeps on giving" conclusion that they, as others, are valuable less for what they do than for who they are must become *even more of a priority* for all parents.

And if for no other reason than naked self-interest, the goal of instilling an I'm OK and so are you outlook in a child should be an essential focus for all parents. This is true because a child so raised has less of a need to perversely assert their worth in a display of will exhibited in a contrary or rebellious manner (Parry 1979). But even more importantly, children internalizing a strong sense of optimism clearly associated with the I'm OK, You're OK outlook are on average less depressed, achieve more, and over their lives are healthier than youngsters trending toward pessimism (Seligman 1991). And just as those outcomes clearly benefit children well into adulthood and beyond, their "My child is successful" gains are equally enjoyed by the prideful parents who raised them.

In the end, for parents wanting their sons or daughters to become well-adjusted and successful adults, isn't a foundational sense of overall OKness *an essential precondition* for any child to have even a reasonable chance to live a self-actualized existence? Thus whether OKness results more from nature or from nurture, there is no better reason for parents to demonstrate unconditional love for their children in the form of I'm OK, You're OK parenting than this.

I'M NOT OK, YOU'RE OK

Even in "good homes," it isn't long before a child is inevitably scolded and criticized. Even in "good homes," the child experiences the discomfort of colic, teething, bellyaches, and hunger when caregivers are slow to respond. Even in "good homes," the child is often confused as to what to do, afraid of things going bump in the night, and clumsy, careless, and forgetful of rules. Even in "good homes," loving and thoughtful parents will instruct, command, and punish a young child, even if it is simply to protect the youngster from harm. And even in "good homes," when children are faulted, penalized, or merely corrected they at least initially don't understand the difference between *doing* bad and *being* bad.

It is because of this pervasive uncertainty that the I'm Not OK, You're OK mindset and its I'm OK, You're Not OK counterpart are sometimes referred to as defensive positions. That is, "their purpose is to defend the child from being flooded with the rage or hopelessness of despair . . . [by maintaining] hope of finding the magic formula that will insure happiness, either through his own efforts or [with] the help of others" (English 1975, 417). Thus at least in their less severe forms, understanding the genesis for either of these "defensive" worldviews may be as simple as realizing that in seeking this happiness-promoting "magic formula," children will adapt their position to complement the behaviors of their principal caregiver, who most often is the mother.

Consequently, it seems likely that in adapting to an overbearing mother, a child will often internalize a passively compliant I'm Not OK, You're OK mindset, and in responding to an indecisive and overanxious mother the child will likely gravitate to a rebellious form of the I'm OK, You're Not OK position (English 1975). But even defending oneself by adopting a complementary position to the primary stroke provider doesn't guarantee unconditional relief from the frustration, ambiguities, self-doubts, and criticisms imposed on the young child by parent directives he has yet to completely follow or thoroughly understand.

To that end, "How dare you disobey me," or "I told you not to touch that hot stove," or "No television for you until you learn to treat me with respect" are emotionally painful lines from the early screenplays of virtually all our stories. Yet, as is widely known but less publicly seen, some early life stories are worse. Far worse.

In some homes, children are raised hearing an incessant drumbeat of their "by the way" failings. Seemingly unable to do anything right, in some homes children are told "You didn't clean your room and *by the way* you didn't . . ." or "You didn't do well in school and *by the way* you didn't . . ." or "You didn't tell me where you were going and *by the way* you didn't . . ." In such homes, criticism and punishment behind closed doors is the norm as are feelings of inadequacy, insignificance, and unwantedness. In such homes, it's a wonder how any children can rise above such confidence-destroying criticisms with even a shred of their self-esteem and original OKness intact.

But even if controlling and punitive parental actions are kept to a minimum, the very nature of children as physically small, relatively unknowing, and entirely dependent often leads them to the only conclusion that makes any sense at all. And frequently that inference is that others, initially defined by and limited to parental stroke providers, *must* be okay and that "I am not." This outlook is inevitably compounded by additional factors dictating that compared to other animals, human infants are especially helpless, reach physical maturity more slowly, and due to the educational, vocational, and economic demands of the modern world, remain dependent on caregivers for a greater percentage of life.

Thus from a child's point of view, such an extended period of neediness virtually guarantees their determination to view others more positively than themselves. For even with marginally attentive parents, if the infant lives past their first birthday, enough parental strokes must have occurred without which the child would not have survived. And thus being so reliant, even this minimal level of nurturance is enough for the helpless child to comparatively view his or her caregivers as all-knowing, all-powerful, and all-OK. Yet however strong this sense of dependency continues to be, by the end of the first year of life the stroke economy of virtually any child takes a turn for the worse.

Inevitably, as the child begins walking at about twelve months of age and no longer needs to constantly be picked up, he or she loses a primary source of physical stroking. No longer receiving the same quantity of bodily strokes once expected and regularly received by being held, cuddled, and nursed, the now-ambulatory child must find substitutes for those contact strokes no longer available.

Such replacements may be offered as parental smiles, frowns, or verbal sounds received as messages and stored "as nonverbal survival fuel to see him [or her] through the longer unstroked intervals of time" (English 1972, 66). However, even for a child fortunate enough to have attentive parents, the overall value of such verbal and nonverbal recognition and approval strokes pales in comparison to the tactile strokes no longer received.

Indeed, if that is so for children of "always there" parents, the stroke economy collapse for children with "barely there" parents is far greater. But whatever the quality of parenting a child experiences, this inevitable decline in strokes combined with the typically restrictive and often-punitive aspects of childhood socialization almost certainly leads to the I'm Not OK, You're OK life outlook as the logical conclusion "of *all* small children" (Harris and Harris 1985, 7). And as the universal position of early childhood, it is this worldview that likely persists most commonly in the general population.

Thus the I'm Not OK, You're OK position likely results from the "*situation of childhood* and not the intention of the parents [that] produces the problem" (Harris 1973, 48). And although hardly ideal in the long term, the child internalizing this position achieves his or her "first mastery in "making sense of life" [and] in solving what Adler called "life's central problem"—the attitude toward others" (Harris 1973, 65).

In any case, if this "I'm not as good as others" position naturally evolves in even enlightened and caring homes, one can only imagine the un-OK burden borne throughout life for children raised where love is rare and anger, criticism, and punishment are the norm. Thus as the likely residue of being a child, any child, the characteristics associated with internalizing this outlook should be at least somewhat familiar to everyone.

The legacy of the I'm Not OK, You're OK life position is therefore a lack of self-esteem and confidence resulting in self-doubt, obsessive approval seeking, "You can't fight city hall" passivity, and a less-than-fulfilling life. And lacking faith in oneself and contaminated by a "whatever will be, will be" mindset, it is easy to see how this frame of reference may also result in endless equivocations. Agonizing ad nauseam like Tevye in *Fiddler on the Roof*, "On the one hand . . . , but on the other . . . ," the only decisions made are not to decide.

As ever-present elevator muzak, the I'm Not OK, You're OK melody plays in the background of one's unconscious until notice is taken of its existence. And that existence is exemplified by feelings of never being attractive enough, smart enough, athletic enough, and good enough. Yet however "enough" is defined, it is always beyond reach in a victim's existence where Wooden Leg, Kick Me, and Schlemiel are among the only games in town.

If someone tells such obsessively insecure people that they're smart, they characterize themselves as stupid. If someone says they're beautiful, they view themselves as ugly. And if someone describes them as strong, they see themselves as weak. As self-effacing "imposters" in whatever they do, life is a charade where smiling is a mask, emotional flagellation is the norm, self-criticism is a daily event, appeasement of and subordination to others is a compulsion, depression is an internally prescribed drug of choice, and withdrawal from others is often the only escape.

Yet in depriving such an un-OK person of even the possibility of gaining confidence-building strokes from others, such a retreat is surely self-defeating. And without sufficient reality-check contact from others, "withdrawn people may develop an elaborate fantasy life centered on wishes that if they become holy enough, wise enough, rich enough, or irresistible enough, they will be OK" (Prochaska and Norcross n.d., 13).

But with the hardcore I'm Not OK, You're OK confidence-challenged worldview still remaining as the backdrop for existence, the same depressive drama will likely continue throughout life unless destructive parental stroking patterns dictate an arguably even more toxic position.

I'M OK, YOU'RE NOT OK

Sometimes referred to as the criminal or paranoid position, individuals internalizing the I'm OK, You're Not OK mindset commonly feel persecuted, victimized, cheated, angry, and superior to others. Confrontational, unwilling to change, often narcissistic, arrogantly grandiose, and overly critical, such "It's not me, it's them" people in looking for suitable scapegoats rarely, if ever, find humble pie.

But that's not all. Those programmed with the I'm OK, You're Not OK outlook habitually provide assistance to those "incapable" of helping themselves, commonly seek targets for leveling games such as Rapo, Blemish, and NIGY, exploitatively succeed at another's expense, and frequently look for a con or "angle" as motives for the behavior of others. In short, such an overly suspicious and self-aggrandizing recipe is all but certain to yield a relationship-damaging cocktail for anyone embracing the game roles of finding-fault persecutor or admiration-seeking rescuer in the boardroom, bedroom, or virtually everywhere else. And when such negative feelings for others become extreme, it is far too often but a small step to bully, rob, brutalize, and even kill "inferiors" when viewing them with a "they are no more important than the gum on the bottom of my shoe" lack of empathy.

Yet as the I'm OK, You're Not OK stance is the antithesis of the I'm Not OK, You're OK mindset so common to childhood, how then does such an arrogant, dictatorial, and contemptuous life position become the "normal" for anyone? Simply put, the origin of this uncommonly negative worldview is likely found in the actions of abusive parents.

There is reason to believe that, at least in its most malevolent incarnations, the I'm OK, You're Not OK life position results from children being physically and/or emotionally oppressed by their caregivers. When mistreatment is a frequent occurrence, a child's safety and comfort can only be found through escape from the source of torment. Once alone, the child self-strokes through rocking or touching themselves and at least in a relative sense begins to heal. This healing translates into an unconsciously understood stimulus-response association that when parents are present there is pain and when alone there is not. And it is this sense of safety, recovery, and relative comfort when separated from his or her source of distress that fuels the child's switch from the depressive I'm Not OK, You're OK outlook to its more pernicious opposite.

Moreover, this incipient I'm OK, You're Not OK mindset is later reinforced by the child's instinct for survival. Likely globalizing the torment from parents as universal threats from others, the child over time begins to adaptively lash out in misguided "I'll get others before they get me" attempts at self-preservation. And so internalizing the best defense as a good offense, innocents are preemptively assailed without conscience.

As a result, when others do not matter, when "the total fault in every situation lies with others" (Harris 1973, 73), when any evidence that others are OK has been paranoically eliminated, and when others are seen as risks in a dog-eat-dog world, morality is hardly an obstacle to harming "those others." And while it is impossible to definitively prove the aforementioned explanation for the I'm OK, You're Not OK mindset, the statistical relationship between childhood abuse and adult criminality is inescapable. In fact, representative of numerous other studies, a 2001 U.S. Department of Justice review of 1,500 cases of child abuse or neglect over time found that childhood maltreatment increased the likelihood of adult arrest for violent crime by 30 percent (Widom and Maxfield 2001).

Additionally, the I'm OK, You're Not OK position may not only directly result from parental mistreatment but may also ensue as its reactive formation and projective side effect. That is, such torment initially leading to doubts about self-worth may later be defended against by an "I am better than others" countervailing grandiosity and by projecting un-OKness onto blameless targets. Thus beginning in early childhood, such positional leveling may be unconsciously adopted by abused children as a strategy to compensate for an otherwise inadequate sense of essential worth. To that end, some believe that "it is not possible to view others as not-OK unless one views at least part of oneself as not-OK" (White 1994, 271).

I'M NOT OK, YOU'RE NOT OK

People programmed with the I'm Not OK, You're Not OK position tend to feel helpless, hopeless, and self-destructive, if not suicidal. It may be described quite simply as the "give up" or "life is not worth living" futile mindset, often resulting in "leave me alone" withdrawal from others and even from life itself.

As such, while the two other un-OK life positions represent a range of severity from relatively healthy to extremely dysfunctional, this most depressive "I can't help myself and you can't or won't help me either" position is "fundamentally pathological" (Harley 2006, 254). In fact, if a chronically pessimistic outlook likely undermines one's immune system so that infectious diseases happen more frequently and the ravages of aging occur earlier and more severely than necessary (Seligman 1991), one doesn't have to be a genius to extrapolate the emotional and physical toll taken by the I'm Not OK, You're Not OK mindset.

Whereas other than for the initial I'm OK, You're OK stance, the aforementioned life positions result from parental stroking patterns, the I'm un-OK and so are you outlook may well result from an ongoing pattern of stroke deprivation. This occurs when for many unfortunate children, survival strokes existing in the first year of life are discontinued and a sense of abandonment is internalized. Thus even without being explicitly stated, the unmistakable message received by those so deprived can be none other than not to exist. And to make matters worse, since the purpose of the Adult ego state is in part to obtain strokes, with none forthcoming it stops developing (Harris 1973).

The emotional path the youngster endures to get to this "Why bother?" position seems clear. When parents provide only minimal care, infants are "trained" to internalize the dependent and insecure I'm Not OK position. Yet when care and stroking continues and is generally humane, children will later come to believe that their parents and, by extension, others are OK. However, because parents who ignore their children are unlikely to be viewed so positively, stroke-deprived youngsters already internalizing an un-OK dependency mindset about themselves understandably extrapolate a malignant but wholly inaccurate view of the wider world as well. And it doesn't much matter that this toxic perception is not reality. *It is the child's reality.*

Accordingly, children who have been denied sufficient stroking will likely consider themselves inadequate for being needy and view their parents as equally without merit for "abandoning" them. As a result, life is lived in a "don't give a damn" hell where they can't help themselves because they are "inferior," and they can't rely on anyone else because others are equally without value. And even if caregivers outside the family later provide strokes, in many instances the damage has already been done. For as with the other life positions, once the primary view of oneself and others is decided upon, reality is selectively interpreted to reinforce and confirm that initial conclusion. This being so, even if caregiving substitutes are well meaning, they will often be viewed as no more OK than the child's neglectful parents.

Thus with seemingly no hope for a better life and with existence defined as unending victimization, the ultra-apathetic, bitter, and/or frequently angry I'm Not OK, You're Not OK individual will, in the extreme, live out an unproductive, nothing matters "self-destructive life of intermittent institutionalization, irreversible substance abuse, senseless homicide, or [even] tragic suicide" (Porchaska and Norcross n.d., 13). But that this most final act of "stop the world I want to get off" desperation is even possible should not be surprising. This is so because however tragic in consequence but perversely understandable in logic, hopelessness as an aspect of depression is "the most accurate predictor of suicide" (Seligman 1991, 126).

I'M OK, YOU'RE OK (ADULT)

Considered by many as the most basic philosophy of Transactional Analysis, the reprise from early infancy of the I'm OK and so are you position is the only outlook that can be decided upon by conscious and rational adult choice. And however difficult to realize and equally hard to maintain, it is self-servingly beneficial for any thinking person to seek this optimistically healthy yet fragile mindset. For in addition to its positive impact on health, if as the principle of reciprocity suggests we attract in others not what we want but what we are, why would anyone understanding this behavioral dynamic logically harm themselves by believing otherwise?

TWELVE

Recognizing Drivers

I'm driven for some reason. But I don't know where I'm going.
—Courtney Love

Because feelings of inferiority and insignificance are so unpleasant, people diminish them by more than playing psychological games, employing defense mechanisms, and, most positively, striving toward an I'm OK, You're OK life position. According to Transactional Analysis, they also unconsciously utilize behaviors that may sound beneficial but when excessive ultimately reduce one's quality of life. Known as drivers, these habitually enacted coping behaviors interpreted in childhood as "how to behave" can, however, also be positive in result if used as a guide rather than a straitjacket in overcoming difficulties, solving problems, diminishing anxiety, or simply feeling better about oneself.

As likely a universal condition of mankind, the use of drivers is thus a balancing act. That is, drivers can be a personal force for good only if in realizing their darker side people harness them as a rational choice "when appropriate, rather than be driven by them by default" (Trubshaw 2011). Yet for many individuals, this is sadly not the case. For in blindly following one or more of these parentally transmitted virtues, the vast majority of uninformed and unaware people are beguiled into believing they are safe, in control, and are behaving in ways conducive to their happiness (Klein 1985; Conway 1978). But clearly they are not.

Referred to as "counterinjunctions" when applied as positively enacted "solutions" to moderate or overcome the esteem-sapping effects of restrictive parental messages such as "Don't Grow Up," "Don't Act," "Don't Be Close," or even "Don't Be Who You Are," drivers are often explicitly transmitted with good intent to children from the Parent ego state of their parents. Accordingly, people tend to obsessively rely on one of these "working styles" (Hay 1993) throughout life as "must do" remedies to feeling less than okay. This is especially so in order to "survive" stressful situations.

Yet because by definition drivers as "If only I . . ." or "As long as I . . ." solutions for un-OKness are regularly taken to extremes, their unbounded result is often far more negative than is their benefit. This is so because feelings of inadequacy are so deeply ingrained in most people that whichever driver is "chosen" as a short-term solution for overcoming a sense of worthlessness, dependency, or incompleteness is invariably never enough.

Caught in a vicious cycle when a driver isn't working to reduce stress or even to significantly curb feelings of inferiority, instead of trying a different approach to provide relief, people often continue being driven but with ever-greater intensity. Thus as with many mood-altering drugs, because "dosage" over time must increase to gain equal effects, those same driver behaviors used to remedy self-doubt are often so exaggeratedly engaged that they become those very behaviors generating additional unhappiness. Accordingly, because such "robbing Peter to pay Paul" driver messages are so obediently and often obsessively followed, releasing their hold on behavior requires Adult awareness, understanding, and oversight.

THE SEVEN DRIVERS

Hurry Up

Those using this "early bird catches the worm" driver seek OKness by multitasking and overscheduling themselves. And in doing so, such "right now" people often described as "Type A" personalities may well blunt the impact of "Don't Be Slow" or "Don't Be Late" injunctions, but the price they pay is high. For in "taking on" too much at once, rushing through work, avoiding procrastination at any cost, and desiring immediate gratification by "getting things done," chronically impatient "hurry up" people are inevitably prone to overlooking details and to making mistakes.

Obsessively looking to cram as much activity as possible into narrow windows of time, "hurry ups" are productive at best and relationally destructive at worst. Moreover, these "never enough time" individuals are extremely uncomfortable with having to wait at restaurants, in traffic jams, and even for people to stop talking. To that end, they routinely interrupt others and will patronizingly add words when ideas are not voiced quickly enough. Chronically impatient, "hurry ups" talk fast, drive fast, and even eat fast. And as often true of other drivers, those internalizing the Hurry Up behavioral imperative frequently become frustrated, annoyed, agitated, and critical when others do not act similarly.

But since drivers also embody the possibility of far more positive behaviors, under the watchful eye of an aware and moderating Adult, those prescriptions for OKness can promote their original intent rather than amplify those very insecurities they were intended to diminish. Thus in the case of the Hurry Up driver, the same unconscious directive obsessively accepting the importance of not "dragging one's feet" must at times also give consent to complete tasks but at a less frenetic pace. And such Adult "get out of jail free" permissions releasing one from the internal tyranny of uncontrolled and controlling drivers are known as "allowers" (Clarkson 1992, 17; Kahler 1977).

As a mechanical governor limits the speed of an engine, allowers limit the speed of out-of-control drivers. These "stop the driver" authorizations are typically phrased as an "It's okay to . . ." or an "I may . . ." statement encouraging Adult oversight and moderation. Thus an allower for the Hurry Up driver might be *"It's okay to* slow down when moving too fast likely results in errors of judgment or execution" or *"I may* occasionally stop, smell the roses, and enjoy the so-called simple pleasures in life." And since when taken to extremes drivers are superficial "lipstick-on-pig" solutions to the negative programming of a not-OK life position and script, identifying them and accepting their corresponding allowers can provide awareness-fueled relief as a guide-for-living "truth that sets one free" (Gere 1975, 285).

But in order to be truly effective as a driver release, an allower should be supported by Adult statements specifically affirming not only what one may do but what one wants, what one is capable of, and most importantly what one *will* do. Typically, these so-called "goer statements" are "I no longer have to . . ." or "I am capable of choosing whether to . . ." or "I will make a conscious decision when to . . ." assertions supporting their allower intent. As such, "goers" as allower-reinforcing "I declarations" provide "get off the dime" motivational direction for escaping the bondage of unrestricted driver behaviors.

Try Hard

Likely responding to either a "Don't Be Weak" or "Don't Fail" injunction, people employing this driver unconsciously believe that if they try hard enough, self-esteem will be protected and "things" will "eventually" work out. However, for many "try harders" this gung-ho attitude is short lived. Rarely completing goals, multiple projects begun with passionate "I'll try" enthusiasm often remain unfinished. Juggling many balls at once as in the game of Harried, one after another is dropped only to start the act anew. Semesters started with revitalized focus soon resemble past terms where lethargy was the norm. Diets begun with the best of intentions dissolve into nonexistent results. New Year's resolutions become yesterday's news. And "turning over a new leaf" as a better parent, spouse, friend, or person inevitably morphs into business as usual surrender.

Yet because those internalizing this driver frequently also try hard to avoid control by others, they sometimes exhibit passive-aggressive behaviors such as dawdling, stubbornness, procrastination, intentional inefficiency, and "forgetfulness" (Hazell 1989). And when failure inevitably results, those internalizing the Try Hard driver, in keeping with its esteem-enhancing theme, not uncommonly prefer blaming circumstances "out of their control" for such outcomes rather than looking in the mirror (Klein 1987).

Beginning early in life in response to "do something" parental demands, this driver is a "Look how hard I'm trying" or an "At least I tried hard" verbal palliative for failure in order to avoid caregiver rejection, maintain approval, and stay at least relatively okay. Yet while it's important to "try hard," in and of itself it may not be enough. Clichéd but true, it is just as important to "try smart." Equally so, it's okay to successfully finish what's been started before "trying hard" at another task. Yet without such awareness, the results of the Try Hard driver often lead to an exercise in futility that Eric Berne referred to as the "bash trap phenomenon."

The bash trap phenomenon is the tendency for some people to solve problems by continually limiting themselves to ineffectual solutions. Again and again, such "trapped" individuals try harder by bashing their heads against the same walls and their fists into the same doors, never realizing why the one won't budge and the other won't open.

Resembling real-life Wily Coyotes in the Road Runner cartoons, "bash trappers," believing that success is just around the corner, erroneously presume that expending increasingly more effort in ill-conceived courses of action will eventually lead to positive outcomes. Yet as for other drivers, when Try Hard is not working "the magic safety is broken. Escalation. Repetition. Frenzy. Chaos erupts. Comfortable coping is past. Gut panic replaces it" (Conway 1978, 346). And in the end, the likely result of such overwrought efforts is that a predictable world of failure is maintained, more obviously effective approaches are rigidly overlooked, and, as previously mentioned, doing the same thing over and over and expecting a different result again becomes as good a definition as any for insanity.

Be Strong

For those internalizing this driver, weakness cannot be tolerated. Often assumed by males to stay OK, feelings are ignored, emotional restraint even in emergencies is valued, massive self-sufficiency is admired, help is rarely sought, and unconquerable resiliency is celebrated. As a likely response to a "Don't Feel" or a "Don't Be Weak" injunction, the "be strong" credo is simple: "Never let anyone see you sweat," and though you may "fall seven times, stand up eight."

With good reason, often relied on during difficult times, those internalizing the Be Strong driver inspire a sense of security in others but are often seen as emotionally flat, critical of playful pursuits, always in control, and directed by a "constipated" Child ego state. But what those receiving help from "be strongs" often don't realize is that in accepting such support, their "saviors" may view them as without backbone and silently scorn their lack of self-sufficiency.

Superficially resembling positively purposeful Adult activity, when "be strong" behaviors regularly result in "spreading oneself too thin," overscheduling, and counterproductive outcomes, the driver rather than the ego state is in control. And while endurance, strength of resolve, and stoically managing one's emotions are often desirable qualities, the Be Strong allower internalizing permission to exhibit vulnerability by at least occasionally leaning on others or by openly expressing one's feelings is no less worthy of embracing.

Be Perfect

This "you can always do better" driver is often the prime motivator of extremely high achievers producing accurate and detailed work. Arising from parental messages questioning "only" a 92 percent on a math test, a three-for-four hitting performance in Little League, or a silver rather than a gold medal in a track meet, "be perfects" are unsatisfiable. But since there is virtually nothing that can be done that will be perfect enough, they cover all bases by offering too much information, equivocating to a fault, criticizing themselves when falling short of perfection, and being obsessively concerned with "What if . . .?" paralysis-by-analysis details.

As far as relationships are concerned, issues frequently arise involving other people's "lower" standards and their indifference for the "right" way to do things. These relational deal breakers are exacerbated still further by demands that friends, family members, and colleagues follow self-righteous guidelines for "proper" conduct. And when that invariably doesn't happen, the "be perfect" reaction is "How can they act as they do?" disbelief or a perfectly self-satisfied "When you want something done right, you have to do it yourself" response.

However, because one can almost always have done better in being more "coloring within the lines" perfect, such "exactly right" people doom themselves to an exactly wrong sense of eternal unhappiness. "Be perfects" are the proverbial puppies chasing their tails. Once perfection seems within reach, it becomes an elusive and virtually unreachable target. And so living lives more of frustration than of joy, for hardcore "be perfects" there can be no such thing as "doing one's best."

Thus for those internalizing this never-satisfied driver, a lack of perfection can only mean one thing, and that is, that they are not okay. This in turn fuels a further escalation of efforts to positively transform a "Don't Make Mistakes" or even a "Don't Be Who You Are" parental injunction. Seeking superior quality with Adult oversight and control can be an admirable goal. However, when excellence is only defined as perfection, that otherwise productive purpose becomes an uncompromising obsession leading to self-discounting frustration when flawlessness is inevitably unrealized.

Nevertheless, for those internalizing the Be Perfect driver, there is an escape from its endless cycle of dictating absolute control over people, events, and themselves. Accordingly, that freedom is gained by allowers accepting that comparative equivalency among differing values in "how things are done" is an acceptable part of the human condition, people have a right to choose "laxer standards" for themselves, and the sun will still rise tomorrow if an error is made or a deadline is not. And perhaps even more importantly, it is essential to realize that in occasionally making even obvious mistakes or in falling short of absolute perfection, being OK can be defined as much as by one's efforts as by one's results.

Be Careful

Overlapping with some behavioral aspects of the Be Perfect driver, those incorporating its Be Careful counterpart similarly exhibit elements of paralysis-by-analysis inaction. But while both drivers share the same "Don't Make Mistakes" mandate and the observable conduct for both may look similar, the underlying motives for each conditional path to OKness are entirely different. That is, while "be perfects" struggle over actions fearing flawed performances, "be carefuls" also limited by a "Don't Take Risks" injunction, agonize over decisions involving change.

After all, in leaving one's comfort zone "lies danger of being rejected, banned, shamed, judged, unloved—or simply the unknown" (Hawkes 2007, 211). Yet in maintaining their status-quo world, "be carefuls" may well guarantee a safe and secure cocoon, but they equally ensure a life without spontaneity, new discoveries, and the joy of self-potency by defeating the insecure person of yesterday for the confident one of tomorrow. For in stating the obvious, without risking "pushing one's envelope" in different and often-difficult directions, growth is all but impossible.

Take It

As with the Be Careful driver, the Take It driver has not as yet gained widespread acceptance among TA theorists. However, embodying elements of the Be Strong and Try Hard drivers, it is worthy to consider "all about me" expressions of excessive materialism, intellectual aggressiveness, narcissism, success at all costs, and bull-in-the-china-shop pushiness as behavioral manifestations of the Take It driver (Tudor 2008).

Also exhibited as bullying behavior, exaggerated competitiveness, and the "I want it now" imperialism of seizing what is desired with little or no concern for the necessities of others, one needn't look far to find evidence of this widespread motivator of behavior. Thus for those directed by the Take It driver, "greed is good" and the spirit of Gordon Gekko is alive and well.

As with other counterinjunctive correctives for self-doubt, the Take It driver is unconsciously internalized as an "If only I . . ." strategy for tempering the effects of parental messages likely including "Don't Be Weak" and perhaps even "Don't Fail." But also like other drivers, in the headlong quest to feel better about oneself, the Take It driver is often followed to extremes, resulting in a never satisfied "It's mine" acquisitiveness and an existence where accomplishment is measured purely by what one has rather than by what one has done.

Please Others

More likely common to those with low self-esteem, a preferring-to-be-led person internalizing this behavioral directive will submissively surrender in obeying authority figures or, in extreme cases, go along with the crowd even if doing so is counterproductive at best and dangerous, immoral, or even illegal at worst. Chronically seeing "which way the wind is blowing," those with the Please Others, "I'm not good enough" driver will at times ride bandwagons wherever they are going and whatever their expense. To that end, "while there is no real danger in surrender itself, there is [real] danger in what it is we surrender to" (Woods 2007b, 238).

In withholding their feelings, "please others" will also agree when they disagree, remain silent when they should speak up, and wear a happy face when feeling anything but. As a puppet on a string moving to the real or imagined whims of others, such people don't realize that relationships will not be undermined by respectfully asking for what is wanted, refusing unreasonable requests, or at least occasionally doing what is best for oneself. In fact, the very act of chronically bending over backward to please others might well damage the very relationships those so eager to comply are struggling to maintain. For as Aesop rightly observed, "Please all, and you will please none."

Because of the emotional and physical importance of compliantly adapting to parental demands during early childhood, the genesis for the "please others" imperative likely predates other drivers and accordingly may well be more common and more resistant to Adult moderation. But whether or not this is so, pleasing others seems to be the foundational driver for the other so-called "working styles." After all, in obsessively maintaining current OKness by obeying any of the other six drivers, aren't we still seeking approval by pleasing those who originally provided instructions on how to do so?

"Please others" are "nice" people. They are helpful, pleasant, sensitive to the needs of others, and will always try to do what's "right." Attempting to obey a "Don't Grow Up," "Don't Question Authority," or even a "Don't Think" injunction and being more concerned with how they are doing than what they are doing (Kahler 1977), such "can't say no" people discount their own needs, obsessively seek approval, chronically fear rejection, and just want to be liked. And perhaps one of the most common methods to increase one's likeability is to obey the Please Others driver through ingratiation.

In all probability, ingratiation is the most universally ulterior technique people use to encourage others to like them. In this approach, positive feelings toward oneself are prompted through insincere tactics including exaggerated flattery, disingenuously rendering gifts and services, falsely showing interest in others, endlessly expressing unmeant "I like or I love you" endearments, and head-nodding conformity to the opinions of those one is courting. For due to a sense of fairness encouraged if not demanded by the principle of reciprocity, few can resist such "please others" brownnosing by refusing to return the favor to the source of such positive strokes.

Undeniably so, ingratiation and its Please Others source are commonly observed and almost universally experienced. Indeed, hardly a day goes by in failing to witness their real-world manifestations displayed by a child to a bully, a worker to a boss, or an enabling and insecure parent to a defiant child. Indeed, so ubiquitous are examples of the Please Others driver that in its less exaggerated forms one rarely takes notice. Yet when excessive, its detrimental or even destructive control over our actions is impossible to ignore.

To that end, arguably some of the best supporting evidence for the existence of the Please Others driver taken to extremes has been observed in a series of experiments conducted by Solomon Asch in 1951, Stanley Milgram in 1961, Philip Zimbardo in 1971, and reports of a nationally publicized series of crimes in 2004.

THE ASCH PARADIGM

In questioning to what extent group pressure fosters conformity in the stated perceptions and opinions of its members, the unknowing subjects of this experiment were placed in a group of seven others who were actually collaborating with psychologist Solomon Asch. Shown a picture of a "standard" line and three additional "matching" lines, all participants were then asked to select the matching line that mostly closely approximated the length of the standard line. After several tests were completed without error, those "in on" the experiment unanimously selected the wrong matching line as a duplicate to the standard line during several of the remaining trials.

And though without artifice the exercise was so easy that for a control group the line-matching error was less than 1 percent, when confederates of Asch uniformly spoke with a scripted voice in wrongly matching the lines, over a third of the 123 unwitting subjects agreed with that obviously incorrect verdict about half the time and 75 percent of subjects conformed to clearly inaccurate group perceptions at least once (McLeod 2008).

When interviewed after the experiment, most of those succumbing to their Please Others driver said that "they did not really believe their conforming answers, but had gone along with the group for fear of being ridiculed or thought peculiar" (McLeod 2008). And as demonstrated in other similar experiments, this behavioral provocation is hardly an anomaly. That is, in response to peer pressure, about *one in every three people* will consistently change their behavior or opinions to ingratiatingly agree with an obviously incorrect judgment of a seemingly unanimous majority in order to avoid standing apart from the group.

Why such spontaneous and often-faulty agreement occurs seems clear. With no tangible benefits for accord or obvious penalties for dissent, conformity, more than disagreement, is its own reward. That is, in surrounding oneself with like-minded stroke-generating allies, mindlessly "going along with the crowd" as an elementally motivated survival mechanism (McRaney 2011) may not be so mindless after all. And if this is so for conformity, it can be no less so for its behavioral mainspring represented by the Please Others driver.

Yet however much the Please Others driver shows up in laboratory experiments or the trivial matters of daily life, its real-world impact is often far more consequential. For when this need to conform infects a social group, business, or governmental body, adversity may well be at hand. And this tendency for members of decision-making teams to reflexively agree with one another at the expense of critical reflection is known as groupthink.

Starkly portrayed in the 1954 novel *Lord of the Flies*, when members of a group protect their leader from confidence-sapping dissent and become unwilling to "ruffle anyone's feathers" in compulsively seeking team harmony, catastrophe looms. In fact, seeking "survival" in support, "people can maintain an unshakable faith in any proposition, *however absurd*, when they are sustained by a community of like-minded believers" (Kahneman 2013, 217; emphasis added).

Thus motivated far more by the Please Others driver, generalized insecurities, and primitive survival instincts than by any objective analysis, subordinates demonstrating misguided loyalty publicly align their views with those of leadership or silently acquiesce to their wrongheaded decisions without comment or protest. Big mistake. For when isolated from contradictory information, such self-censorship leads to a group's inflated sense of moral correctness, unjustified confidence, an illusion of invulnerability, and a diminished ability to reverse faulty decisions before they yield calamitous results.

But groupthink is far more than an interesting quirk of human nature. Reticent group members protecting organizational cohesion by refusing to question, sublimating doubts, and withholding alternatives, prompt huge and all-too-real costs. Thus among historical mishaps and misfortunes too numerous to mention, a groupthink-fueled false consensus may well have resulted in the sinking of the Titanic, the Bay of Pigs invasion, the Vietnam War, the Watergate scandal, the Jonestown mass-suicide tragedy, and the space shuttle Challenger disaster. And even more recently, the weapons of mass destruction rationale to invade Iraq in 2003 and the almost comically bad website launch of the Affordable Healthcare Act in 2013 may have also resulted from a look-the-other-way blindness induced by submission to the groupthink dynamic of human behavior.

But that's not all. In addition to groupthink's conformity-imposing influence on relatively innocuous social gatherings, meetings at work, and far more serious conclaves in government, one may additionally speculate how much it currently impacts terrorist groups. Likewise, one also has to wonder what role "do what you're told" compliance played in state-sponsored terrorism's most horrific example in modern history. And in seeking to better understand the Holocaust less than twenty years after World War II, Stanley Milgram of Yale University sought to answer the second of those questions.

THE MILGRAM EXPERIMENTS

Similar to the research of Solomon Asch a decade earlier, the Milgram experiments also dealt with the power of situations to foster conformity. However, while Asch's work focused on group influence as a motivational force, Milgram's research instead centered on submission to the will of authority figures in contributing to the most sinister ends of all.

On the surface, the question Milgram sought to answer seemed straightforward enough. Would seemingly typical Americans obey, as many Germans had done during World War II, the orders of an authority figure even if such compliance meant suffering to those they had no justifiable reason to harm? Or would the subjects of the experiment refuse an authority's demands to inflict pain on others, thus at least suggesting that the compulsive obedience leading to the systematic slaughter of more than six million people was a uniquely Germanic character flaw? And with the horror of the Holocaust still fresh in everyone's mind, some undoubtedly believed this latter explanation to be true. However, those so inclined would soon realize how very wrong they were.

Conducted at Yale University, the design of Milgram's original experiment on obedience was deceptively simple. Two people at a time were told by a lab-coated "technician" that one person would be the "learner" and the other the "teacher" in a behavioral study on memory and learning. In a rigged selection process, "teachers" were chosen from a group of forty adult males recruited after responding to advertisements calling for paid volunteers to participate in a research project directed by the school's psychology department.

After the rationale for the experiment was further explained, each "learner" was strapped into a chair, and an electrode, said to be connected to a shock generator, was attached to his or her wrist. After experiencing a sample shock as proof of the generator's authenticity, the "teacher," now sitting before a control box in an adjacent room, was told to read a list of word pairs to the "learner" via a microphone hookup connecting both subjects. The seemingly genuine control box contained a row of thirty switches, from 15 to 450 volts, with descriptors ranging from "Slight Shock," to "Moderate Shock," to "Danger: Severe Shock," to "XXX," implying the possibility of death.

Once the entire word list was read, learners were asked to select the second word in each pair among three other possible choices. Additionally, teachers were instructed to shock learners in progressively higher voltages for each word pair error and that doing so would cause no "permanent tissue damage." And although increasingly strident screams of pain were heard with each successively higher jolt of electricity, the real shock was that the electricity generating machine was fake, the screams had been prerecorded, the "learner" was an actor-collaborator of Stanley Milgram, and, though criticized by some, the results of the experiment provided suggestive evidence that one might not have to go to Germany to staff a concentration camp. For those comprehensively extrapolating the results of Milgram's research to the "real world," the conclusion was that blindly-willing-to-obey sadistic guards could likely be found in any medium-sized American town.

With no actual authority over the subjects of Milgram's study other than the perceived authority its elaborate staging implied, it was initially predicted that "teachers" *who could quit at any time* would begin to disobey orders to shock learners at about 120 volts, the level at which there was the first verbally dramatized indication of pain. It was further predicted that only 4 percent of the teachers would reach 300 volts and only one in a thousand would administer the highest voltage. Yet in experiments duplicated elsewhere, "with no limiting factor preventing the teacher from delivering the maximum intensity of the shock . . . [other than] compassion for another human being" (Harris 1973, 285), *none* stopped short of a 300 volt shock, and *65% reached the maximum of 450 volts* when told to do so.

Interestingly, Milgram's experiments are not only a textbook example of the destructive power possibility of the Please Others driver operating without even minimally potent Adult oversight but, not surprisingly, also demonstrate the harmful effects of equally unbridled and ultracompliant adapted Child ego states. As expected, the experiment's "teachers" often spoke to "learners" from their controlling Parent states. Yet becoming ever more distressed as the pain they were seemingly inflicting increased, their comments directed to the authority figure "technician" were undeniably expressed from clearly tormented yet passively accepting Child ego states.

In point of fact, when obeying demands to render punishment to others, the adapted Child for more than half of Milgram's subjects was in control, and the Adult was nowhere to be found. As one clearly distressed "teacher" replied when asked why she continued to inflict pain on her learner: "I had to do it. You said so" (Thompson 1976, 132; Milgram 1974). And it is this response and others like it that are both troubling yet hopeful: troubling because free to cathect the Adult at any time, the choice for most of the experiment's participants was a less-than-humane version of the adapted Child, yet hopeful because of TA's optimistic emphasis on strengthening the Adult to ultimately determine the "right" thing to do.

Clearly, Milgram's experiments demonstrated that in failing to monitor Parent messages to blindly obey authority figures and overly adapted Child fears fueling submission to do so, the Adult ego state of almost two-thirds of the "teachers" was literally "asleep at the switch." And though numerous other experiments have also yielded evidence demonstrating the power of the Please Others driver in fostering compliance to the destructive demands of others, none is arguably more famous than a study taking place at a California university in 1971.

THE STANFORD PRISON SIMULATION

Originally designed by Stanford University professor Philip Zimbardo as a two-week simulation experiment on prison life, twenty-four white, middle-class male college undergrads were chosen to participate. These participants had been selected after enduring extensive psychological testing and were judged to be law abiding, emotionally stable, and physically healthy. In a word, those who were selected were rather "ordinary" young men. Yet, what took place in the basement of the Stanford University psychology building was anything but ordinary. For as in the Milgram experiments, participants all too willingly became overwhelmed by a situation in which the norms of acceptable behavior were soon undermined by an artificially constructed reality.

Completely by chance, fifteen of the student volunteers were chosen as "guards" and the remaining nine were assigned as "prisoners." The "guards" worked in standard, eight-hour shifts while the "prisoners" lived in the "jail" round-the-clock. And though the roles of prisoner and guard were selected randomly, shortly after the experiment started these rather typical college students began to "live" their assigned roles. As a result, their behaviors changed in very obvious and disturbing ways.

Since the situation called for a status difference between the jailers and the jailed, "guards" soon became all-powerful, hostile, and often sadistic, and "prisoners" morphed into passive, obedient, and child-like targets of maltreatment. And though the "guards" had been told that they could not physically harm the "jailbirds," with at least the tacit approval of "Prison Superintendent" Zimbardo, their torment was unrelenting.

Armed with wooden batons, full uniforms, and mirrored sunglasses, formerly "nice guy" guards demanded that "prisoners" obey creatively abusive and capriciously imposed rules without question. Failure to fully comply led to a loss of privileges including opportunities to read, write, or to converse with other "detainees." This loss of privileges soon escalated to a loss of "permission" to wash, sleep, and even eat. Passively accepting such arbitrary and artificially enacted indignities, "inmates" were also coerced to clean toilets with their bare hands, compelled to do exercise, required to relinquish their mattresses, subjected to sexual humiliations, and forced to endure "solitary confinement" in an unlit closet. And even though their actions were closely monitored by the prison's putative authority figure Zimbardo, a full third of the "guards" came to exhibit genuine sadistic tendencies.

After thirty-six hours, one "prisoner" began to cry uncontrollably and to exhibit disordered thinking and severe depression. Within days, several other "inmates" developed similar stress-related symptoms. And when five traumatized prisoners were released shortly thereafter, it became obvious that the study had gotten out of hand. Accordingly, the simulation was terminated after "only" six days. Even so, it was clear what driver had impacted its outcome in which students pleased each other by dutifully role-playing a simulation, abusive "guards" pleased their "Superintendent" by "maintaining security," and "prisoners" pleased their captors by passively accepting such treatment.

Clearly, the disturbing outcome of the Stanford Prison Experiment supports the truism that under certain circumstances even seemingly "good" people can change into conforming role players capable of immorality, violence, and insensitivity to the suffering of others. And one need look no further than the Abu Ghraib prison scandal of 2004 to know that such disturbing behaviors are still too little an exception and too often front-page news.

Just as God's favorite angel, Lucifer, is said to have "fallen from grace" and was transformed into Satan, people can also cross the line between good and evil. This tendency for certain situations to provoke conversion in seemingly virtuous people from compassion and morality to the "might makes right" darkness of violence and injustice is thus not coincidentally known as the "Lucifer Effect" (Zimbardo 2007).

However, due to a nearly universal sense of "I'm not as good as others" insecurity and the equally universal dictates of the Please Others driver, only relatively few people can completely overcome the inclination to thoughtlessly obey orders or to "follow the herd." Only a rare person will risk losing position, prestige, or strokes by "swimming upstream." Only a supremely secure person can withstand the corrupting power of some situations without moral impairment. And only a confident, courageous, and "OK person" can routinely resist submitting to blind and often-destructive acquiescence.

Yet because such noble people are still too uncommon, one needn't rely on academic experiments, long-ago events, or faraway "aberrations" to witness real-world and recent confirmation that mindless and seemingly incomprehensible "please others" compliance remains alive and well. As such, reflexive surrender to the destructive directives of misguided leaders and unbalanced authority figures remains a familiar outcome in gangs, cults, terrorist groups, and in the following example at, of all places, a fast food restaurant.

THE "MCDONALD'S HUMILIATION"

In April 2004 a man falsely identifying himself as a police office called a McDonald's eatery in Mount Washington, Kentucky, claiming that a suspect in a recent theft was an eighteen-year-old female employee. Speaking to the assistant manager who was also female, the "officer" instructed her to escort the teenager into the restaurant's office, lock the door, and look for contraband by ordering the young woman to strip. And when after an hour of acting on those orders the assistant manager needed to return to her behind-the-counter duties, she was told that her fiancée could take over.

Apparently no more willing to stop the madness than his future wife, the fiancée complied with over-the-phone instructions to require the still-nude adolescent to dance, exercise, and submit to a spanking (McRaney 2011). Over three hours later and only after forcing the embarrassed and shivering young employee to perform a sex act did the dehumanizing insanity mercifully end.

Thus for anyone believing that the "please others" imperative to blindly obey authority figures is an experimental anomaly or a historical oddity from the "distant past," just ask the young victim of the Kentucky prank call scam if that is indeed so. For as a result of her ordeal, the innocent target of the "McDonald's Humiliation" required antidepressants, underwent therapy for posttraumatic stress disorder, and abandoned plans to attend college.

Sadly however, there is more to the story. During the police investigation of the hoax, it was discovered that in the prior decade *at least seventy* similar prank calls had been made by a man claiming to be a detective or police officer to fast food restaurants and grocery stores in some thirty states. But that's still not all. In several of those instances, employees also complied with unconfirmed phone instructions, initiated strip searches, asked few questions, and offered no more resistance than the overly compliant and emotionally traumatized targets of such abominations.

With that in mind, the aforementioned examples involving blind-faith acceptance of groupthink errors on the one hand and authority figure directives on the other were not mentioned to highlight the power of the Please Others driver by minimizing the power of situations to influence behavior. Indeed, the field of social psychology is devoted to the study of environmental circumstances acting as profoundly impactful motivators of human conduct. But while there is little doubt that environmental pressure influences behavior in disturbing and often destructive ways, one can't help but wonder if this would be as frequently so if not for the Please Others driver and its I'm Not OK wellspring.

Obviously, the potent influence of situations is very real in dictating both positive and negative actions. However, just as obviously, we are not powerless to behave morally in the face of environmental pressure. Yet in rationalizing one's questionable behavior as due to irresistible "circumstances beyond our control" and equally questionable conduct of others as the fruit of character flaws, we predictably justify reprehensible conduct with Wooden Leg explanations providing relief for situation-specific guilt and omnipresent doubt. Thus for insecure people, this "fundamental attribution error" provides false but esteem-enhancing clarity for human conduct. That is, when others act badly, it is due to moral and behavioral weakness. But when I behave badly, "There was nothing else I could have done."

But make no mistake. Whatever the situation, whatever the power of misguided groups or misleading authority figures, whatever alibi we manufacture to excuse our actions, and whatever the Please Others driver compels us to do, what we surrender to is inarguably still our choice and ours alone.

THIRTEEN

Interpreting Scripts

If you don't design your own life plan, chances are you'll fall into someone else's plan. And guess what they have planned for you? Not much.

—Jim Rohn

Just as some computer programs run silently in the background, ready to be launched when they are called for, psychological scripts operate similarly by positively or negatively directing human behavior. Yet however restricting or elevating a script may be in furnishing a "default setting" for fulfilling one's destiny, it provides a sense of security "and control . . . [in moving] forward into the future even if the end of the road is not in sight" (English 1977, 289). Undeniably so, a life with a predictive sense of direction is preferable to an existence fraught with uncertainty. And it is equally undeniable that without even knowing the term "lifescript" as yet uncoined, Alfred Adler, in discussing a child's creation of a fantasized link to later life, seemed to be saying much the same thing.

> It is the actual inferiority of the child, his insecurity, his helplessness and weakness that necessitates the exploring of possibilities and gathering of experiences in order to create a bridge into a future where he will not be helpless, insecure, and weak, but, instead, big and powerful, and where he will find satisfactions of all kinds. The consequence of this bridge is the most important achievement of the child's mind. (Adler 1959, 47; Wilson 1975, 119)

Thus as a frame of reference "bridge" in satisfying security needs for a stable and predictable world, a script is an unconscious program or story of how one's life will unfold in which the main character is compelled to create daily "episodes" that fit the overall prologue, climax, and if tragic the catastrophic theme of the narrative. Moreover, these serialized "installments" often include a cast of characters chosen and manipulated by the "star of the show" to further the overall story.

To illustrate, a man with a script based on a "women are gold diggers" theme may choose partners reinforcing that perception, a woman whose script is based on an "I'm a princess" motif will frequently prefer men validating her "others should do for me" role, and a person of either sex enacting an "I am oppressed" story will likely select a "supporting cast" confirming that belief. And as in psychological games and televised dramas, a favored role of victim, persecutor, or rescuer often continues in an endless season of reruns until the final curtain is drawn.

The larger point is that a script may not dictate the life a person consciously desires but instead what a person unconsciously drives it to become. Hence whatever the plot of the story decided upon early in life, it will often evolve as "the psychological force which propels the person toward his destiny, regardless of whether he fights it or says it is his own free will" (Berne 1973, 32). And for better or worse, that parentally inspired destiny launching us into "patterns of behavior in which we always seem to elicit a certain response from others, or end up in similar situations" (Trubshaw 2011), is known as the script payoff.

Colloquially known as the "curse" when parental script messages negatively foretell how a child's life will unfold, such directives have an enormous impact as self-fulfilling prophecies. This is so because as with the Pygmalion or placebo effects, there is little doubt that a person's expectations and their more direct manipulation of another's conduct have enormous influence in generating anticipated behaviors. And if this is undeniably so in limited-access relationships such as among teachers and students, doctors and patients, or researchers and subjects, the power of parental actions and expectations to affect the quality of a child's life is far greater. After all, if a mother or father can make a child miserable with a frown or their injury "better" by "kissing the boo-boo," there is little behaviorally that their explicit or implicit messages can't impact.

Consequently, a child told "You will never amount to anything," or "You'll end up like your deadbeat older brother," or with greater finality "Just drop dead" will have their future almost certainly compromised before it even begins. To that end, when the negative expectation "curse" is decreed in dozens, hundreds, or perhaps thousands of transactions, there is ever less hope for the child other than to end up an addict, an indigent, a mental patient, or to die early and alone.

But however common such an unappealing menu of calamitous destinies may be, and however potent early messages are in determining a life story's final outcome, the script-handicapped child is *still* not doomed to a dysfunctional existence. For even accepting Maslow's formulation inferring safety and security as an elemental need for a predictable world, "it is *precisely because life scripts are so predictable* that they can be brought into awareness and redecided, which makes change possible" (Clarkson 1988, 211; emphasis added). Moreover, as few people exclusively interpret everything in terms of events occurring during early childhood, thoughtful and well-motivated adults can continually reinvent themselves as a result of more recent experiences.

But that's not all. Even high-risk youngsters have exhibited enormous resiliency based on genetic endowment, chance encounters with powerful mentors, their own strength of will, and, perhaps even more importantly, the inherent adaptability of the human brain. As such, whether the child's impediments come from "social ideology, poverty, a pathological family environment, or stressful life experiences, the plastic potential of the brain offers the promise for positive and corrective change" (Thomas and Chess 1980, 28; Cornell 1988, 271). Thus already containing more neural connections than stars in the Milky Way, the brain's ability to create and link additional neurons in response to new ways of thinking (Marx 2013) offers possibilities for a better life whatever the toxicity or strength of one's script.

Existing on a continuum, a script can therefore promote a health-inspiring story that updated as required will positively direct and inform a person's life, a self-constructed prison that can be limiting and self-defeating, or more commonly any place in between (Newton 2006; Cornell 1988). That said, although a script frequently has negatively restrictive effects, as an organizing framework for how life will develop it can be, albeit far less often, closer to a continually evolving and minimally defined performance than an uneditable screenplay.

But whether a script ultimately becomes a guide or a prison, parents provide their children with its first draft as directives on how best to survive in the world. Positive or negative, such edicts may include such "truths" as "Work hard," Get good grades," "Always trust your instincts," "Rich people will screw you," "Poor people cannot be trusted," or "Stay among your own kind." Additionally, an individual's primary script may be parentally supplemented by memes that if incorporated into a child's life story become an "episcript" collection of various negative beliefs, feelings, expectations, goals, and conduct.

Often unconsciously assumed early in life, such an episcript "package" of someone else's pathologies attaches itself as an ultimately harmful but unwittingly accepted addition to a child's already well-established script. And because the episcript's vulnerable recipient often experiences it as an unalterable obligation to be faithfully implemented, maladaptive behaviors as metastasizing cancers become increasingly pervasive, resistant to removal, and damaging in virtually all instances (English 1996).

Because one's script is such an all-encompassing organizing force, it is therefore not surprising that the factors and events leading to its creation are no less all-encompassing. To that end, "somewhere between the ages of four and seven" (English 1977, 288), an individual's projected story of life is aligned with and largely determined by unconscious, pervasive, and omnipresent perceptions of oneself and others.

Thus in accord with a child's life position, scripts initially emerge as the Little Professor's interpretation of and reaction to internal and external events (Woollams and Brown 1978) in which the child navigates between his own needs and caregiver limits frustrating their satisfaction. And since a primary need in children, and for that matter adults, is to gain greater insight into existence, scripts as frame of reference expectations about life are originally written as a little person's "explanatory narrative that gives meaning to the past, provides a problem-solving blueprint for the present, and predicts the future" (Newton 2006, 186).

Young or old, people are strongly motivated to understand the meaning of life, how the world works, and their place within that reality. To that end, one's script is a self-created story helping to make sense of it all because "it involves the maps and models of the world that a person creates and the patterns he or she then projects onto the environment" (Allen and Allen 1988, 285). Thus in a sense, children are not scripted. In unconsciously formulating patterned responses to caregiver guidance on gaining desirable outcomes from them and from the larger world, they unknowingly script themselves (Goulding and Goulding 1978).

> We receive and process information constantly about who we are; how others see us; who or what we are like; what the big people predict for us; what happens to people like us [and] what the norms, expectations and precedents are in our family. This information comes through what we hear from our care-givers and others, what we observe happening in our world, and through stories, television, films and videos, which offer us a range of characters to choose from in our attempt to answer the question "What happens to someone like me?" (Barrow, Bradshaw, and Newton 2001, 55)

Thus formulating the infinitely important decision of one's identity is likely initiated as an unconscious survival strategy response adapting to pressures and expectations from the home environment well before the youngster is competently able to do so. These pressures and expectations leading to immaturely decided character traits "are crystallized . . . into script roles" (Jongeward and James 1971, 7), which as double-edged swords are a blessing in providing the reassurance of a predictable world and frequently a curse in dictating enslavement within a self-limiting identity.

So for many if not most people, "the way we experience our existence for the rest of our lives is largely determined by the foundations we create while we are still helpless" (Levin 1985, 60; Cornell 1988, 277). The result, as Oprah Winfrey once observed, is that "often we don't realize who we're meant to be because we're so busy trying to live out someone else's ideas."

The calculus of such self-perpetuating bondage is simple. Since security is a basic human need and familiarity provides security, behaviors from the past are repeatedly orchestrated in the present to recreate familiar feelings confirming one's life position and overall script decision. So whatever the long-term consequences, once our story is decided upon, predictability-assuring repetition compulsion drives actions to reinforce and confirm our initially formulated construction of reality.

Yet whether the story is good or bad, there is an emotionally comforting value in such script-inspired consistency "freeing us to work within limitations much like the small curbs along the highway bring comfort to the wearied driver" (Allen and Allen 1988, 286). Without a script providing constancy, control, and security-blanket comfort to the seeming chaos of the world, understanding reality would require more information to be continually processed than it already does. And because of this, making choices about daily conduct would be even more stressful and overwhelming than it already is.

But however positive a script's value in diminishing such change-related stress may be, it is more than equaled by its potential cost. For just as games are artificial structures limiting relational intimacy, nonwinning scripts are similarly constructed systems inhibiting self-actualization and impelling chronic patterns of dysfunctional and often destructive behaviors.

Thus in an endless cycle of repeating performances, without knowledge of a script's existence or without belief that it can be rewritten, one's story, if toxic, becomes an unseen director crippling potential by demanding the same failing show to continue. This is so because long before the Adult is fully functioning, the Child takes all the information he or she has received and "decides, once and for all, that *that is the way life is*. The Child then goes about setting things up so that life always comes out the way its decision has preordained" (Meininger 1973, 70). And later into adulthood, we rarely question whether the "normal" of our predictably scripted world is the only way to define existence. But clearly, it is not.

Later, upon entering the wider world at about age five, the initial draft of the child's story is edited as a strategy governing responses to social challenges met early in life including friendships, schooling, and relationships with the opposite sex. These "tests" of the youngster's preparation for social living "may reinforce the life script or cause it to be adjusted in positive or negative directions" (Mitchell 2011). And this fine-tuning of the script will likely be further influenced both in and outside the home by key experiences promoting or discouraging the full emergence of the child's innate abilities.

> Children are, therefore, born automatically into a great predicament because there is always a discrepancy between the possibilities of what they could become and what they are permitted to achieve. This discrepancy can be enormous—some children are born and their potential

> is immediately snuffed. Other children may be allowed quite a wide range of development. (Steiner 1974, 65)

Thus because genetic endowment sets one's potential while upbringing largely determines the extent to which that potential is realized, our possibilities are often compromised by parents who decide our future long before we can question, counter, or even understand what they're doing. At the very least, such parentally imposed fates when negatively restrictive may diminish or even completely sabotage fulfillment of a child's genetic destiny. And at most, such dictates undermine even the possibility of self-actualization.

But the mix of heredity and environment provided by parents is not alone when imparting the foundation for one's script. Other significant people, most notably grandparents, can also play an important role in how a child's life will unfold. And this is so whether the child has a significant relationship with "grandma" and "grandpa" or even whether they are alive or not.

Obviously, if living and playing a highly visible and hands-on role in the life of a child, the scripting impact of grandparents will be significant. However, if through death or distance grandparents do not directly interact with their grandchildren, their injunctions, permissions, attributions, and modeling of how to conduct life will *still* be transmitted by the child's parents as intermediaries in a transgenerational process of script passing that has been referred to as the "family parade" (James 1984).

This "parade" need not be unpleasant, and it may well be positive or even comically trivial as the following story illustrates:

> A bride served baked ham, and her husband asked why she cut the ends off. "Well, that's the way mother did it," she replied. The next time his mother-in-law stopped by, he asked her why she cut the ends off the ham. "That's the way my mother did it," she replied. And when Grandma visited, she, too, was asked why she sliced the ends off. She said, "That's the only way I could get it into the pan." (James and Jongeward 1971, 103)

But far more seriously, whether messages are passed directly or in absentia from grandparents to their grandchildren, if they are growth-inhibiting and dysfunctional they can negatively impact generations yet to come. Yet if messages are growth-promoting and healthy, their influence reverberating through the years will likely serve to positively ghost-write scripts for winners yet unborn.

Moreover, because heredity largely determines what you *can* be, and environment frequently determines what you *will* be, if caregiver messages, transgenerational or otherwise, are humane, rationally directed, and unconditionally loving, genetic capabilities play a larger role in the character of one's script. And as previously mentioned, such thoughtful and supportive child-rearing recognizes the power "crystallizing" and "paralyzing" milestones have in amplifying or diminishing a youngster's innate potential.

Significant and positive confidence-building childhood events encouraging one's specific abilities to more fully express themselves are crystallizing experiences. Thus in praising and supporting a child's talents, parents are also enabling already-existing aptitudes to reach levels unlikely to occur without such recognition. As a result, the child's self-esteem grows as does the realization that the environment can be positively manipulated to ensure the flowering of specific gifts within an overall fulfilling life story. And with a self-reinforcing feedback loop of recognition fueling confidence, confidence promoting achievement, and achievement fueling further recognition and confidence, it should not be surprising that anyone gaining widespread acclaim in a particular endeavor as an adult often "decided" that script very early in life.

In contrast, significant and negative confidence-shattering childhood events discouraging one's specific abilities to even partially express themselves are referred to as paralyzing experiences. When parents ignore or criticize such special talents, their discounts reinforce a commonly internalized I'm Not OK life position, which leads to shame, doubt, fear, and a crippling of potential. And with such emotional burdens to overcome, there is far less likelihood that incipient abilities can emerge as evidence of a positive life story. There is thus little value for a child hitting the jackpot of the genetic lottery if parents either refuse to validate or even destroy their winning ticket.

Yet whichever set of experiences, crystallizing or paralyzing, one encounters in childhood, there is no doubt that they can profoundly alter the path of one's existence. And the reason this is so is a deceptively simple explanation known as the "law of effect."

Formulated by American psychologist E. L. Thorndike, the law of effect states an uncomplicated and obvious truth. Namely, actions that are encouraged are likely to continue while those that are ignored or punished are unlikely to be repeated except randomly. Thus because a child's life story initially results from parental pressure in which certain behaviors are explicitly or implicitly promoted and others are not, if parents as a child's behavioral models are unfulfilled, insecure, externally oriented, and pessimistic, "they will pass on their loser's programming, and if they are winners, then they will pass on that kind of program" (Berne 1973, 39). And knowledge of how people learn virtually ensures that result.

At its simplest level, learning involves a causal interaction between the learner and the environment. That is, an experienced event is followed by a period of reflection. Almost as a scientist, it is during this period that a person thinks consciously or otherwise about the event, relates it to the outcomes of similar experiences, and, in an effort to gain desired if not always desirable results, draws predictive conclusions that either confirm past responses or call for a change in behavior.

Thus because such "experiential learning [is] the basic human process/adaptation which appears in many forms from babyhood to old age" (Newton 2006, 191), there is little doubt that in order to please parents, young children will initially internalize whatever self-defining script messages their "all-knowing and all-powerful" caregivers offer as the conforming and conditionally stroked path to "the most favorable result." But as so painfully obvious, it very often isn't.

However, because knowledge of one's script can provide insight into counterproductive daily conduct and a "going nowhere" destiny, such awareness as a motivating force is the first step toward positive change. And script recognition shouldn't be all that difficult to accomplish. Obviously, an objective evaluation of "How have I been acting?" or "How have I been doing?" is as good a place as any to begin.

Is my life going well? Am I happy with my health, my job, and with my relationships? If not, what steps have I taken or will I take to improve my situation? Is my life unexciting or without direction? Do I feel like I'm aimlessly drifting and powerless to change the status quo? Have I made bad choices and continue to do so leading to detrimental or destructive outcomes?

Yet if the script is still unclear, distilling experience into a concise description of "failing at everything," "drugging myself to death," "waiting for Prince Charming," "looking for respect," "taking care of others," "expecting Santa Claus," "born to lose," or, far more positively, "achieving my dreams" should further clarify how one's story is unfolding. But often the most accurate method revealing the shorthand blueprint of one's existence is to ask a single question regarding the end of life. And that question is, "What will your last words be?"

While honestly examining the quality of life, the choices made leading to that assessment, and summarizing the ultimate conclusion of one's story with a deathbed question are all useful bottom-line approaches to identifying one's script, answering additional queries related to childhood can also provide clarity. Resembling a self-administered form of psychoanalysis as a means to possibly uncover highly significant early-life events, such questions found in *Transactional Analysis in Brief* and other TA sources include:

- What is your earliest memory?
- What is the family story about your birth?
- How were you named? What is your nickname?
- What was your favorite childhood fairy tale or story, what was its theme, and are you imitating any of its characters as a model for your life? (Because a person's favorite myth or fairy tale is likely

related to their life script, this question may be particularly illuminating).

- What were the nicest and worst things that your parents often said to you? Also, how did your parents describe you and who did your parents say you took after?
- What do you know or have heard about your grandparents?
- If you continue along your current path, what will your life be like in five and ten years?
- If you could change anything about yourself, what would it be?
- How long do you expect to live?
- What do you want most out of life?
- What will your tombstone say?

Although there are numerous types of scripts, often preordaining much of life from early childhood, at the simplest level there are four basic blueprints unconsciously guiding where one is going in life and the path likely taken to get there. Embodying "varying degrees of constructiveness, destructiveness, and nonproductiveness" (Jongeward and James 1973, 3), they are the winner, loser, banal, and hamartic scripts.

WINNER SCRIPTS

For a person fortunate enough to be the main character in a winner's script, the story is extremely optimistic, exciting, and at times even inspirational. Such an internally oriented individual approaches their fullest potential by honestly and effectively manipulating reality to generate positive strokes through legitimate achievement on their life's journey toward a self-actualized conclusion. But because implicit in a winner's script is an I'm OK, You're OK center of perceptual gravity, there are equal or greater advantages still.

As mentioned in chapter 11 and elsewhere, the benefits of such an underlying winner's script foundation of continual optimism may well be a healthier and longer life. This is so because such a hopeful outlook implies that "events arousing negative affect are approached with confidence that the future holds something positive and better, thus internally generating a positive emotional state that mutes the adverse [physical] effects of the prolonged arousal of negative emotion" (Danner, Snowden, and Friesen 2001, 805).

More precisely, while those with loser scripts typically describe misfortune as permanent rather than temporary, pervasive rather than specific, and attributable to personal and immutable character flaws rather than to correctable mistakes, innocent oversights, or unavoidable happenstance, winners view failure in exactly opposite terms (Seligman 1991). And although the bad news is that only one group of explanations for failure leads to resilience, optimism, and hope, and the other to a figurative and literal dead end, the good news is that those following a nonwinning script can indeed learn to see themselves and the world more positively.

Summing up, a winner internalizes a sense of freedom and growth, follows a self-actualized agenda, and envisions a moral, productive, and joyous destiny. For this reason, the creator of such a "be all you can be" script authors positive goals as the hero of their own story.

LOSER SCRIPTS

In the unhappy narrative of a loser's script, the main character continually sets himself up for failure and depression through "rackety" behaviors. The lead in this drama plays the "unlucky" victim buffeted by the cruel winds of fate where control is elusive, success is rare, personal responsibility is a foreign concept, positive goals are nonexistent or unrealized, and despair is the emotion du jour. That this is so should not be surprising. For excepting the winner's script, the primary "drama triangle" roles of rescuer, persecutor, and victim found in psychological games are also enacted in stories of life. And equally not surprising, the most commonly accepted role for the "star" in a loser's script is victim.

Although there are numerous versions of loser scripts, among the most common subtypes or themes include those dictating a life of loneliness, confusion, dependency, or little pleasure. Referred to as the "loveless," "mindless," "powerless," and "joyless" scripts (Steiner 1974), an individual is either unable to develop intimate relationships, feels incapable when coping with life's inevitable problems, is passive when facing obstacles, or rejects natural Child exhilaration without which life is less worth living. And as for other unfulfilling scripts, each of these depressing screenplays is largely dictated by parental messages and reinforced throughout life by a contaminated, impotent, or simply unaware Adult ego state.

To that end, the sabotaged relationships of a loveless script theme might well be fostered by "Don't Be Close" or "Don't Trust" parental directives in collusion with an Adult contaminated by a "No one is any good" Parent and an "Either are you" Child ego state. And "Don't Think" or "Don't Succeed" edicts promoting a mindless script's lack of awareness and control are likely supported by an all-too-willing Adult infected by insecure Child feelings of inadequacy and depression.

Furthermore, a "Don't Act" message internalized when a youngster is repeatedly "rescued" by parents doing for the child what the child could easily do for himself can't help but further a powerless script. And a "Don't Lose Control" injunction fostering a lack of spontaneity, fun, and excitement in a joyless script remains unchallenged by a disabled and ineffective Adult corrupted by an overly powerful Parent demanding the straight-and-narrow of a paint-by-number existence.

Clearly, just as there is a correlation between specific parental injunctions and their negatively prompted loser scripts, there is an equally likely alignment between loser scripts and certain life positions. That is, it would be difficult to envision an existential frame of reference other than an arrogantly superior form of I'm OK, You're Not OK for an unhappy and self-isolating loveless script. Equally so, there is little question that the self-doubt and chronic neediness of a mindless or powerless script corresponds to an I'm Not OK, You're OK frame of reference. And finally, one would be hard-pressed to believe that the stroke-deprived futility of a joyless script could emerge from any other than an I'm Not OK, You're Not OK outlook on the world.

BANAL SCRIPTS

As the story followed by most people, the banal script is not particularly exciting or interesting. It is a languishing-in-life tale lacking freshness where the protagonist plays it safe, just exists day-to-day, accepts someone else's goals, and strives for nothing more than a rationalized "it could be worse" settling-for-mediocrity nonwinning existence. For those following this well-regulated, "one foot in front of the other," "dime-a-dozen" storyline, the mantra is both simple and redundant. Life is unfulfilling and seemingly meaningless *but* "At least I didn't totally fail" or "At least I'm not completely destitute," or "At least most people don't appear to hate me." And seemingly referring to such "at leasters," Truman Capote once remarked that "Life is a moderately good play with a badly written third act."

Not realizing what is possible or what could be accomplished, profound happiness, satisfaction, and certainly self-actualization are rarely if ever achievable for those refusing to leave the status quo safety of unexceptional existences. It's not that people internalizing banal scripts are seen as unsuccessful. On the contrary, by all appearances they may be viewed as "having it all together." However, fearing failure they settle for what is rather than what could be. They run as fast as they can to stay in the same place. And even when things are going relatively well, they obsessively worry "waiting for the other shoe to drop." As a result, those internalizing banal scripts "have no more than a glimpse . . . that their potentialities as human beings have . . . been betrayed and defeated" (Steiner 1974, 118).

HAMARTIC SCRIPTS

From Aristotle's tragic hero who commits a ruinous error, this most severe form of loser's script is authored by those walking blindly and relentlessly toward their own destruction. Exposed to toxic attributions and injunctions early in life, the script's protagonist inevitably comes to the attention of police, lawyers, doctors, or morgue attendants. This is so because the plot of a hamartic script calls for the main character to become an unstoppable force of nature in breaking the law, abusing drugs, ignoring health problems, and doing whatever else it takes to irresistibly speed toward oblivion on the highway to hell.

But whatever script one unconsciously follows, since the mother is typically a child's primary caregiver, she becomes the main source for the "material" from which the seminal or "primal protocol" script is written. As a result, the evidence a youngster unconsciously employs to author their story is most often a powerful combination of maternal stroking patterns, commands, behavioral modeling, injunctions, permissions, and attributions describing who the child is and what he or she will likely become.

Even if commonly delivered as less-than-obvious communications, these life story messages are extremely powerful in that "human beings are deeply affected by and submissive to the will of the specific divinities of their household—their parents—whose injunctions they are impotent against as they blindly follow them through life, sometimes to their self-destruction" (Steiner 1974, 64). Thus for many people, a script outline implanted in early childhood remains largely unchallenged long after its parental author is writing no more. And in echoing throughout life, this blueprint for destiny "acts like a computer tape or a player-piano roll, which brings out the responses in the planned order long after the person who punched the notes has departed the scene" (Berne 1973, 65–66).

However, all such script messages are not equal. Certainly, disapproving communications often carry more weight than their positive counterparts. But whether positive or negative, their potency is dependent on the age the child internalizes them, their frequency, and whether each parent reinforces the other in their delivery. Additionally, if script-promoting messages occur during a time of great turmoil in the home from a divorce, an illness, or a death, their power may well be greater still (Woollams and Brown 1978).

Yet whatever the power of parental communications in directing and defining one's life, without Adult awareness of a script's existence and the possibility of exchanging one story for another, its narrative will inescapably be reinforced by behaviors carrying the plot to its ultimate conclusion. And as an actor chooses a "method" for the dialogue's delivery or a conductor decides on the arrangement of a musical score, people unconsciously select a primary time-structuring style supporting their nonwinning life story from a menu including never, always, until, after, almost, and open-ended script patterns (Woollams and Brown 1978).

These duration-specific programs often aligned with complementary drivers have predictive value in coloring how a script will unfold and, as they are time or event centered, whether a script will continue or be terminated. As such, Adult awareness of script-enacting styles and their motivating drivers is an important precondition for replacing a nonwinning story with one directing far more positive outcomes.

NEVER PROGRAM

A Never script pattern is followed by a person "never" finishing tasks, goals, dreams, or at times even sentences. Beginning many projects but finishing few, such a "try hard" or "hurry up" person experiences life seemingly "doomed" to failure in which "one's ship never comes in," there is "never enough time" for personal desires, and success is always just beyond reach.

However, as might be expected, anyone following a Never program is no innocent bystander in their script drama. Such individuals are "never" fulfilled in relationships, "never" successful in their careers, and "never" satisfied with their lives for a reason. And that reason is that whenever happiness is within reach, they sabotage themselves rather than edit their script to ensure a better ending.

ALWAYS PROGRAM

Whereas a Never script program manifests itself by an inability to complete or even start projects, an Always program contrastingly results in an inability to stop playing losing hands in one's job, one's relationships, or in virtually any other aspect of life. "Sticking to one's guns" in "biting the bullet," bash trappers exhibiting this extremely common pattern become increasingly fearful to change a failing course of action in order to begin another that might end just as badly. In a damned if you do and damned if you don't, "You made your bed now lie in it" world, the "grin and bear it" author of an Always program is overly cautious and likely directed by a Be Strong or Be Careful driver.

UNTIL PROGRAM

Goal-driven individuals following the Until program have difficulty rewarding themselves or enjoying life until a task or project is "flawlessly" completed. Unable to "play" *until* "some day" when work is done, a goal is accomplished, or an achievement is reached, happiness is continually deferred fulfilling the needs of children, home, job, ailing parents, or one's self-imposed and unsatisfiable expectations.

For such individuals, life is an endless series of prices paid and obstacles overcome without satisfying one's Child until it is too late for any reward other than a bed in a nursing home and an unhappy sense of martyrdom. And even in the short-term, Be Perfect and Be Strong motivated Until programmers can't sit still to enjoy a movie, a meal, or even sex until one last thing is put away, attended to, or is done. The reason for such rigidity is clear. And that is, suffering "must" always precede joy.

AFTER PROGRAM

Ever vigilant "waiting for the boom to be lowered," the After program for script enactment fosters the fear that as good as things are, joy will be short-lived and heartaches are sure to follow. On a daily basis, this theme for living "is illustrated by a consistent pattern of fun, then atonement, joy, then misery; or pleasure followed by pain" (Woolams and Brown 1978, 229). In a "chickens will always come home to roost" existence, "Christmas was fun but now the bills come due" and "Time off was a blast but tomorrow it's back to my lousy job."

For those internalizing an After program, enjoyment is fleeting and future happiness is always just around the corner *but only* after stoically accepted payments in "be strong" suffering are made. It's not that a conscious or semiconscious choice is made to defer rewards until the "piper is paid" as in the Until program. Rather in the After timetable, life will *inevitably* offer a "whatever can go wrong will go wrong" sucker punch as some cosmic homeostasis meant to balance the scales of pleasure and pain *whatever* one does.

This rarely living-in-the-moment After mindset is sometimes exhibited by beginning sentences positively and ending them with a "but" followed by a negative note. Hence for such "Debbie and Donald Downer" individuals, even the most enjoyable experiences are tempered by a sense of dread often experienced as vacation is ending and school, work, and "jumping through hoops" responsibility is just around the corner.

ALMOST PROGRAM

As in the myth of Sisyphus, an Almost program promotes a "try hard" existence in which an individual almost but never quite reaches his or her goals. Also known as an "Over and Over" program, it doesn't matter whether one's dreams include fulfillment in the arts, employment, or love. As success draws near, "shooting oneself in the foot" results in an endless series of self-sabotaged failures and "almost did but didn't" disappointments.

Certainly less dismal than a script limited by a Never timetable, an Almost program does "allow for" at least a measure of success. That is, when a job promotion was "on the table," getting too friendly with Jack Daniels resulted in being "passed over" for the position. When desired admission into an Ivy League university was within reach, cheating on a final exam resulted in a talented student's "thanks but no thanks" letter of rejection. When the achievable goal was Fortune 500 employment, failing to show up for a job interview forced an insecure executive to remain at her dead end job. And when interest and ability suggested playing professional baseball was possible, achievement for an unmotivated athlete with star potential stopped *almost* at that objective as well.

OPEN-ENDED PROGRAM

Enacting one of the other script styles early in life until the pattern ends with a major event such as the beginning of an empty nest or the end of a career, an Open-Ended program originates in a lack-of-direction vacuum of "Now what?" confusion, "Remember when?" memories, and rudderless despair. For many in the supposed golden years of life, one door closing does not presuppose another opening. And sadly, with no further script programming directives as a guide, people internalizing an Open-Ended theme in passively hoping for Shangri-la are instead more likely to find a rapidly approaching end of days.

While the Open-Ended pattern is an equal opportunity source of despair and favors no driver over others, women accepting traditional sex-role definitions often experience that theme earlier in life than spouses not enduring such despondency until retirement. Culturally programmed as primary caregivers for their children, such women in failing to develop their own talents, interests, and career paths often feel depressed and without purpose when their children leave home to begin lives of their own.

This is so because we often define ourselves by what we do rather than by who we are. And when what we do dramatically changes, until a new identity is created we often feel disoriented and lost. Thus in living a Sleeping Beauty style script, women who have "slept" through years of family sacrifice without actualizing their full potential (Jongeward 1972) would surely benefit by setting new goals and redefining themselves.

However, as for many things in later life, the Open-Ended program typically seen as a negative and inevitable precursor to "pushing up daisies" needn't be viewed that way. In fact, for people script-bound as the dutiful parent or breadwinner from early adulthood through late middle age, the lack of structure for an Open-Ended script pattern in their "golden years" can finally provide the freedom to answer the "What Now?" question.

But whether one's remaining time is filled with regret and depression or is seen as an opportunity for personal growth and reinvention, the open-ended response to the Open-Ended program must come from within. As such, the cure for age-related despondency must be a self-initiated permission to "please oneself" (Erskine and Selzer 1977) by reaching for the brass ring of self-actualization, whatever its positively written definition, rather than squandering a second chance at fulfillment when answering the "What Now?" question with no answer at all.

Yet however negative a script may be, under what conditions it was reinforced, or how it is carried out, because freedom not powerlessness is one's birthright it needn't be a preordained and self-imposed prison without options and from which there is no escape. For while the earlier a script is authored and the longer it remains unquestioned the more difficult it is to undo, its story once seemingly etched in granite can still be revised as if written in sand.

Thus despite the deterministic power of scripts, freedom is not unreachable. However, in order to rewrite one's story by silencing or at least reducing the self-talk of parental directives, an empowered and perceptive Adult must fashion an antiscript generated by an epiphanous event, idea, or philosophy commonly known as a spellbreaker or internal release. For in the final analysis, while the bell of past events can never be unrung, one's Adult no longer need listen.

Admittedly, reinventing oneself by writing another script is no easy task. Yet however difficult it may be, the catalyst for exchanging negative script-bound inertia for a more positive future can occur at any time and may take a variety of forms. It could surface as an obvious-to-others momentous occurrence such as a near-death experience illuminating what really is important, a friend's casually spoken advice to be happy "without being perfect," exposure to a "heart-of-the-matter" philosophy that change is possible, or even the overheard comments of a stranger about fears conquered or challenges overcome. But however the script's spell is broken, only by doing so can the antiscript declaration of one's independence be successfully written.

Originating from within, antiscripts are supported by consciously decided directives that constructively contradict growth-inhibiting mottos, slogans, injunctions, or attributions recorded in one's Parent ego state. For example, a "Just accept things" theme embedded in a banal script can be replaced by a message intrinsic to winner's script such as "Positive goals will confidently be pursued with effort, determination, and resilience." Or with Adult awareness, a "you'll never amount to anything" Parent recording consistent with going-nowhere scripts can confidently be replaced by a proclamation that "the losing in this family stops with me" or that "I will succeed through a willingness to work hard and accept responsibility for my actions." In any case, as a defiantly authored "I no longer am going to do what I'm *supposed* to do" replacement program for an uninspired or tragic original story, the writing of an antiscript is a necessary step toward a more fulfilling life.

Thus a script need not be destiny. However, since what isn't acknowledged is unlikely to be changed, a redecision to draft a more positive narrative begins with Adult identification of one's current script, a willingness to author *and sustain* an antiscript despite Child fears to maintain a predictable yet unhappy existence, and the confident energy to become the leading man or woman in a new story. And once summoned, such an irresistible energy described by Nietzsche as the "undimmed eye of the sun" will rise from the universal drive for freedom to become all one is capable of being.

FOURTEEN

Gaining Freedom

To be free is to have achieved your life.
—Tennessee Williams

Much like a muscle, the Adult ego state "increases in strength with exercise" (James and Jongward 1971, 241). Such exercise involves an open-mindedness to new ideas through formal education supplemented by a daily challenging of past beliefs through a dispassionate and ongoing analysis of personal experience. And in so pursuing an ever-more-accurate perception of reality, an empowered Adult increases freedom to abandon self-imposed limits of the past by choosing to look at oneself and the world anew.

But even if complete choice and freedom are illusions, even if we are limited in realizing or transcending our past, and even if one's sense of reality will always be inexact, we all have the ability as self-focused "cognitive therapists" to more objectively question our here-and-now reality. And that process of personal enlightenment begins by asking the right questions.

In an ideal sense, the reality-testing Adult is quick to ponder and slow to certainty when continually asking "What assumptions have I made?" "How do I really know what I know?" "Have I fairly considered other points of view?" Or "Have I rushed to judgment without sufficient evidence to do so?" But if one is going to enlist Adult support in gaining freedom, still other questions need be asked: "Are my beliefs, actions, and feelings appropriate and effective in the current reality or are they based on outdated Parent and Child messages?" "Is my Adult imposing its will on unsound Parent and Child recordings, or, being contaminated, is it the other way around?" "Is my impulsive Child's need for instant gratification harming me?" "Is my controlling Parent sabotaging my relationships?" "What am I telling myself that is leading to unhappy or unsuccessful outcomes?" And ultimately, "What is most important?"

But whatever questions are asked, an individual possessing a potent and energized Adult ego state internalizes a self-aware world in which perceptions are relative, constants are rare, unconditional truth is often fool's gold, critical thinking is the norm, and an "appreciation of uncertainty is [viewed as] a cornerstone of rationality" (Kahneman 2013, 263). And although such premises seem self-evident, since questioning one's comfortable reality is anything but comfortable, for many their use is far less so.

Yet difficult as such questioning may be, since growth is inseparable from change, "if people become aware of their transactional behavior, in particular their games and the underlying script, they would, by application of Adult control, be able to modify their lives in a positive direction" (Steiner, The Transactional Analysis Corroboration Research Project).

With this self-enhancing goal in mind, it is important to realize that to see things from multiple perspectives, to withhold judgments, to impartially estimate probabilities, and to objectively weigh evidence is the foundation for Adult behavior. When reflecting on questions, the critical-thinking Adult speaks the language of "I think" or "It is likely" or "The evidence suggests" rather than the language of absolute certainty, which is absolutely often wrong. It understands that there is a world of difference in stating that something is "possibly" or even "probably" so than in making ex-cathedra pronouncements implying an all-knowing and often-contaminated monopoly of truth. And above all else, it realizes, as did Socrates, that with few exceptions "the only true wisdom is knowing that you know nothing."

The empowered Adult well recognizes the danger of clinging to an ineffective past by not asking the "right" questions. But it also understands that even if such questions are asked, evidence may be unknowingly manipulated to gain answers that are antithetical to personal growth or are inconsistent with objective reality. Thus when proof is "cherry picked" to support deeply embedded and often-irrational narratives, the Adult remains in a self-imposed "not knowing what one doesn't know" prison where "being right" temporarily protects self-esteem but impairs decision-making, *whatever* questions are asked. To that end, one such flaw in cognitive processing, sometimes referred to as the "fallacy of positive instances," is more commonly known as "selective perception."

Whenever people unknowingly or semiconsciously notice things that confirm their point of view and ignore whatever contradicts that outlook, they are selectively perceiving reality. That is, in "building a case" for what is believed, we often interpret, accept, and internalize only stimuli supporting our perceptions among a much larger array of possibilities. For example, after many events happening in a day, a depressed person will only focus on unpleasant experiences in order to "confirm" that "one can never catch a break." Or, lacking awareness, a prejudiced person will reflexively only focus on "evidence" that reinforces their intolerance and will deny, distort, or ignore any information challenging such bias.

That said, the allegorical story of a superstitious man who wore a copper bracelet to keep lions away comes to mind. "When told that there were no wild lions in the city where he lived, he was elated to learn that the bracelet was working so well" (Getty 1976, 438).

We all have confidently evaluated our "carefully" proofread written work as "without error" only to later discover numerous and ultimately obvious mistakes. Yet, how could this be unless we often perceive the world as we want or expect it to be rather than how it really is? We all have debated the relative merits of books, movies, music, sports teams, and presidents. How could this be if "objective reality" was not so "objective" after all? Even visually, we have all argued the comparative "hotness" of supermodels, the best color for our living room walls, and whether an image from Mars shows an intelligently designed human face or a naturally created rock formation. How could this be unless we often choose to believe what we want to believe and choose to see what we want to see?

Even the well-known Rorschach inkblot test is based upon the different ways we all visualize reality. How could this be unless we often only perceive what we subjectively infer, what we've been environmentally "programmed" to notice, or what we are genetically or biochemically predisposed to see? Thus undeniably, as producers of our own reality shows, selective perception is the tool of choice in conforming the wider world to preconceived and often narrow-minded points of view. And if further confirmation was needed of this all-but-universal tendency to irrationally accept false conclusions based on selectively perceived evidence, the following "proof" miraculously associating two tragedies from American history should end all doubt.

> Few people haven't heard of the supposed connection between the assassinations of Abraham Lincoln and John F. Kennedy. Without chronicling the numerous similarities between those two events, their coincidental parallelisms are often portrayed as evidence in linking them in an unexplainable or even mystical way. But often unrealized is that almost anything can be proved by selectively perceiving certain evidence to the exclusion of obvious contradictions.
>
> True, there *are* many similarities between the murders of these two Presidents. However, there are infinitely more differences than likenesses in the crimes. Yet by selectively perceiving evidence of two events separated by 100 years and innumerable contrasts, the case is made "proving" an interesting set of coincidences is far more than that. (Bright 2013, 47–48)

But whether for events in the wider world or for those of the most personal nature, selective perception is more than simply "stacking the cards" by unthinkingly paying greater attention to evidence supporting deeply held perceptions. It also involves a "confirmation bias" of *actively* seeking, exaggerating, and highlighting any experiences, facts, or memories confirming well-defended convictions (Wason 1960) and ignoring, devaluing, or discrediting evidence refuting or even challenging them. This cognitive distortion of more forcefully challenging information not fitting deeply held perceptions than questioning information supporting one's assumptions (Kunda 1990) almost guarantees continuation of beliefs whatever their absurdity or harm. Summed up by the late Stanford University psychologist Leon Festinger, "A man with a conviction is a hard man to change. Tell him you disagree and he turns away. Show him facts and figures and he questions your sources. Appeal to logic and he fails to see your point" (Mooney 2011a).

While the cognitively biased mechanisms sustaining fossilized thinking are selective perception and confirmation bias, self-delusion is taken to another level by motivated reasoning. That is, in efforting to arrive at predetermined conclusions, many individuals not only pigeonhole people, places, and things in irrationally constructed boxes, but in selectively evaluating reality they also ignore irrefutable evidence and airtight logic by *aggressively justifying* indefensible points of view. And it is such confirming what-one-already-knows "reasoning" supported by like-minded allies and defensively tortured rationalizations that may well produce the biggest delusions of all. It is thus not surprising that when fueling up our intellectual tanks from similarly contaminated sources, we can do little other than to self-satisfyingly arrive at the same comfortably familiar yet undeniably fictionalized destinations.

But however sure of things we may claim to be, one would think that often being mistaken about the simplest and/or most personally important of things would be a potent cure for hubristic certainty. Surely, after being wrong about one's career, marriage, football team, and even where one's car keys have been placed, it would seem that there shouldn't be much that one *should be* sure about. But for people confidently claiming positivity about events, ideas, or the behavior of others they could rationally not possibly know for certain, even reasonable doubt is obviously not the case.

Emotionally defensive to contrary evidence and armed with a sense of self-assurance that only claiming a monopoly on truth can provide, the tail of beliefs for such sure-about-everything people wags the dog of evidence rather than the other way around. And while such flawed reasoning matters little in guiding opinions of movies, music, books, or a referee's decision during an athletic contest, disregarding contradictions to beliefs concerning problems facing one's country, its next leader, or the appropriateness and effectiveness of our own behavior matters much.

The origin for selective perception, confirmation bias, and motivated reasoning is the very source once posited by Adler, Maslow, and Berne for much of what we say, believe, feel, and do. That is, for many, if not most, people, challenges to beliefs are also challenges to self-esteem. As such, the more fragile one's self-concept the more emotionally threatening contradictory information becomes and the more resistant one is to objectively viewing such data. Thus with relatively few exceptions, the esteem-enhancing desire to be "right" devalues conflicting evidence and deactivates common sense.

Still another reason why fight-or-flight reflexes are not only applied to threats from predators but from conflicting information as well (Mooney 2011a) is that confronting two opposing thoughts, what we believe is right and what credible evidence conclusively demonstrates as right, is psychologically uncomfortable. As mentioned previously, this cognitive dissonance motivates people to reduce such discomfort by ignoring or degrading evidence challenging one's perceptions while blindly embracing practically any reassurance of existing beliefs. Common to intractable conspiracy theorists, Holocaust deniers, members of the Flat Earth Society, moon landing doubters, and politically motivated "objective" pundits, such close-mindedness virtually guarantees that "undeniable truth" will often be sacrificed for undeniable ignorance.

Moreover, in seeking the safety and security of a predictable world so important to Maslow's hierarchy of needs, it's easy to understand why people continue believing what is already "known." Thus as with Dorothy, the fear of not being in Kansas anymore imprisons us in a "don't confuse me with the facts" status quo. Never realizing that beliefs may be based on exceptions to reality rather than on reality itself, that a few samples of evidence may only coincidentally mirror a larger truth, and that virtually anything can be "proved" by selectively narrowing one's focus, we fail to challenge the past and live in an invented universe of our own design.

But winning arguments simply by making debating points is a Pyrrhic victory. For in doing so, we often neglect an essential struggle to emancipate the Adult to question outdated Parent beliefs and Child fears limiting our freedom to see the world more realistically and become more of who we are capable of being. And it is for this self-limiting reason that Voltaire was right in noting that "a state of doubt is unpleasant, but a state of certainty is ridiculous."

Yet challenging archaic Parent attitudes and Child behaviors presupposes awareness of such obsolete recordings and the need for a continual monitoring of their occurrence. And this awareness begins with the Adult question of "Which ego state is now active?" It is by the very process of asking this question and answering "That is my Parent" or "That is my Child" that an autonomous, potent, and hypervigilant Adult initially seizes greater control of life (Harris 1973).

Thus the wherewithal to reprogram the Parent and Child ego states must begin by recognizing and questioning their recordings in light of current reality. And it is only through such reprogramming that the wider reality can be challenged through "the establishment of and embarking upon a new course in the direction of goals arrived at by the Adult" (Harris 1973, 170).

With the possible exception of a decontaminated Adult supported by an internally oriented responsibility mindset, little is more important on one's journey toward self-actualized freedom than creating a goal-driven improvement contract. Such a covenant sets positive, specific, and reasonable objectives, what one is willing to do to achieve them, what changes will be evident when the contract is satisfied, *and* a commitment to regularly measure and share progress along the way.

In fact, "nothing further can be accomplished until you have firmly decided on something you want to change and are willing to stick to that decision" (Meininger 1973, 133). In agreeing, Alfred Adler tersely insisted that "we cannot think, feel, will, or act without the perception of some goal" (Adler 1929, 3; Wilson 1975, 118). Assuredly, without positive goals as the necessary "why" of efforts, self-doubt and status-quo inertia will speak as "why not" rationalizations guaranteeing law of least effort inaction.

> In an admittedly small 2010 study conducted by Dr. Gail Matthews at the Dominican University of California, the benefits of adult goal setting were strongly suggested if not confirmed. By *simply thinking* about goals participants hoped to realize within a four-week period, almost half reported successfully achieving them. When another group was asked to write their goals, the rate of success rose to 61 percent. A third group accompanying their written goals with an action plan to accomplish them and who also shared their aspirations with a friend reported an achievement rate of 64 percent. And when a last group was asked to contact that friend with a weekly progress report, the goal accomplishment success rate increased to 76 percent. (Bright 2013, 88; Lee 2010)

Additionally, breaking down or "chunking" such commitments to larger goals into smaller, more manageable steps encourages confidence and is an effective antidote to "all at once" procrastination, anxiety, and Child-authored "I'll never be able to do this" negative thinking. An effective approach to realize such incremental goal-inspired change is to embrace the strategy of making small improvements day after day, leading over time to ever greater progress. "This continuous drive for self-improvement to not only exhibit 'swing for the fences' growth on a daily basis but to continually *move those fences further back*" (Bright 2013, 127), is expressed in the Japanese practice of betterment without end known as kaizen.

Yet however goals are accomplished, a potent Adult is an indispensable resource in challenging counterproductive "I'm not good enough" self-talk that undermines motivation, perseverance, and ultimately success. Only the Adult can reflect on unfounded self-doubt by recounting past examples of "I can't do this" fears that ultimately proved groundless. Whether it was learning to drive, the first day of a class where course requirements seemed insurmountable, or navigating unclear responsibilities and unknown office politics on a just-accepted job, we all have stories of mastery once seemingly "beyond reach" becoming an easily accomplished new normal. And if such pessimistic thoughts were without merit in the past, why should they be any less baseless today?

But the power of setting goals extends beyond elevating one's commitment toward their realization. At a minimum, it should also include a daily mindfulness to notice supportive ideas that without such focus would likely have "flown under the radar" (Bright 2013; Locke and Latham 2002). And that shouldn't be all that difficult to do. For anyone seriously committing to a goal knows, it naturally prompts a hyperawareness attracting environmental stimuli serving its fulfillment. To that end, once a specific goal is firmly internalized, wherever one looks one discovers what is looked for.

> A well-publicized example of this phenomenon was said to have occurred in 2004 for Facebook creator Mark Zuckerberg. During the initial stages of designing what became a worldwide sensation, when a friend asked him if a particular female student was "available," Zuckerberg, portrayed as barely paying attention to the question, instantly realized that adding "relationship status" to Facebook would springboard his Internet brainchild to unimagined popularity. Yet without his goal of creating a social networking site as a magnet for randomly generated supportive ideas, his friend's "boy meets girl" question would have meant little.
>
> Then again, one doesn't need to be a *Time* magazine "Person of the Year" or a young billionaire to realize the power of goals in stimulating creativity. Ideas bolstering creative endeavors are "out there" for the taking, and goals as lightning rods "entice" such ideas by increasing sensitivity to receiving them. Or like a net trolling for fish, goals allow irrelevant ideas to pass through while snaring more important prey. Thus in defining genius, Thomas Edison was only partially right. For as much as perspiration undoubtedly led to his inventive breakthroughs, goal setting "attracted" or "caught" the inspirations without which such insights would less likely to have occurred. (Bright 2013, 87)

However, goal setting does more than inspire creativity for making money or conceiving the "next big thing." Specifically, envisioning elements of a better life can also serve as goals in reaching that destination. And as with more everyday aims, once such life objectives are visualized they, too, will elicit seemingly random environmental stimuli illuminating paths toward their realization. Moreover, goals provide the daily and long-term "What should I do now?" activating self-talk without which apathy and aimlessness are likely to occur.

We all know the feeling of lying in bed on a Saturday morning drifting in and out of sleep until a "want to" or "need to" goal pops into our head. Whether we "must" clean the house because our beloved mother-in-law is coming for a visit, the kids need to be dropped off at soccer practice, or, with time running out, holiday shopping has to be done, we all know that after such thoughts enter our minds it is difficult if not impossible to go back to sleep. As a result, we are likely to get out of bed and plan our day around accomplishing whatever tasks need attention. Clearly, goals drive behaviors.

As Eric Berne observed, "A loser doesn't know what he'll do if he loses, but talks about what he'll do if he wins. A winner doesn't talk about what he'll do if he wins, but *knows* what he'll do if he loses." And in actuating such "knowing-what-to-do" purpose when things don't go well, people who set self-improvement goals and create plans to achieve them become winners by gaining a greater sense of confidence, control, and responsibility for how they'll face the rest of their lives. And besides, setting positive life goals and efforting their accomplishment often replaces humdrum feelings of boredom and "why bother" aimlessness with a greater sense of excitement, anticipation, and focused meaning to existence.

However, empowering the Adult to ask the "right" questions, think critically, question Parent and Child recordings, and set goals based on such rethinking still does not guarantee freedom toward a more self-actualized existence. Since even self-aware people *really know* virtually nothing about virtually everything, even an enlightened Adult's willingness to consider as much evidence *refuting* its views as in confirming them only assures movement *toward* truth.

Indeed, scientists aware of cognitive biases and *deliberately* seeking to disprove their own hypotheses with additional research can *still* accept false conclusions. Thus in attempting to make good decisions, even a voice-of-reason Adult can make poor judgments when filtering an infinite amount of data, infinitely limited by experience and at times by contamination, of which it is often infinitely unaware.

But knowing that probability not certainty in perceiving reality is all that is possible should not stop the Adult's search for truth. To that end, however small the amount of what can really be seen and known, seeking an ever-closer approximation of reality, compared to an unexamined life, is certainly a goal worth pursuing. For although a fully enabled Adult can *still* lead to success *or* failure, at the least its empowerment makes positive change possible.

However, gaining freedom implies more than a potent and decontaminated Adult processing answers to the "right" questions with immunity from selective perception, confirmation bias, and motivated reasoning. Gaining freedom also demands an internally oriented sense of responsibility where in the arguably overstated words of Ernest Hemingway "Every damn thing is your own fault, if you are any good." Indeed, the autonomy of being answerable for one's actions and feelings "is the ultimate goal in transactional analysis" (James and Jongeward 1971, 263).

And while many might question Hemingway's all or nothing quote in quantifying personal accountability, one thing *is* undeniable. Freedom is impossible if dependent upon others for one's moods, miseries, or self-esteem. This being so, in order to live a life of diminished suffering we have to "understand our role as the creator of our pain; our own mind causes our problems, not other people, not the world out there" (Tolle 1999, xiv). And by continually denying responsibility for our internal world, we are doing little other than to foolishly relinquish power over our lives to something or someone else.

> No one can say something producing hurt, rage, insecurity, or doubt in someone unless the person experiencing those emotions had similarly criticized themselves. Thus in stimulating those emotions, verbal "assaults" remind us that more work needs to be done in overcoming our inner demons by changing what we don't like about ourselves or to be more accepting of who we are. In that, the person blamed for our unpleasant emotions is more teacher than attacker. (Bright 2013, 50)

Of course, events or others can "invite" us to think and act in certain ways, but where is it written that we must accept that invitation? As a slave to others, one cannot be master of oneself. And this realization is the first step toward gaining freedom.

In looking back on life, is it possible that fulfillment can result from something other than striving to maximize one's capabilities? Is it possible that contentment may not be found by forging intimate relationships, raising moral and self-sufficient children, building a satisfying home life or career, or in making a creative or altruistic contribution to the world? And is it possible to someday look back at the landscape of life and never ask whether the world has been better for one's existence? Of course it's possible (Bright 2013, 134).

Perhaps Robert Louis Stevenson was wrong in his claim that becoming all we are capable of being "is the only end of life." Perhaps in observing that "the powerful play goes on, and you may contribute a verse," Walt Whitman was equally mistaken. "And perhaps 'be all you can be' is nothing more than an idealized and unreachable Madison Avenue slogan based on the existential psychobabble of a long dead psychologist. For if so, and a meaningful life can be found elsewhere than a kaizen-inspired journey toward self-actualization, there is nothing wrong with that"

(Bright 2013, 134). However, betting that eventual "How did I come to this?" regret will not follow failing to at least endeavor one's potential is a dangerous and not easily reversible wager.

> In reviewing life, people typically reach their final years questioning whether existence has been generally meaningful, productive, and successful. If believed so, a person experiencing a sense of having written their verse accomplishment is better prepared to live their remaining years without remorse and in relative peace. However, if looking back and seeing a selling-oneself-short history filled with squandered opportunities, unrealized talents, wasted years, and paradise lost, many people believing it is too late to change are instead filled with self-condemnation and despair. (Bright 2013, 134)

It is one thing when it's too late to find another route by turning around in a seemingly endless traffic jam. It is quite another in reviewing one's life to feel equally trapped in a journey without escape, without alternatives, and without joy. Yet despite what many people feel and how many others behave, we are not trapped. Indeed, rather than condemning oneself to walk a narrow path when the road is endlessly wide, rethinking everything provides an infinity of choices in how to experience the world. And failing to realize this is to diminish the only life one will ever know.

As such, it is never too early to realize that failing to look ahead, seeking excuse rather than possibility, imposing subjective limits on potential, accepting one's negative script without question or struggle, and engaging the game of life timidly not to lose rather than to win will likely result in unsatisfying outcomes. And "while existence passes by with all the subtlety of an onrushing locomotive, each day, each moment is yet another opportunity to begin anew the journey toward a more productive, enriching, and true to oneself future" (Bright 2013, 134).

After all, isn't freedom as Camus observed "nothing but a chance to be better?" And with life relentlessly hemorrhaging away, why wait to exercise that "being better" freedom? For clichéd but true, once acknowledged that life is inexorably winding down, is it not so that the wise does at once what the fool does at last? A fulfilling life need not only be for "other people." With that in mind, the question you must first answer is: "Why not for you as well?"

Shortly before leading his men into battle against the Aztecs in 1519, Hernando Cortes scuttled his ships. Making retreat impossible, the conquistador motivated his men to the task of survival by sending a clear message that there was no turning back. Much of life is like that. As existence has no dress rehearsals, at life's end there will be no encore nor return for a second chance. Thus above all things, one must find the courage to save oneself by scuttling one's internal ships of finger-pointing, irresponsibility, and magical thinking. There are no "do-overs" and there is no Santa Claus. The Easter Bunny and the Tooth Fairy don't exist, and the story of one's life can only be edited by its leading man or woman.

Yet even though such an internally focused mindset does not guarantee a "being all one can be" optimistically lived existence, the freedom to build the world one wants begins with a looking-in-the-mirror sense of accountability and control. Contrastingly, the glass half empty path to dysfunction, despair, and lost possibilities begins with an externally driven "It's not me" outlook, all but guaranteeing self-sabotage and drift. As undeniable for some and as painful for others to accept, with few exceptions *it is you*.

Life is all about priorities and choice. Thus you alone have the power to prioritize a "seize the day" sense of urgency in rethinking everything by accepting responsibility for the quality of your existence. You alone can regain the infinite possibilities of childhood by reclaiming your autonomous self free from the dictates and expectations of others with a limited choice of roles to play. You alone have the power to recognize that every defense you use, every racket you accept, and every game you play gets you further from the freedom to rescript a life well lived. And you alone can be carried by your self-imposed current or can triumph by imposing a more favorable one. It is entirely your call.

Your final question is thus simple. Will excuses win in dictating a life of unfulfilled potential or will *you* win in directing a life toward more fully realized possibilities? And only you can decide that in answering that "What will you be?" question, there is no better time than now.

Appendix

Ego State Recognition Exercises

In order to gain greater ability in identifying ego states, consider completing the following recognition exercises. However, before doing so, remember that in real-world situations words alone do not always accurately indicate ego states. Body language, voice tone, and situational context must also be weighed in order to most precisely identify an individual's Parent, Adult, or Child.

Directions: In the space provided after each statement or question, identify each of the following reactions as most likely emerging from the Parent, Adult, or Child ego state. (Answers are on page 198.)

1. Always ask for help when you don't understand. _____
2. I'm gonna go to the dance no matter what! _____
3. What is your evidence? _____
4. I wish it would snow! _____
5. Just shut up! _____
6. (unemotionally) Have you made an attempt to change? _____
7. You're acting stupid as usual! _____
8. (sadly) What's wrong with me? _____
9. Why doesn't everybody leave me alone? _____
10. What are the facts? _____
11. The weather looks like it's improving. _____
12. This happens to me all the time! _____
13. (unemotionally) No, I can't agree. _____
14. Don't be ridiculous! _____
15. Don't worry dear. I'll fix it for you. _____
16. How shall I begin that presentation? _____

17. How did you arrive at that conclusion? _____
18. I hope this medicine cures my acne! _____
19. Kids today are lazy and irresponsible! _____
20. Perhaps we should just agree to disagree. _____
21. Spelling always counts! _____
22. You'll do it because I said so! _____
23. In my opinion, you are inviting more problems by behaving that way. _____
24. Everybody else is going! Can't I go, too? _____
25. Pride goeth before the fall. _____
26. How dare you talk to me that way! _____
27. Mine is better than yours! _____
28. It is 4:30 p.m. _____
29. Come on now, you must try harder! _____
30. That behavior is vulgar and disgusting! _____
31. I wonder when the test will be. _____
32. Always respect you elders! _____
33. (unemotionally) I think you'd be better off ignoring that comment. _____
34. (unemotionally) Here's something that will likely make you feel better. _____
35. Would you be willing to discuss our disagreement in order to arrive at a solution we both feel good about? _____

Directions: Considering each situation, identify responses as Parent, Adult, or Child.

A pupil is disruptive during a lesson. Possible teacher responses include:

36. I worked so hard on the lesson and you've ruined it! It's not fair. I'm upset and now I have a headache. _____
37. That does it! Wipe that smile off your face! You can spend the next two nights in detention! _____

38. (calmly) When you talk during a lesson, it is difficult for me to do my job. If this behavior continues, I'll be forced to ask you to leave the room. _____

39. At the moment, you are likely heading down the wrong road. How can you stop that from happening? _____

An attractive new employee is assigned to your department.

40. Be careful of strangers! You can't tell a book by its cover! _____

41. I wonder where he/she is from? _____

42. I'm sure that he/she won't like me! _____

You come home and see a luscious piece of chocolate cake on the kitchen counter.

43. I want to eat it all! _____

44. I shouldn't eat that! _____

45. I wonder how many grams of fat that cake contains? _____

A coworker suddenly faints.

46. I'll call an ambulance for help. _____

47. He/she shouldn't have gotten so drunk last night! _____

48. Poor thing. She must really be sick. _____

49. Everyone will think it was me who got him/her upset! _____

An acquaintance gives you an unexpected compliment.

50. It's about time that fool showed me some respect! _____

51. Wow! I feel great! _____

52. Does he/she expect a compliment in return? _____

At work, you notice that smoke is seeping under your office door.

53. I wonder what is burning? _____

54. It would be a good idea to stay calm. _____

55. I better get outta here quick! _____

56. People should be more careful! _____

A parent is not satisfied with his/her child's grades in school.

57. Have you asked your teacher for help? _____

58. If I've told you once, I've told you a hundred times: your grades must improve! _____

59. Your teacher is an idiot! _____

In the market, you see someone stealing food.

60. I'm afraid to say anything! _____

61. Theft probably causes the price of food to rise. _____

62. He/she should be ashamed of him-/herself! _____

A colleague at work finds you smoking a cigarette in a no-smoking area.

63. I sure could use a drag on that cigarette! _____

64. Only fools smoke! _____

65. (unemotionally) Are you aware of the rules against smoking in this area? _____

An unexpected meeting is called for at work.

66. We should have an agenda before every meeting! _____

67. Doesn't my idiot boss have anything better to do? _____

68. If my boss thinks I'm going to sit here for an hour, she is nuts! _____

A shapely woman walks into a restaurant wearing a provocative outfit.

69. Wow! She is so hot! _____

70. Anyone with a shred of decency wouldn't dress that way! _____

71. What need is she satisfying by dressing like that? _____

72. I'm surprised there is so little reaction to that outfit. _____

A teacher responds to a student who has questioned her competency during class.

73. I can see that you are very angry with me, and I'd like to discuss this further after class. _____

74. You make me want to quit teaching! _____

75. It's about time you grew up! _____

EGO STATE RECOGNITION ANSWERS

1. P
2. C
3. A
4. C
5. P
6. A
7. P
8. C
9. C
10. A
11. A
12. C
13. A
14. P
15. P
16. A
17. A
18. C
19. P
20. A
21. P
22. P
23. A
24. C
25. P
26. P
27. C
28. A
29. P
30. P
31. A
32. P
33. A
34. A
35. A
36. C
37. P
38. A
39. A
40. P
41. A
42. C
43. C
44. P
45. A
46. A
47. P
48. P
49. C
50. P
51. C
52. A
53. A
54. A
55. C
56. P
57. A
58. P
59. P
60. C
61. A
62. P
63. C
64. P
65. A
66. P
67. P
68. C
69. C
70. P
71. A
72. A
73. A
74. C
75. P

TRANSACTION RECOGNITION EXERCISES

Identify the following transaction types as either Complementary, Crossed, or Ulterior (Answers are on page 202).

1. Stimulus: "I think you're great!"
   Response: "I like you, too!"

Transaction Type: ____________________

2. Stimulus: "Let's get drunk!"
   Response: "Grow up!"

Transaction Type: ____________________

3. Stimulus: "Kids are just awful today!"
   Response: "I don't have any evidence of that."

Transaction Type: ____________________

4. Stimulus: (calmly) "Did you hide my newspaper?"
   Response: (calmly) "I put it where you lost my car keys."

Transaction Type: ____________________

5. Stimulus: (scowling) "Last week didn't you say that you'd look for work?"
   Response: (averting eye contact) "Perhaps I did."

Transaction Type: ____________________

6. Stimulus: "Where the hell have you been?"
   Response: "Wouldn't you like to know?"

Transaction Type: ____________________

7. Stimulus: "Those poor people have suffered so much after the tsunami!"
   Response: "Yes, it's a tragedy how much they've lost!"

Transaction Type: ____________________

8. Stimulus: "Clean up after yourself!"
   Response: (without emotion) "When would you like me to begin?"

Transaction Type: ____________________

9. Stimulus: (winking) "When is the meeting?"
   Response: (licking lips) "It is at three o'clock."

Transaction Type: ____________________

10. Stimulus: "Those people are all so stupid."
   Response: "I haven't noticed that."

Transaction Type: ____________________

11. Stimulus: (without emotion) "I need to finish that project today."
   Response: "Why do you always leave things for the last minute?"

Transaction Type: ____________________

12. Stimulus: "I'm sick and tired of listening to your problems!"
   Response: (without emotion) "Don't do it then."

Transaction Type: ____________________

13. Stimulus: "Those teachers assign too much work!"
   Response: "Yeah. They should remember what it's like to be a student."

Transaction Type: ____________________

14. Stimulus: (calmly but scowling with arms folded) "I thought you said the job would be done by now."
   Response: (looking down) "I thought so, too."

Transaction Type: ____________________

15. Stimulus: "I feel terrible!"
   Response: "That's because you stupidly hang out too much with your drunken friends!"

Transaction Type: ____________________

16. Stimulus: "Those teenagers from that town are uncontrollable!"
   Response: "Yeah. They're all animals!"

Transaction Type: ____________________

17. Stimulus: "Why does everyone hate me?"
Response: "Is it possible you've contributed to this situation?"

Transaction Type: ____________________

18. Stimulus: "Do you know where the dictionary is?"
Response: "Can't you remember anything?"

Transaction Type: ____________________

19. Stimulus: "Our boss is a fool!"
Response: (thoughtfully) "What is your biggest complaint about him/her?"

Transaction Type: ____________________

20. Stimulus: "Stop talking nonsense!"
Response: "You're the idiot, not me!"

Transaction Type: ____________________

TRANSACTION RECOGNITION ANSWERS

1. Complementary
2. Crossed
3. Crossed
4. Ulterior
5. Ulterior
6. Complementary
7. Complementary
8. Crossed
9. Ulterior
10. Crossed
11. Crossed
12. Crossed
13. Complementary
14. Ulterior
15. Complementary
16. Complementary
17. Crossed
18. Crossed
19. Crossed
20. Crossed

References

Adler, A. 1929. *The Practice and Theory of Individual Psychology*. London: Routledge and Kegan Paul.

———. 1931. *What Life Should Mean to You*. Boston: Little, Brown and Company.

Adler, K. 1964. "Life Style in Schizophrenia." In *Essays in Individual Psychology*, edited by K. Adler and D. Deutsch. New York: Grove Press.

Allen, J. R., and B. A. Allen. 1987. "To Find/Make Meaning: Notes on the Last Permission." *Transactional Analysis Journal* 17 (3): 72–81.

———. 1988. "Scripts and Permissions: Some Unexamined Assumptions and Connotations." *Transactional Analysis Journal* 18 (4): 283–93.

Atasoy, O. 2013. "You Are Less Beautiful Than You Think You Are." *Scientific American*. http://www.scientificamerican.com/article/you-are-less-beautiful-than-you-think/.

Bader, E., and J. K. Zeig. 1976. "Fifty-Seven Discounts." *Transactional Analysis Journal* 6 (2): 133–34.

Ball, J. D. 1978. "TA and RET." *Transactional Analysis Journal* 8 (1): 19–22.

Barnes, G., ed. 1977. *Transactional Analysis After Eric Berne: Teachings and Practices of Three TA Schools*. New York: Harper's College Press.

Barrow, G. 2007. "Wonderful World, Beautiful People: Reframing TA as Positive Psychology." *Transactional Analysis Journal* 37 (3): 206–9.

Barrow, G., E. Bradshaw, and T. Newton. 2001. *Improving Behaviour and Raising Self-Esteem in the Classroom*. London: David Fulton Publishers, Ltd.

Bary, B. B., and F. M. Hufford. 1990. "The Six Advantages to Games and Their Use in Treatment." *Transactional Analysis Journal* 37 (3): 206–9.

Beck, M. 2013. "I'm Not Okay, You're Not Okay!" *The Oprah Magazine*, December, 55–56, 58.

Belbenoit, R. 1938. *Dry Guillotine*. New York: E. P. Dutton & Company.

Berne, E. 1961. *Transactional Analysis in Psychotherapy*. New York: Ballantine Books, Inc.

———. 1963. *The Structure and Dynamics of Organizations and Groups*. Philadelphia: J. B. Lippincott.

———. 1964a. *Games People Play*. New York: Grove Press.

———. 1964b. *Principles of Group Treatment*. New York: Oxford University Press.

———. 1973. *What Do You Say After You Say Hello?* New York: Bantam Books, Inc.

Bexton, W. H., W. Heron, and T. H. Scott. 1954. "Effects of Decreased Variation in the Sensory Environment." *Canadian Journal of Psychology* 8 (2): 70–76.

Blacklidge, V. Y. 1976. "The Nature and Nurture of the Natural Child." *Transactional Analysis Journal* 6 (3): 246–52.

Bloom, P. 2010. "The Moral Life of Babies." *The New York Times Reprints*, May 5. http://www.nytimes.com/2010/05/09/magazine/09babies-t.html?pagewanted=all&_r=0.

"Born Good? Babies Help Unlock the Origins of Morality." *60 Minutes*. CBS. July 28, 2013. Web Transcript. http://www.cbsnews.com/news/babies-help-unlock-the-origins-of-morality/.

Boulton, M. 1977. "Parental Injunctions: Witch Messages Masquerading as Nurturing Parent Messages." *Transactional Analysis Journal* 7 (1): 10–14.

———. 1978. "The Nurturing Parent and Social Issues." *Transactional Analysis Journal* 8 (2): 117–20.

Boyce, M. 1978. "Twelve Permissions." *Transactional Analysis Journal* 8 (1): 30–32.

Breen, M. 1973. "Supplemental Parenting of the Kick Me Player." *Transactional Analysis Journal* 3 (1): 40–46.

Bright, N. 2011. "Reality Television: Like it or Not, it Reflects Who We Are." *South Florida Sun-Sentinel.com*, July 24. http://articles.sun-sentinel.com/2011-07-24/news/fl-brightcol-oped0724-20110724_1_reality-joe-millionaire-temptation-island.

Bright, N. 2013. *Those Who Can: Why Master Teachers Do What They Do*. Lanham, MD: Rowman & Littlefield Publishers, Inc.

Brown, J. 1970. "A Behavioral Analysis of Masochism." *Journal of Experimental Research in Personality* 4:60–65.

Calcaterra, N. B. n.d. "Eric Berne M.D." http:www.ericberne.com/transactional-analysis/.

Capers, H., and L. Goodman. 1983. "The Survival Process: Clarifications of the Miniscript." *Transactional Analysis Journal* 13 (3): 142–48.

Caracushansky, S. 1980. "Self-Actualization and Cure." *Transactional Analysis Journal* 10 (4): 322–25.

Carroll, R. T. 2003. "Motivated Reasoning." http://skepdic.com/motivatedreasoning.html.

Chapman, A. 1995–2012. "Eric Berne's Transactional Analysis-Early TA History and Theory." http://www.businessballs.com/transact.htm.

Cheney, W. D. 1973. "The Ego-Defensive Function of Life-Scripts." *Transactional Analysis Journal* 3 (3): 11–15.

Choy, A. 1990. "The Winner's Triangle." *Transactional Analysis Journal* 20 (1): 40–46.

Clarkson, P. 1988. "Script Cure? A Diagnostic Pentagon of Types of Therapeutic Change." *Transactional Analysis Journal* 18 (3): 211–19.

Clarkson, P. 1992a. "In Praise of Speed, Experimentation, Agreeableness, Endurance, and Excellence: Counterscript Drivers and Aspiration." *Transactional Analysis Journal* 22 (1): 16–20.

Clarkson, P. 1992b. "The Interpersonal Field in Transactional Analysis." *Transactional Analysis Journal* 22 (2): 89–94.

Clarkson, P. 1993. "Bystander Games." *Transactional Analysis Journal* 23 (3): 158–72.

Cole, M. 1984. "How to Make a Person Passive-Aggressive or the Power Struggle Game." *Transactional Analysis Journal* 14 (3): 191–94.

Conway, A., and P. Clarkson. 1987. "Everyday Hypnotic Inductions." *Transactional Analysis Journal* 17 (2): 17–23.

Conway, N. V. 1978. "Drivers and Dying." *Transactional Analysis Journal* 8 (4): 345–48.

Corey, G. 2009. "Transactional Analysis." For Web Tutor *Theory and Practice of Counseling and Psychotherapy*, 8th ed.

Cornell, W. F. 1988. "Life Script Theory: A Critical Review from a Developmental Perspective." *Transactional Analysis Journal* 18 (4): 270–82.

Costello, R. K. 1976. "Consolidating Injunctions." *Transactional Analysis Journal* 6 (1): 52–56.

Crichton, E. 2007. "Transactional Analysis: Ego States—What They Are and How to Diagnose Them." *Australian Journal of Clinical Hypotherapy and Hypnosis*, April. HighBeam (1P3-1283039351).

Danner, D. D., D. A. Snowden, and W. V. Friesen. 2001. "Positive Emotions in Early Life and Longevity: Findings from the Nun Study." *Journal of Personality and Social Psychology* 80 (5): 804–13.

"Delaying Gratification." *American Psychological Association*. www.apa.org/helpcenter/willpower-Gratification.pdf.

Del Casale, F. 2001. "Supporting Terminally Ill Patients and Their families Using Refocalization Psychology and Transactional Analysis." *Transactional Analysis Journal* 31 (3): 182–88.

Dell, P. 1986. "In Defense of Lineal Causality." *Family Process* 25:513–21.

De Quintero, L., and D. Boersner. 1982. "Specific Strokes for Specific Needs." *Transactional Analysis Journal* 12 (4): 309–13.

Dieser, R. B. 1997. "Empirical Research on Attribution Theory." *Transactional Analysis Journal* 27 (3): 175–80.

Dolor, R. G. 2014. "Loneliness is Deadlier than Obesity Among Elderly People, Study Warns." *Tech Times*, February 17. http://www.techtimes.com/articles/3523/20140217/loneliness-is-deadlier-than-obesity-among-elderly-people-warns-study.htm.

Dyer, W. 1976. *Your Erroneous Zones*. New York: Funk & Wagnalls.

Dyer, W. 2009. *Excuses Begone! How to Change Lifelong, Self-Defeating Thinking Habits*. Carlsbad, CA: Hay House, Inc.

Ellis, A. 1993. *Die Rational-Emotive Therapie* [Reason and Emotion in Psychotherapy]. Munchen: Pfeiffer (original published in 1962).

English, F. 1969. "Episcript and the 'Hot Potato' Game." *Transactional Analysis Bulletin* 8:77–82.

———. 1971. "Strokes in the Credit Bank for David Kupper." *Transactional Analysis Journal* 1 (3): 27–28.

———. 1972. "Sleepy, Spunky and Spooky." *Transactional Analysis Journal* 2 (2): 64–67.

———. 1975. "I'm OK—You're OK (Adult)." *Transactional Analysis Journal* 5 (5): 416–19.

———. 1977. "What Shall I Do Tomorrow?: Reconceptualizing Transactional Analysis." In *Transactional Analysis After Eric Berne: Teaching and Practices of Three TA Schools*, edited by G. Barnes, 287–347. New York: Harper's College Press.

———. 1988. "Whither Scripts?" *Transactional Analysis Journal* 18 (4): 294–303.

———. 1996. "Berne, Phobia, Episcripts, and Racketeering." *Transactional Analysis Journal* 26 (2): 122–31.

———. 1998. "On Receiving the 1997 Eric Berne Memorial Award for Hot-Potato Transmissions and Episcripts." *Transactional Analysis Journal* 28 (1): 10–15.

Ernst, K. 1972. *Games Students Play*. Millbrae, CA: Celestial Arts.

Erskine, R. G., and T. Selzer. 1977. "Open-Ended Scripts: A Second Chance for Women." *Transactional Analysis Journal* 7 (4): 294–97.

Fine, M. J., and J. P. Poggio. 1977. "Behavioral Attributes of the Life Positions." *Transactional Analysis Journal* 7 (4): 350–56.

Frank, J. 1974. "Adapted and Critical Parent." *Transactional Analysis Journal* 4 (4): 8–9.

Frederickson, B. L. 2007. "The Broaden and Build Theory of Positive Emotion." In *The Science of Well-Being*, edited by F. A. Huppert, N. Baylis, and B. Keverne, 217–40. Oxford: Oxford University Press.

Freud, S. 1933. *New Introductory Lectures on Psycho-Analysis*. New York: W. W. Norton & Company.

Gellert, S. D. 1975. "Drivers." *Transactional Analysis Journal* 5 (4): 422–29.

Gere, F. 1975. "Developing the OK Miniscript." *Transactional Analysis Journal* 5 (3): 285–89.

Getty, R. E. 1976. "Reward, Reinforcement and Recognition: A Comparative Analysis." *Transactional Analysis Journal* 6 (4): 437–41.

Ghose, T. 2013. "Why We're All Above Average." *LiveScience*, February 6. http://www.livescience.com/26914-why-we-are-all-above-average.html.

Gladfelter, J. 1977. "Enjoying Every Minute." In *Transactional Analysis After Eric Berne: Teaching and Practices of Three TA Schools*, edited by G. Barnes, 394–424. New York: Harper's College Press.

Gladwell, M. 2008. *Outliers: The Story of Success*. New York: Little, Brown and Company.

———. 2009. *What the Dog Saw and Other Adventures*. New York: Little, Brown and Company.

Glende, N. 1982. "Get Sick as an Escape Hatch." *Transactional Analysis Journal* 12 (3): 197–98.

Gobes, L. 2001. "Ego States—Metaphor or Reality." In *Volume of Selected Articles from the Transactional Analysis Journal, 1981–1990*, 274–76. Oakland, CA: International Transactional Analysis Association.

Gormly, J. B. 1984. "Training in Powerlessness During Transitional Life-Events." *Transactional Analysis Journal* 14 (2): 140–44.

Goulding, R. L., and M. M. Goulding. 1978. *The Power is in the Patient: A TA/Gestalt Approach to Psychotherapy*. San Francisco: TA Press.

Graff, R. A. 1976. "A Game Transactional Analysts Play." *Transactional Analysis Journal* 6 (3): 263–67.

Gregoire, J. 2004. "Ego States as Living Links Between Past and Current Experiences." *Transactional Analysis Journal* 34 (1): 10–29.

Hamlin, J. K., K. Wynn, and P. Bloom. 2007. "Social Evaluation by Preverbal Infants." *Nature Publishing Group* 450 (22): 557–60.

Harley, K. 2006. "A Lost Connection: Existential Positions and Melanie Klein's Infant Development." *Transactional Analysis Journal* 36 (4): 252–69.

Harris, T. A. 1973. *I'm Ok-You're Ok*. New York: Avon Books.

Harris, T. A., and A. B. Harris. 1985. *Staying Ok*. New York: Avon Books.

Hartman, C., and N. Narboe. 1974. "Catastrophic Injunctions." *Transactional Analysis Journal* 4 (2): 10–12.

Hawkes, L. 2007. "The Permission Wheel." *Transactional Analysis Journal* 37 (3): 210–17.

Hay, J. 1993. *Working it Out at Work*. Watford: Sherwood Publishing.

Hazell, J. W. 1989. "Drivers as Mediators of Stress Response." *Transactional Analysis Journal* 19 (4): 212–23.

Heron, W. 1957. "The Pathology of Boredom." *Scientific American* 196 (January): 52–56.

Hesterly, S. O. 1982). "Gimmicks Useful Inner Cues in Avoiding Games." *Transactional Analysis Journal* 12 (2): 144–46.

Hine, J. 1990. "The Bilateral Nature and Ongoing Nature of Games." *Transactional Analysis Journal* 20 (1): 28–39.

Hobbs, G. W. 1984. "Magister Dixit." *Transactional Analysis Journal* 14 (3): 174–79.

"Holism: The Body/Mind Connection." 2001. *International Wellness Directory*. http://www.mnwelldir.org/docs/healing/bodymind.htm.

Holloway, W. H. 1972. "The Crazy Child in the Parent." *Transactional Analysis Journal* 2 (3): 32–34.

Holloway, W. H. 1977. "Transactional Analysis: An Integrative View." In *Transactional Analysis After Eric Berne: Teachings and Practices of Three TA Schools*, edited by G. Barnes, 169–221. New York: Harper's College Press.

Holtby, M. E. 1973. "You Become What I Take You to Be: R. D. Laing's Work on Attributions as Injunctions." *Transactional Analysis Journal* 3 (4): 25–28.

Horwitz, A. 1982. "The Relationship Between Positive Stroking and Self-Perceived Symptoms of Distress." *Transactional Analysis Journal* 12 (3): 218–22.

Hughes, R. L. 1978. "Is the Little Professor Right?" *Transactional Analysis Journal* 8 (2): 120–23.

Jacobs, A. 1997. "Berne's Life Positions: Science and Morality." *Transactional Analysis Journal* 27 (3): 197–206.

James, J. 1984. "Grandparents and the Family Script Parade." *Transactional Analysis Journal* 14 (1): 18–28.

James, M. 1986. "Diagnosis and Treatment of Ego State Boundary Problems." *Transactional Analysis Journal* 16 (3): 188–96.

James, M., and D. Jongeward. 1971. *Born to Win: Transactional Analysis with Gestalt Experiments*. Reading, MA: Addison-Wesley.

Jaoui, G. 2001. "Stages for Success." In *Volume of Selected Articles from the Transactional Analysis Journal, 1981–1990*, 207–10. Oakland, CA: International Transactional Analysis Association.

Joines, V. 1982. "Similarities and Differences in Rackets and Games." *Transactional Analysis Journal* 12 (4): 280–83.

Jones, J. V., and W. J. Lyddon. 2000. "Cognitive Therapy and Empirically Validated Treatments." *Journal of Cognitive Psychotherapy*, January 1. HighBeam (1P3-1474560861).

Jongeward, D. 1972. "What Do You Do When Your Script Runs Out?" *Transactional Analysis Journal* 2 (2): 78–80.

Jongeward, D., and M. James. 1973. *Winning With People: Group Exercises in Transactional Analysis*. Reading, MA: Addison-Wesley.

Kahler, T. 1975. "Drivers: The Key to The Process of Scripts." *Transactional Analysis Journal* 5 (3): 280–84.

Kahler, T. 1977. "The Miniscript." In *Transactional Analysis After Eric Berne: Teachings and Practices of Three TA Schools*, edited by G. Barnes, 222–56. New York: Harper's College Press.

Kahneman, D. 2013. *Thinking, Fast and Slow*. New York: Farrar, Straus and Giroux.

Karpman, S. B. 1968. "Fairy Tales and Script Drama Analysis." *Transactional Analysis Bulletin* 7 (26): 39–43.

Karpman, S. B. 2009. "Sex Games People Play: Intimacy Blocks, Games, and Scripts." *Transactional Analysis Journal* 39 (2): 103–16.

Klein, M. 1985. "Ten Personality Types." *Transactional Analysis Journal* 15 (3): 224–31.

Klein, M. 1987. "How to be Happy Though Human." *Transactional Analysis Journal* 17 (4): 152–62.

Koren, M. 2014. "Average Americans Think They're Smarter Than the Average American." *National Journal*, May 12. http://www.nationaljournal.com/domesticpolicy/average-americans-think-they-re-smarter-than-the-average-american-20140512.

Kuijt, J. 1980. "Differentiation of the Adult Ego State: Analytical Adult and Experiencing Adult." *Transactional Analysis Journal* 10 (3): 232–37.

Kunda, Z. 1990. "The Case for Motivated Reasoning." *Psychological Bulletin* 108 (3): 480–98.

Laing, R. D. 1971. *The Politics of the Family and Other Essays*. New York: Pantheon Books.

Lammers, W. 1994. "Injunctions as an Impairment to Healthy Ego State Functioning." *Transactional Analysis Journal* 24 (4): 250–54.

Lankford, V. 1988. "The Parent Ego State from a Reparenting Perspective." *Transactional Analysis Journal* 18 (1): 47–50.

Lee, J. 2010. "Students Can Benefit From Goal-Setting." *The Daily Bruin*, October 15. http://www.dailybruin.com/article/2010/10/students_can_benefit_from_goalsetting.

Lehrer, J. 2009. "Don't! The Secret of Self-Control." *The New Yorker*, May 18. http://www.newyorker.com/reporting/2009/05/18/090518fa_fact_lehrer?currentPage=all.

Leveson, V. 2011. "Know Thyself to Know How to Deal With Others." *New Zealand Herald*, May 21. HighBeam (1G1-256880169).

Levin, P. 1985. *Becoming the Way We Are: A Transactional Guide to Personal Development*. Wenatchee, WA: Directed Media.

Lieberman, M., L. Yalom, and M. Miles. 1973. *Encounter Groups: First Facts*. New York: Basic Books.

Linley, P. A. 2007. "Leveraging Business Performance Through Strengths." Presentation given at the *Positive Psychology, Well-Being and Business Conference* sponsored by the University of East London, November 8. London, United Kingdom.

Little, R. 2006. "Ego State Relational Units and Resistance to Change." *Transactional Analysis Journal* 36 (1): 7–19.

Locke, E. A., and G. P. Latham. 2002. "Building a Practically Useful Theory of Goal Setting and Task Motivation: A 35-Year Odyssey." *American Psychologist* 57 (9): 705–17.

Loria, B. R. 2001. "The Parent Ego State: Theoretical Foundations and Alterations." In *Volume of Selected Articles from the Transactional Journal, 1981–1990*, 246–53. Oakland, CA: International Transactional Analysis Association.

Loria, B. R. 2003. "Whither Transactional Analysis: Obsolescence or Paradigm Shift." *Transactional Analysis Journal* 33 (2): 192–200.

Mart, L., T. Nichols, and M. Cantrell. 1975. "Parent Shrinkers Revisited." *Transactional Analysis Journal* 5 (3): 259–63.

Marx, P. 2013. "Mentally Fit." *The New Yorker*, July 29. http://www.newyorker.com/magazine/2013/07/29/mentally-fit.
Maslow, A. 1943. "A Theory of Human Motivation." *Psychological Review* 50 (4): 370–96.
Maslow, A. 1968. *Toward a Psychology of Being*. New York: Van Nostrand Reinhold Company.
Maslow, A. 1954. *Motivation and Personality*. New York: Harper and Row Publishers, Inc.
McCormick, P. 1973. "TA and Behavior Modification: A Comparison Study." *Transactional Analysis Journal* 3 (1): 10–14.
McCormick, P. 1977. *Social Transactions*. Stockton, CA: Vanguard Press.
McLeod, S. A. 2008. "Asch Experiment." *Simple Psychology*. http://www.simplypsychology.org/asch-conformity.html.
McRaney, D. 2010. "You Are Not So Smart: A Celebration of Self Delusion." June 23. http://youarenotsosmart.com/2010/06/23/confirmation-bias/.
McRaney, D. 2011. *You Are Not So Smart*. New York: Penguin Group.
Meininger, J. 1973. *Success Through Transactional Analysis*. New York: The New American Library, Inc.
Melzack, R. 1965. "Effects of Early Experience on Behavior: Experimental and Conceptual Considerations." In *Psychopathology of Perception*, edited by P. H. Hoch and J. Zubin, 271–99. New York: Grune and Stratton.
"Memory Wizards." *60 Minutes*. CBS. April 20, 2014. Web Transcript. http://www.cbsnews.com/news/Memory-wizards-60-minutes/.
Mescavage, A., and C. Silver. 1977. "Try Hard and Please Me in Psychological Development." *Transactional Analysis Journal* 7 (4): 331–34.
Milgram, S. 1974. *Obedience to Authority*. New York: Harper and Row.
Mills, R. 1986. "Psychological Variables Related to Life Satisfaction of Older People." *Transactional Analysis Journal* 16 (2): 132–36.
Milner, B. 1977. "Memory Mechanisms." *Canadian Medical Association Journal* 116 (12): 1374–76.
Mitchell, G. 2011. "Alfred Adler & Adlerian Individual Psychology." http://www.mind-development.eu/adler.html.
Mooney, C. 2011a. "The Science of Why We Don't Believe Science." May/June. http://www.motherjones.com/politics/2011/03/denial-science-chris-mooney.
Mooney, C. 2011b. "What is Motivated Reasoning? How Does it Work? Dan Kahan Answers." May 5. http://blogs.discovermagazine.com/intersection/2011/05/05/what-is-motivated-reasoning-how-does-it-work-dan-kahan-answers/#.VGoylTTF_w0.
Morris, F. E., and D. G. Morris. 1982. "The Love Bind." *Transactional Analysis Journal* 12 (4): 284–87.
Mossman, H. 1981. "Games Bureaucrats Play: TWIC." *Transactional Analysis Journal* 11 (2): 171–72.
Mountain, A., and C. Davidson. "Transactional Analysis." *Mountain Associates*. http://businessballs.com/transactionalanalysis.htm.
Napper, R. 2009. "Positive Psychology and Transactional Analysis." *Transactional Analysis Journal* 39 (1): 61–74.
Newell, S., and D. Jeffery. 2002. *Behaviour Management in the Classroom: A Transactional Analysis Approach*. London: David Fulton Publishers.
Newton, T. 2006. "Script, Psychological Life Plans, and the Learning Cycle." *Transactional Analysis Journal* 36 (3): 186–95.
Novellino, M. 2000. "The Pinocchio Syndrome." *Transactional Analysis Journal* 30 (4): 292–98.
Novellino, M. 2005. "Transactional Analysis: Epistemological Foundations." *Transactional Analysis Journal* 35 (2): 157–72.
Novey, T. 1980. "I Am OK and You Are OK. 95% = Cure." *Transactional Analysis Journal* 10 (2): 135–39.

Novey, T. 2002. "Measuring the Effectiveness of Transactional Analysis: An International Study." *Transactional Analysis Journal* 32 (1): 8–24.

Novey, T. 2006. "Myth and Measurement." *Transactional Analysis Journal* 36 (3): 180–85.

Obbes, J. 2011. "Transactional Analysis." *Philippi Trust South Africa*, November 28. http://philippitrustsa.blogspot.com/2011/11/transactional-analysis.html.

Oller-Vallejo, J. 1994. "Using Attributive Strokes to Differentiate Natural Traits." *Transactional Analysis Journal* 24 (3): 185–88.

Orten, J. 1972. "Contributions to Stroke Vocabulary." *Transactional Analysis Journal* 2 (3): 8–10.

Orten, J. D. April 1975. "Indirect Validation and Script." *Transactional Analysis Journal* 5 (2): 142–43.

"Our Dark Hearts: The Stanford Prison Experiment." *PsyBlog*, September 6, 2007. http://www.spring.org.uk/2007/09/our-dark-hearts-stanford-prison.php.

Parry, T. A. 1979. "To Be Or Not To Be Ok: The Development of the Child Ego State." *Transactional Analysis Journal* 9 (2): 124–130.

Penfield, W. 1952. "Memory Mechanisms." *A.M.A. Archives of Neurology and Psychiatry* 67:178–98.

Pittman, E. 1984. *Transactional Analysis for Social Workers and Counsellors*. London: Routledge and Kegan Paul.

Priya, R. U. 2007. "Transactional Analysis and the Mind/Body Connection." *Transactional Analysis Journal* 37 (4): 286–93.

Prochaska, J. O., and J. C. Norcross. (n.d.). "Transactional Analysis." http://academic.cengage.com-resource_Uploads/downloads/0495007773_57098.pdf.

"Public Policy Implications of the New Science of Mind." *Charlie Rose Brain Series 2 Episode 13*. PBS. March 7, 2013. Web Video. http://www.charlierose.com/watch/60190667.

"Restaurant Shift Turns Into Nightmare." *ABC News*. November 10, 2005. http://abcnews.go.com/Primetime/story?id=1297922&page=4.

Robertson, E. 2013. "Stress DOES Have an Impact on Cancer: Anxiety Switches on a Gene That Speeds up the Spread of the Disease." *Mail Online*, August 23. http://www.dailymail.co.uk/health/article-2400784/Stress-DOES-impact-cancer-Anxiety-switches-gene-speeds-spread-disease.html.

Rosenfeld, I. 1999. *Live Now Age Later*. New York: Warner Books, Inc.

Samuels, S. 1971. "Stroke Strategy: The Basis of Therapy." *Transactional Analysis Journal* 1 (3): 23–24.

Saul, H. 2013. "New Study Finds Health Kick Can Reverse the Ageing Process." *The Independent*, September 17. http://www.independent.co.uk/news/science/new-study-finds-health-kick-can-reverse-the-ageing-process-8821542.html.

Schachter, S. 1994. "Leon Festinger 1919–1989: A Biographical Memoir by Stanley Schachter." *National Academy of Sciences*: 97–110.

Schaffer, H. R. 1965. "Changes in Developmental Quotient Under Two Conditions of Maternal Separation." *British Journal of the Society of Clinical Psychology* 4:39–46.

Schlegel, L. 1998. "What is Transactional Analysis?" *Transactional Analysis Journal* 28 (4): 269–87.

Seaton, G. J. 1952. *Isle of the Damned*. New York: Popular Library.

Seligman, M. P. 1991. *Learned Optimism*. New York: Alfred A. Knopf.

Seligman, M. P. 2011. *Flourish*. New York: Free Press.

Shaley, I. 2012. "Early Life Stress and Telomere Length: Investigating the Connection and Possible Mechanisms: A Critical Survey of the Evidence Base, Research Methodology and Basic Biology." *Bioessays*, November. http://www.ncbi.nlm.nih.gov/pubmed/22991129.

Simmons, C. H., and K. Sands-Dudelczyk. 1983. "Children Helping Peers: Altruism and Preschool Environment." *The Journal of Psychology* 115 (2): 203–07.

Sinpetru, L. 2013. "Gene Switched on by Stress Speeds Up the Spread of Cancer." *Softpedia*, August 24. http://news.softpedia.com/news/Gene-Switched-On-by-Stress-Speeds-Up-the-Spread-of-Cancer-377951.shtml.

Smith, R. H. 2013. *The Joy of Pain: Schadenfreude and the Dark Side of Human Nature*. New York: Oxford University Press.
Solis, O. R. 2004. "Some Thoughts on the State of the World from a Transactional Analysis Perspective." *Transactional Analysis Journal* 34 (4): 341–46.
Sprietsma, L. C. 1978. "A Winner's Script Apparatus." *Transactional Analysis Journal* 8 (1): 45–51.
Stafford, T. 2013. "Are We Naturally Good or Bad?" *BBC Future*, January 14. http://www.bbc.com/future/story/20130114-are-we-naturally-good-or-bad.
"Stanford Prison Experiment." *Wikipedia*. http://en.wikipedia.org/wiki/Stanford_prison_experiment.
Steiner, C. 1971. "The Stroke Economy." *Transactional Analysis Journal* 1 (3): 9–15.
———. 1974. *Scripts People Live: Transactional Analysis of Life Scripts*. New York: Grove Press.
———. 1981. "Acceptance Statement from Claude Steiner on Co-Winning the Eric Berne Memorial Scientific Award for the Stroke Economy." *Transactional Analysis Journal* 11 (1): 6–9.
———. 1997. "Transactional Analysis in the Information Age." http://www.claudesteiner.com/tainfo.htm
———. 2001. "Emotional Literacy." In *Volume of Selected Articles from the Transactional Analysis Journal, 1981–1990*, 136–47. Oakland, CA: International Transactional Analysis Association.
———. 2003. "Core Concepts of a Stroke-Centered Transactional Analysis." *Transactional Analysis Journal* 33 (2): 178–81.
———. 2007. "Stroking: What's Love Got to Do With It?" *Transactional Analysis Journal* 37 (4): 307–10.
———. "The Transactional Analysis Corroboration Research Project." http://www.emotional-literacy.com/corro.htm.
Steinfeld, G. J. 1998. "Personal Responsibility in Human Relationships: A Cognitive-Constructivist Approach." *Transactional Analysis Journal* 28 (3): 188–201.
"Strip Search Prank Call Scam." *Wikipedia*. http://en.wikipedia.org/wiki/Strip_search_prank_call_scam.
Summerton, O. 2000. "The Development of Game Analysis." *Transactional Analysis Journal* 30 (3): 207–18.
Swede, S. 1978. "OK Corral for Life Positions." *Transactional Analysis Journal* 8 (1): 59–62.
Swenson, W. M., J. S. Pearson, and D. Osborne. 1973. *An MMPI Source Book: Basic, Item, Scale, and Pattern Data on 50,000 Medical Patients*. Minneapolis: University of Minnesota Press.
Terlato, V. 2001. "The Analysis of Defense Mechanisms in the Transactional Analysis Setting." *Transactional Analysis Journal* 31 (2): 103–13.
"The Gift of Endless Memory." *60 Minutes*, December 16, 2010. CBS. Web Transcript. http://www.cbsnews.com/news/the-gift-of-endless-memory/.
Thomas, A., and S. Chess. 1980. *The Dynamics of Psychological Growth*. New York: Brunner/Mazel.
Thompson, H. O. 1976. "An Example of Ego States." *Transactional Analysis Journal* 6 (6): 131–32.
Tolle, E. 1999. *The Power of Now*. Novato, CA: New World Library.
Trimble, W. E. 1977. "Script Profiles: Three Ways to OK-ness." *Transactional Analysis Journal* 7 (4): 300–02.
Trubshaw, J. 2011. "Transactional Analysis: Supporting People Through Rapid Change." *Tinder Consulting*, January 23. http://www.tinderconsulting.com/Transactional-Analysis-supporting-people-through-rapid-change.html.
Tudor, K. 2008. "Take It: A Sixth Driver." *Transactional Analysis Journal* 38 (1): 43–57.
Vallejo, J. O. 1986. "Withdrawal: A Basic Positive and Negative Adaptation in Addition to Compliance and Rebellion." *Transactional Analysis Journal* 16 (2): 114–19.

Vandra, A. 2009. "Mechanisms for Transmission of Ulterior Transactions." *Transactional Analysis Journal* 39 (1): 46–60.
Wason, P. C. 1960. "On the Failure to Eliminate Hypothesis on a Conceptual Task." *Quarterly Journal of Experimental Psychology* 12 (3): 129–40.
Watzlawick, P., J. H. Beavin, and D. D. Jackson. 1967. *Pragmatics of Human Communication: A Study of Interactional Patterns, Pathologies and Paradoxes.* New York: Norton.
White, T. 1994. "Life Positions." *Transactional Analysis Journal* 34 (4): 269–76.
Widom, C. S., and M. G. Maxfield. 2001. "An Update on the Cycle of Violence." *Research in Brief,* January. U.S. Department of Justice, National Institute of Justice.
Wilson, F. R. 1975. "TA and Adler." *Transactional Analysis Journal* 5 (2): 117–22.
Woods, K. 2000. "The Defensive Function of the Game Scenario." *Transactional Analysis Journal* 30 (1): 94–97.
———. 2002. "Primary and Secondary Gains from Games." *Transactional Analysis Journal* 32 (3): 190–192.
———. 2007a. "The Stroking School of Transactional Analysis." *Transactional Analysis Journal* 37 (1): 32–34.
———. 2007b. "Surrender as a Group Norm." *Transactional Analysis Journal* 37 (3): 235–39.
Woollams, S. 1977. "From 21 to 43." In *Transactional Analysis After Eric Berne: Teachings and Practices of Three TA Schools,* edited by G. Barnes, 351–79. New York: Harper's College Press.
———. 1978. "The Internal Stroke Economy." *Transactional Analysis Journal* 8 (3): 194–97.
Woollams, S., and M. Brown. 1978. *Transactional Analysis.* Dexter, MI: Huron Valley Institute Press.
Woollams, S., M. Brown, and K. Huige. 1976. *Transactional Analysis in Brief.* Ann Arbor, MI: Huron Valley Institute.
Wyckoff, H. 1971. "The Strike Economy in Women's Scripts." *Transactional Analysis Journal* 1 (3): 16–20.
Zalcman, M. J. 1990. "Game Analysis and Racket Analysis: Overview, Critique, and Future Developments." *Transactional Analysis Journal* 20 (1): 4–19.
Zechnich, B. 1976. "NIGYSOB Revisited." *Transactional Analysis Journal* 6 (2): 173–76.
Zimbardo, P. 2007. *The Lucifer Effect: Understanding How Good People Turn Evil.* New York: Random House.

Index